CURRENT PHILOSOPHICAL ISSUES

Essays in Honor of Curt John Ducasse

Publication Number 657

AMERICAN LECTURE SERIES®

A Monograph in

The BANNERSTONE DIVISION *of*
AMERICAN LECTURES IN PHILOSOPHY

Edited by

MARVIN FARBER
Distinguished Service Professor
State University of New York
at Buffalo

It is the purpose of this Series to give representation to all important tendencies and points of view in Philosophy, without any implied concurrence on the part of the Editor and Publisher.

Photograph by Imogen Cunningham, San Francisco

Curt John Ducasse

CURRENT PHILOSOPHICAL ISSUES

Essays in Honor of Curt John Ducasse

Compiled and Edited by

FREDERICK C. DOMMEYER, Ph.D.
Department of Philosophy
San Jose State College
San Jose, California

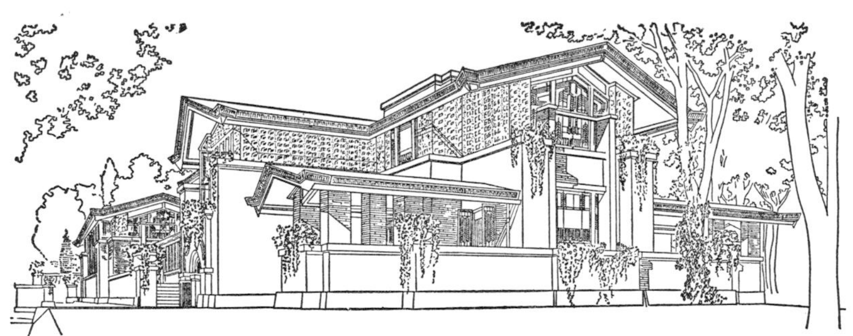

CHARLES C THOMAS • PUBLISHER
Springfield • Illinois • U. S. A.

Published and Distributed Throughout the World by

CHARLES C THOMAS • PUBLISHER

BANNERSTONE HOUSE

301–327 East Lawrence Avenue, Springfield, Illinois, U. S. A.

NATCHEZ PLANTATION HOUSE

735 North Atlantic Boulevard, Fort Lauderdale, Florida, U. S. A.

Library of Congress Catalog Card Number: 66–16796

With THOMAS BOOKS *careful attention is given to all details of manufacturing and design. It is the Publisher's desire to present books that are satisfactory as to their physical qualities and artistic possibilities and appropriate for their particular use.* THOMAS BOOKS *will be true to those laws of quality that assure a good name and good will.*

Printed in the United States of America

K–8

LIST OF CONTRIBUTORS

ALICE AMBROSE, M.A., Ph.D., Ph.D. (Cantab.), LL.D. (Hon.), *Fellow, University of Wisconsin; Alice Freeman Palmer Post-doctoral Fellow, Wellesley College; Marion Kennedy Student, Newnham College, Cambridge University; Sophia and Austin Smith Professor of Philosophy, Smith College; Formerly, Faculty, University of Michigan.*

CHARLES A. BAYLIS, A.M., Ph.D., *Sheldon Travelling Fellow (Harvard), Cambridge, Paris and Hamburg Universities; Professor and Chairman of Philosophy, Duke University; Formerly, Faculty, Brown University; Formerly, Professor and Chairman of Philosophy, University of Maryland; Guggenheim Fellow and Senior Fulbright Scholar, Oxford University; Formerly, Vice President Eastern Division, American Philosophical Association; Formerly, Vice President of the Association for Symbolic Logic.*

PETER A. BERTOCCI, A.M., Ph.D., *Professor of Philosophy and Chair of Borden Parker Bowne Professor of Philosophy, Boston University; Fulbright Scholar, Italy and India; Formerly, Faculty and Chairman of Philosophy, Bates College; Formerly, Secretary and President, American Theological Society; Formerly, Secretary and President, Metaphysical Society of America; Formerly, Member Executive Committee, Eastern Division of the American Philosophical Association.*

BRAND, BLANSHARD, A.M., B.Sc., Ph.D., Litt.D. (Hon.), L.H.D. (Hon.), LL.D. (Hon.), *Sears Scholar, Harvard University; Rhodes Scholar, Oxford University; Emeritus Professor of Philosophy, Yale University; Visiting Professor, Columbia University, and University of Minnesota; Honorary Fellow, Merton College, Oxford University; Formerly, Professor and Chairman of Philosophy, Yale University; Formerly, President, Eastern Division of the American Philosophical Association; Formerly, Carus Lecturer, Gifford Lecturer, Hertz Lecturer, British Academy, Howison Lecturer, Adamson Lecturer, Manchester University; W. B. Noble Lecturer, Dudleian Lecturer, Harvard University; Matchette Lecturer, Wesleyan University.*

RODERICK M. CHISHOLM, A.M., Ph.D., *Professor of Philosophy, Brown University; Visiting Professor, Harvard University, University of California, University of Graz, Princeton University, University of Alberta, University of Illinois, and University of Southern California; Member, American Academy of Arts and Sciences; Formerly, Chairman of Philosophy, Brown University; Formerly, Vice President, Eastern Division American Philosophical Association; Formerly, Member Executive Committee, American Philosophical Association.*

FREDERICK C. DOMMEYER, Ph.D., *Department of Philosophy, San Jose State College, San Jose, California; Formerly, President of Creighton*

Philosophical Club; Tully Cleon Knoles Lecturer in Philosophy at the University of the Pacific.

MARVIN FARBER, Ph.D., *from Harvard University, graduate work at Berlin, Freiburg and Heidelberg Universities; Dr. h.c. from Université de Lille. Sheldon Fellow, Parker Fellow; Distinguished Professor of Philosophy, State University of New York at Buffalo. Formerly on faculty of Ohio State University; Formerly Chairman of Philosophy and Acting Dean of Graduate School at University of Buffalo; Formerly Professor and Chairman of Philosophy at the University of Pennsylvania; Editor,* Philosophy and Phenomenological Research; *President, Eastern Division of the American Philosophical Association; Former President, International Phenomenological Society; Guggenheim Fellowship.*

CHARLES HARTSHORNE, A.M., Ph.D., *Sheldon Travelling Fellow, Harvard University; Professor of Philosophy, University of Texas; Visiting Professor, Stanford University; Exchange Professor, New School for Social Research; Fulbright Lecturer, Melbourne and Kyoto Universities; Terry Lecturer, Yale University; Formerly, Faculties, University of Chicago and Emory University.*

MORRIS LAZEROWITZ, Ph.D., *Fellow, University of Michigan; Alfred H. Lloyd Post-doctoral Fellow, Harvard University; Sophia and Austin Smith Professor of Philosophy, Smith College; Fulbright Lecturer, Bedford College, London.*

EDWARD H. MADDEN, M.A., Ph.D., *Professor of Philosophy, State University of New York at Buffalo; Formerly, Faculties, University of Connecticut and San Jose State College; Visiting Professor, Amherst College.*

A. I. MELDEN, A.M., Ph.D., *Professor and Chairman of Philosophy, University of California (Irvine); Ford Foundation Fellow; Formerly, President, Pacific Division, American Philosophical Association.*

HENRY H. PRICE, M.A., B.Sc., LL.D. (Hon.), Litt.D. (Hon.), *Professor Emeritus, Wykeham Professor Logic and Honorary Fellow of New College, Oxford University; Visiting Professor, Princeton University and St. Andrews; Flint Visiting Professor, University of California (Los Angeles); Formerly, Assistant Lecturer, Liverpool University; Formerly, Fellow and Lecturer in Philosophy, Trinity College, Oxford University; Formerly, President, Society for Psychical Research, London; Formerly, Gifford Lecturer, Aberdeen University.*

RONALD E. SANTONI, M.A., Ph.D., *Canadian Government Overseas Scholar, University of Paris; Church Society for College Work Post-doctoral Faculty Fellow, Yale University; Associate Professor, Denison University; Formerly, Faculties, University of the Pacific, and Wabash College.*

VINCENT TOMAS, M.A., Ph.D., *Guggenheim Fellow; Professor and Chairman of Philosophy, Brown University; Visiting Professor, University of Minnesota, Northwestern University, Harvard University, Yale University, and Dartmouth College.*

DEDICATION

In the light of his significant contributions to philosophy and to his fellowmen, these essays are respectfully dedicated to Professor Curt John Ducasse.

PREFACE

THE EDITOR of this collection of philosophical essays in honor of Professor Ducasse found himself from the outset called upon to make a number of difficult decisions. Should he specify in advance definite topics for the contributors to discuss? Should the contributors be limited to consideration of ones or others of Professor Ducasse's views? Or should they be left free to write on any philosophical question they chose? Again, from whom should contributions be invited or received? Only from former students in Professor Ducasse's courses? Or, more broadly, from philosophers that happened to be known to the editor or to his advisors to have specially interested themselves in certain of Professor Ducasse's writings?

These and many other such questions perplexed the editor without his being able to come to hard and fast decisions about them. In the end, each of the contributors did write on a philosophical topic of his own choosing, on which he felt that he had something of importance to say. And what the contributors had in common was an interest in Ducasse and his work.

It turned out that some of the contributors had at one time, like the editor himself, been students in courses conducted by Ducasse. Professors Baylis, Chisholm, Melden, Santoni and Tomas fall in this category. The other contributors—Professors Ambrose, Bertocci, Blanshard, Farber, Hartshorne, Lazerowitz, Madden and Price—have been valued friends and sometimes close associates of Ducasse, most of them over periods of many years.

The editor is deeply indebted to all of these philosophers since their efforts and high competence are what make this volume possible. In one or two cases, the contributed papers were written in the face of personal difficulties. One author, for instance, because of impending medical attention, wrote a somewhat shorter paper than he had earlier intended to do.

This volume owes much in addition to Professor Marvin Farber as editor of the Charles C Thomas, Publisher *American Lectures in Philosophy* series. The present volume is in this series, and its preparation was under Dr. Farber's general editorship. In this supervisory capacity, he has been of great assistance to the present writer, always being cooperative and helpful, and at the same time openly attentive to the many suggestions which came from a variety of sources.

Thanks are sincerely offered also to Mr. Payne Thomas of *Charles C Thomas, Publisher,* and to his helpful staff.

FREDERICK C. DOMMEYER

San Jose State College

INTRODUCTION AND BIOGRAPHICAL DATA

I

Introduction

THIS VOLUME has been prepared by its authors in honor of Professor Curt John Ducasse who, for more than half a century, has been intimately associated with professional philosophy in America.

His distinguished career as a teacher[1] and his many publications[2] testify objectively to his worth. Yet, as Morris Cohen has written in *American Thought*[3] about Ducasse, such unattached philosophers "who own no allegiance to school or party like stray dogs run the danger of going unnoticed."

Ducasse has been "an intellectual stray." Cohen was correct in his estimate of Ducasse in this regard. For Ducasse, once he discovered himself philosophically, left the well-worn trails and struck out on his own through the philosophical brush.

In the light of this fact, one might inquire why Ducasse has failed to gather disciples about him and why he is not the leader of a *new* school of philosophy. For it is certainly true that Ducasse has never had a following and that he has not founded a philosophical system.

The answer to the above query is obvious enough if one understands Ducasse's conception of philosophy and is also aware of the manner in which he has consistently applied his metaphilosophy to the solution of philosophical problems. He has conceived of philosophy as a species of knowledge, i.e., as a branch of science, whose special subject matter is to be investigated with the same methodological rigor as the subject matters of the physical and biological sciences.

That Ducasse has not had followers is a tribute to his clear

[1] See Appendix A for the *Academic History of Curt John Ducasse.*

[2] See Appendix B for the *Publications of Curt John Ducasse.*

[3] *American Thought* (Glencoe, Ill.: The Free Press, 1954), p. 323.

elucidation of these metaphilosophical intentions, and also a sign of the discernment of his readers who, understanding him, saw the incongruity which his having "disciples" would constitute. The existence of disciples in Ducasse's case would have testified only to his having failed to communicate his view to his readers.

A traditional religionist or a dogmatic philosopher may have disciples. But the philosopher, functioning as Ducasse would have him, could no more have followers than could a physicist. Ducasse requires of the philosopher that he have a regard for the facts, that he clarify his terms and that he state his hypotheses and theories precisely. He demands also that these theories be verified by an empirical test and that both the consequences and presuppositions of theories be clearly delineated.

True, the subject matter of philosophy is different from that of any of the other sciences. More will be said about it later. But what philosophy provides concerning it must be genuinely knowledge; not esoteric doctrines that would remain untestable.

To point out that Ducasse has had no disciples is not, however, to assert that he has had no influence on American philosophers. His students, both undergraduate and graduate, his colleagues and his many friends have felt the impact of his acute, critical mind, of his thorough analyses of philosophical terms, and of his witty and friendly puncturing of philosophical balloons filled with hot air. It betrays no secret to say that many of Ducasses's ideas show up in the writings of others. But they do so not because they have Ducasse's *Imprimatur* on them but because there is merit in them.

There is much more to be said than this, however. Ducasse, over the years, has striven to practice what he has preached. The result has been over one hundred articles and a number of books, in which he has shed light on difficult philosophical questions, such as those of the analysis of causality, beauty, reality, truth, knowledge, good, sensing, mind, body, etc. Without doubt, Ducasse's Carus Lectures,[4] which in the *Encyclopedia Britannica's* yearly supplement for 1952,[5] were referred to as one of the most important philosophical publications of the year (1951), provide the

[4] *Nature, Mind, and Death* (La Salle, Ill.: The Open Court Publishing Company, 1951).

[5] See p. 555.

climactic expression of his philosophic reflections. Yet, his many articles and his other books have also had their effects on American philosophy and philosophers. The references to such articles, and to his books, in the writings of others, and the inclusion of selected parts of his writings in books of readings in philosophy testify to the high valuation of them by professional philosophers. The lectures he has delivered under established lectureships at several universities, as well as the visiting professorships he has held, are additional indications of the esteem Ducasse has enjoyed among his philosophical colleagues.

Ducasse's intellect has not been and is not bound by convention. His interest in the philosophy of religion, and in the philosophical and parapsychological problems associated with the question of survival after bodily death, as well as his many articles on psychical research, are evidence for the independence of his thought. And by moving into some of these "questionable" areas of scholarly interest, Ducasse has shed light on certain of the problems of men, as distinguished from the problems of philosophers. There are many persons, with no pretensions to scholarship, who have read and appreciated Ducasse's reflections on the problem of survival after bodily death. The sterile character of so much of contemporary philosophy stands in bleak contrast to the warm interest in the concerns of human beings, which is evident in Ducasse's writings.

But Ducasse has brought into those "off-beat" areas the same scholarly integrity, the same high regard for the facts and the same clarity of thought that have marked his work in the more usual fields of academic endeavor. One need only read his book [6] on the problem of survival after bodily death to realize how careful is his consideration of that issue. It is a model of clarity in both the philosophical and parapsychological parts of the problem.

Whatever the ultimate value of Ducasse's many contributions to philosophy may be, one cannot help admiring his persistent and conscientious effort to make philosophizing a knowledge-yielding enterprise. Certainly, if it is not this kind of enterprise, there are some among us who would no longer bother with it.

[6] *The Belief in a Life after Death* (Springfield, Ill.: Charles C Thomas, Publisher, 1961).

II

A Brief Intellectual History of Ducasse

A. 1881–1930

Strange as it may seem, Ducasse managed to spend the first twenty-four years of his life in blissful ignorance of philosophy. Born on July 7, 1881, in Angouleme, France, and educated first in the *Lycée* of Bordeaux and later at Abbotsholme School (England), Ducasse obtained a substantial part of his early education through a study of Latin and Greek. Had he continued with this classical curriculum, he would have become acquainted eventually with the ancient philosophies of Greece. But he abandoned this classical program, turning to a study of mathematics and science in order to prepare himself for admission into the civil engineering program at the *École Centrale*. Illness, however, frustrated Ducasse's new aim and, after a year in Paris, he went to Mexico City to work in a dry goods store.

Ducasse's work in mathematics, however, left its mark on his intellect. He wrote of this study: "I . . . remember becoming clearly conscious some years later that the mathematical, and in particular the geometrical, modes of thought were . . . colouring my reasoning processes on other subjects, inclining me to seek order, clearness, and objectivity." [7]

Another habit of Ducasse's thought, stemming in this instance from the influence of one of his teachers in England, Dr. Cecil Reddie, is that of initiating each inquiry with an exact statement of "the matter in doubt," or the *dubitatum* as Ducasse likes to call it in his classes. This notion is somewhat reminiscent of John Dewey's requirement that the "problematic situation" must be defined before the remaining steps of an act of thought can most usefully occur. It is obvious, however, that Ducasse did not borrow his idea of the *dubitatum* and its definition from Dewey, but rather brought it from England.

Business was not for Ducasse. After two years in Mexico, without discovering for himself either a special interest or taste for

[7] *Contemporary American Philosophy* (New York: Macmillan Company, 1930), p. 301.

any vocation, Ducasse came to New York City, but this great city provided for him no relief from the frustration he found in the business world. It was there, however, that Ducasse stumbled across a work in philosophy for the first time in his life. It was a rather obscure work by a Hindu scholar, Bhagavan Das, entitled *The Science of Peace* and dealing with the relation of the Individual to the Absolute. Only one chapter of it, however, gained Ducasse's attention: the chapter setting forth some of the views of Berkeley, Hume, Kant, Fichte, Schelling and Hegel. Thus began the kind of interest which thereafter gave direction to Ducasse's life.

It was not long after his interest in philosophy had been stimulated that Ducasse left New York City for the Pacific Coast. Of this change, he writes: ". . . in a few months, finding my dislike of business pursuits growing at the same rate as my preoccupation with philosophical questions, I entered the University of Washington." [8]

He entered there in the fall of 1907 with senior standing, because of his work at the French *Lycée,* and was graduated *magna cum laude* the following June, 1908, with an A.B. degree. He stayed on at Washington, receiving his M.A. degree in 1909. During the 1909–'10 academic year, Ducasse was a graduate assistant there in philosophy and psychology. He then went to Harvard for 1910–'11 and 1911–'12, receiving the Ph.D. degree there in 1912.

At the University of Washington, Ducasse was influenced by both Professor W. Savery (philosophy) and Professor H. C. Stevens (psychology). He was impressed by the critical mindedness of Savery and by his dismissal of the pretentious and empty words which, as Ducasse said, pass in some quarters for philosophical thought. From Stevens, whom Ducasse assisted in a psychology research problem, he obtained an insight into the "tireless patience, painstaking care, and scrupulous scientific honesty that characterized his procedures in research . . ." [9]

At Harvard, Ducasse did a large part of his work with Professor Josiah Royce. Of this contact with Royce, Ducasse later wrote:

[8] *Ibid.,* p. 302.

[9] *Ibid.,* p. 303.

> His unaffected and kindly but impressive personality, his powerful constructive intellect, the extraordinary range and thoroughness of his learning, and the genius which enabled him to find for even remotely abstract logical considerations the most concrete and living illustrations, all made upon me a profound and lasting impression, the effect of which, although not easy to analyze in detail, has been far-reaching.[10]

Ducasse arrived at Harvard with an already developed interest in several modern philosophers. The train of thought which had had most impact upon his mind at this time—when he was beginning his studies at Harvard—was idealistic in nature. He had been much attracted to the point of view which, like many another young student of philosophy, he found in Berkeley's idealism. Through Berkeley, however, Ducasse had moved on to the scepticism of Hume, and Hume had led him to Kant. He then found a temporary resting place in Schopenhauer's philosophy. When he got to Harvard, Ducasse was convinced of the "essential soundness" of Schopenhauer's philosophical system.[11]

It might be said parenthetically that these early interests in classical modern philosophy were never obliterated from Ducasse's outlook. In the years that followed, his classroom teaching displayed continuing interest and knowledge in depth of both Hume and Schopenhauer. It was obvious to his students that Ducasse had made careful and prolonged studies of these two philosophers and that he still found value in various aspects of their views.

But at Harvard, Ducasse's idealistic position was first challenged by the neo-realism of Professor Ralph B. Perry. Ducasse's ultimate response to this challenge was an experience somewhat reminiscent of Paul's conversion to Christianity on the road to Damascus though, in Ducasse's case, his insights were not into the truth of a religion. Neither did he suffer a temporary blindness as had Paul. On the contrary, his insights were philosophic and relativistic in nature, and intellectually illuminating.

Ducasse's more immediate response to the challenge of Perry's realism was to write a paper for presentation to Perry's seminar. His paper was designed of course to refute Perry and to defend himself. About this, Ducasse wrote:

[10] *Ibid.*, pp. 303–304.
[11] *Ibid.*, p. 304.

On that, to me, memorable occasion I defended my idealistic positions fiercely, and remained unconvinced of any unsoundness in them. On the other hand, I could not at the time clearly perceive the defect which I believed existed in the position of Professor Perry, and I resolved to examine his published articles with care before the next meeting of the seminary.[12]

It was a few days after these events that Ducasse had an experience that dramatically altered his entire direction philosophically and provided him with the key to the view that he spent the rest of his professional career modifying, correcting and developing. It is perhaps best to have this crucial experience described in Ducasse's own words, so important was it in his philosophic life.

He writes:

> I was at home quietly reading some book . . . when suddenly a most vivid and luminous insight came to me that neither idealism, nor realism, nor any other metaphysical position could, in the nature of things, be either refuted or proved. . . . it proved to be but the beginning of some forty-eight hours of the most extraordinary state of mind I have ever experienced. It was as if the key-log of a jam on some river had suddenly given way. All my previous philosophical ideas seemed to be loosened from their moorings, and to rearrange themselves in new relations together with countless others, unthought of before, that came tumbling in their train. For nearly two days, with hardly any sleep or food, and in a state of the highest exaltation, I worked feverishly, yet not fast enough to put down anything more than bare reminders of the seemingly numberless ideas which kept crowding into my consciousness. But alas! these reminders mostly proved quite inadequate to recall the ideas they were meant to fix, when later in a soberer mood I returned to them with that purpose.[13]

Despite Ducasse's inability to recapture all of his insights, there remained from his experience several of them: (1) no ontology is capable of proof or disproof; (2) that being so, an ontology is logically arbitrary and represents no more than "taste, whim, or temperament of its upholder;" (3) that therefore the

[12] *Ibid.*, p. 304.
[13] *Ibid.*, pp. 304–305.

only proper attitude toward ontologies is one of tolerance since these differences represent only "differences of sheer taste, such as exist, for example, in wines or in foods." [14] Ducasse thus concluded that ontologies are relative to extra-logical factors and that these are of necessity at the foundations of metaphysical systems. Similar relativistic analyses forced themselves upon Ducasse applicable to such other fields of philosophy as epistemology, ethics, aesthetics, etc. Ducasse, following Royce's suggestion, called his view "Philosophical Liberalism." [15]

From this vantage point, Ducasse was led to a reformulation of his conception of philosophy. Whereas he had earlier viewed philosophy in a traditional way, taking ontology and other philosophical disciplines "seriously," i.e., in absolutistic terms, he now began to see the faultiness of this conception and the need for a scientific reconstruction of philosophy. He began to view the ultimately distinctive subject matter of philosophy as consisting of values. But it was not the concern of the philosopher to apply value-terms to facts (this is the task of the critic). It was rather his task "to supply exact knowledge of the meaning of . . . value-predicates . . ." [16] The vague intuitive understanding we have of such terms must be transformed through philosophical analysis into "explicit and accurate knowledge of their meaning." [17] As Ducasse writes more fully:

> It is philosophy alone which scientifically investigates the meaning and the varieties of possible subjects of application of such predicates of criticism as true, valid, clear, right, good, beautiful, sublime, etc.; and this task involves a good deal more than would appear at first sight. For instance, with regard to the predicate True, it involves not only analysing its meaning accurately, but also analysing the import of such modifiers of it as Necessarily, Certainly, Possibly, Probably.[18]

But philosophical analysis requires even more than this, for

> . . . it involves also a classification of the logical kinds of entities of which truth can be predicated—that is to say, of propositions, and an accurate account of each kind. This means

[14] *Ibid.*, p. 305.
[15] *Ibid.*, p. 305.
[16] *Ibid.*, p. 306.
[17] *Ibid.*, p. 306.
[18] *Ibid.*, p. 306.

> an analysis of all such fundamental categories as Causation, Teleology, Space, Time, Identity, Substance, and so on. Nothing short of all this constitutes an adequate instrument of epistemic criticism and the fashioning of that instrument, and of corresponding instruments of aesthetic, ethical, and other types of criticism is the task of philosophy.[19]

Such problems as the origin of life, of matter and of mind are not within the domain of philosophy but rather of natural science. But the predicate "real," in certain of its applications, is a value-predicate and hence its analysis is part of the business of philosophy. Thus is ontology saved for philosophy by Ducasse.

It is obvious that the analysis of value-predicates and of the category of subjects relevant to each, as the task of philosophy, brings the philosopher close to the facts of language. Ducasse is fully aware of this and makes explicit reference to that fact in his 1930 statement to which reference has been made. As he says: "The language-facts which are philosophy's data consist of common phrases where the particular term which happens to be under scrutiny is, not talked about, but used, and used in a manner admittedly correct." [20] It is clearly language *uses* that Ducasse has in mind. Obviously, such value terms as right, good, beautiful, etc., may be misused, but the cases of their misuse are not the data of philosophy. On the other hand, the admittedly correct, or acceptable, uses are philosophical data. That Ducasse has not discarded his relativism by turning the problems of philosophy into semantic issues is clear. After all, a word such as "real" may have several different uses, each of them correct. Also, the use of a word may change over a period of time. Or, one group may correctly use a word in one way, and another group correctly use the same word in another way. Relativism and the accompanying tolerance still have their places in Ducasse's view that the data of philosophy are language-facts.

B. 1930 to the Present

There is no doubt about the fact that Ducasse had, by 1930, developed the essentials of his metaphilosophy. True, these essen-

[19] *Ibid.*, p. 307.
[20] *Ibid.*, pp. 309–310.

tials were to be corrected, modified and developed, but the 1930 outlook of Ducasse is clear and guiding. By 1941, however, Ducasse had written his book on philosophy as a science.[21] In this work, Ducasse again explicitly asserts that philosophy is "a knowledge-seeking enterprise." [22] Common to all the sciences (and philosophy is a science) are the requirements that propositions be formulated without ambiguity, that they be carefully verified and that their consequences and presuppositions be meticulously scrutinized.[23]

These requirements make only more explicit what Ducasse held earlier. He is now, however, much clearer about the subject matter of this science called philosophy. Ducasse now makes a distinction [24] between the primitive and the derivative facts of a science. "The primitive facts of a given science are those which, for it, are beyond question. They are, on the one hand, the facts about which the science asks its very first, most elementary questions, and on the other hand, the facts—of the same general kind—to which the science ultimately appeals in testing the validity of its hypotheses." [25] But the derivative facts of a science "are those discovered as a result of the attempt to answer, about its primitive facts, the kind of questions that distinguish an enterprise of the sort called scientific from enterprises of other sorts." [26]

What ultimately distinguishes one science from another, Ducasse holds, is the nature of its primitive facts. In the case of philosophy, its primitive facts are appraisals or valuations. Such appraisals are beyond question in that they occur; they are facts in that sense. Ducasse had by 1941, however, refined his conceptions and he is then careful to distinguish such primitive appraisals as constitute the ultimate subject matter of philosophy from other kinds of appraisals. Appraisals to be primitive must be spontaneous, particular and formulated.[27] Primitive appraisals cannot

[21] *Philosophy as a Science: Its Matter and Method* (New York: Oskar Piest, 1941).

[22] *Ibid.,* p. 113.

[23] *Ibid.,* pp. 114–115.

[24] *Ibid.,* p. 118.

[25] *Ibid.,* p. 118.

[26] *Ibid.,* p. 119.

[27] *Ibid.,* p. 140.

therefore be generalizations, i.e., inferences; cannot be imitations and cannot be unformulated. This latter requirement means that such appraisals must be stated and thereby available for public examination. Examples of primitive appraisals are such statements as: "This act is wrong," "This ought to be done," etc. From such kinds of primitive appraisals, Ducasse says, one can generalize, e.g., that "stealing is wrong," or that "murder is evil," etc. Such empirical generalizations as these would be analogous, Ducasse holds, to such generalizations in natural science as "glass is brittle" and "wax melts when heated," etc. Scientific theorizing in philosophy (which is a science) would use such generalizations for purposes of "discovering premises from which these empirically discovered generalizations could have been deduced, and from which others empirically confirmable can be deduced." [28]

It is not our purpose here to criticize Ducasse's metaphilosophy.[29] Suffice it to say that in his Carus Lectures of 1951 he gives his conception of philosophy a form which makes some of the earlier criticisms inapplicable. In his Carus Lectures, Ducasse now again says that the subject matter of philosophy consists of "directly observable facts." [30] These facts are, however, described differently in this later view. Ducasse now writes:

> those observable facts can consist only of *other evaluative statements by P, but ones that are beyond question.* And an evaluative statement by P is beyond question if and only if it constitutes a 'definition-by-type,' i.e., a standard example, of what P means by 'having value V,' as distinguished from what he means by 'having value W' opposite of V.[31]

Continuing, Ducasse says:

> A collection of such statements, constituting a representative sampling of P's standard applicative usage of 'moral' and 'im-

[28] *Ibid.*, p. 176.

[29] See Arthur E. Murphy's "Ducasse's Theory of Appraisals," *Philosophy and Phenomenological Research*, Vol. XIII, No. 1, September, 1952, pp. 1–14. Also, in the same Journal, Frederick C. Dommeyer's "A Critical Examination of C. J. Ducasse's Metaphilosophy," Vol. XXI, No. 4, June, 1961, pp. 439–455.

[30] *Nature, Mind, and Death* (La Salle, Ill.: The Open Court Publishing Company, 1951), p. 36.

[31] *Ibid.*, p. 37.

> moral,' is the kind of datum, and the only kind, from which it will be possible to obtain inductively a definition of what 'to be moral' means as applied by P. Such statements, then, are the data of the primitive theoretical problems of philosophy. *They are the primitive, initial, empirically basic facts of philosophy,* which it is the task of philosophical reflection to construe. Hence *they constitute the subject matter which ultimately differentiates philosophy from the other systematic knowledge-seeking enterprises.*[32]

"P" may, of course, be a person or a group of persons.

It is clear from the above that Ducasse holds the theoretical problems of philosophy to be semantical. The predicates "true" or "false," or "good" or "bad," are not applicable to either the primitive appraisals of his 1941 view or the paradigmatic valuations of his 1951 version. But it is from such "standard" valuations that generalization and theory are possible about such value-predicates as "true," "good," "beautiful," "moral," etc.

It is clear that Ducasse's is a sophisticated view of philosophy in which he became aware early that the philosopher has no pipe line to deity, and that he is neither a prophet nor a seer. With marked insight, Ducasse saw that the philosopher's "traditional" task, though misunderstood by many, could be accomplished *after a fashion* by going to the language-facts, by utilizing scientifically the publicly stated paradigmatic valuations. What else is there that the philosopher could do, unless he wants entirely to abandon the "traditional" role of philosophy? Some have done that and, in substance, turned philosophy into a study of grammar of sorts. Others, closer to the "traditional" pattern of philosophy, interest only those who are content with ambiguities, unclear statements and ultimately, nonsense. If one wishes to stay within the classical vocation of the philosopher and make philosophy the knowledge-yielding activity that the great classical philosophers intended it to be, then Ducasse has something to offer. He has something to offer in that he is aware of the defects of classical philosophy but yet provides a way to do the task of such philosophy in a satisfactory manner, i.e., after the manner of the sciences. Professor A. E. Murphy was correct when he said in his article earlier re-

[32] *Ibid.,* pp. 37–38.

ferred to that Ducasse's philosophy "merits closer study than it has so far received." [33]

Ducasse's two most important philosophical insights have probably been these, namely, (1) that, in cases where "real" is not used as meaning "exists," "real" is then a value term; and from this follows Ducasse's "ontological liberalism" as regards metaphysical "positions"; and (2) that Causation is basically a relation between concrete events, and does not presuppose causal laws, but rather entails them if the same sorts of events ever recur; and that Causation is the irreducibly *triadic* relation between *Cause, Effect, and Circumstances,* which scientific experiments contemplate.[34] When this is fully realized, all kinds of artificial puzzles evaporate. For example, certain acts may be moral in the circumstances in which Eskimos live, which would be immoral in the circumstances existing in the United States, because their social effects are different: good in the Eskimo circumstances, but bad in the United States circumstances.

III

Some Other Contributions of Ducasse

There are some contributions of another sort that Ducasse has made to philosophy, and which ought to be noted in an introduction of this kind.

Probably very few professional philosophers would know at this late date that Ducasse had a major hand in establishing the Pacific Division of the American Philosophical Association.

Mrs. Mabel Ducasse, wife of Professor Ducasse, recently turned up a letter written to her in the latter part of April, 1924, by her husband from San Francisco when on his way home to Seattle from the meeting of the Western Division of the American Philosophical Association held April 17, 18, and 19 at the University of Chicago. In this letter, Ducasse had written: "I have just returned from Berkeley, where I had lunch with Adams and Loewenberg. The latter suggested that we organize a Pacific Division of the

[33] See p. 1.

[34] See Ducasse's *Causation and the Types of Necessity* (Seattle, Wash.: University of Washington Press, 1924).

American Philosophical Association, and we constituted ourselves a committee of organization, with myself as chairman."

Loewenberg and Ducasse had been friends at the Harvard University Graduate School, and it was this friendship that had led Ducasse to stop off and visit him on his way home to Seattle. During this visit, Ducasse had told Loewenberg how stimulating he had found the A.P.A. meeting at Chicago, deploring however the fact that the meetings of the Western Division were so far from the West Coast.

Upon Ducasse's return to Seattle, he wrote to a number of influential West Coast philosophers. The results were soon coming. In the March, 1925, issue of *The Philosophical Review* (p. 209) is the following statement: "The recently organized Pacific Division of the APA held its first meeting at the University of California Nov. 28 and 29, 1924." Professor Harold Chapman Brown addressed the meeting on: *The Material World—Snark or Boojum.* At the meeting, a constitution was adopted and officers were elected for the following year.

At the Pacific Division APA meeting on November 27 and 28, 1925, Ducasse read a paper entitled *A Liberalistic View of Truth.* At the business meeting, he was elected Secretary-Treasurer for the following year, with H. W. Stuart of Stanford as President and J. Loewenberg as Vice-President.

C. J. Ducasse was also a moving spirit in the establishing of the *Journal of Symbolic Logic* and the Association for Symbolic Logic.[35]

The initial event was a conversation early in 1934 between Ducasse and Charles A. Baylis. The latter was then an assistant professor in the Philosophy Department at Brown University where Ducasse was then a professor and chairman of the department.

Baylis had been an unusually able student in logic both at the University of Washington and at Harvard. Both Ducasse and Baylis knew of the need for such a Journal and Association as they had in mind, but they were aware also of the financial and technical problems entailed by their goal.

[35] See *The Journal of Symbolic Logic,* Vol. 27, No. 3, Sept., 1962, pp. 255–258; and Vol. 28, No. 4, Dec., 1963, p. 279.

A meeting was held on April 26, 1934, at the Harvard University Faculty Club. Baylis acted as secretary and wrote up the minutes of the meeting. The meeting was attended by: Professors C. A. Baylis, A. A. Bennett, C. J. Ducasse, P. Henle, E. V. Huntington, H. S. Leonard, Wm. T. Parry, W. V. Quine, and H. M. Sheffer. A. N. Whitehead and C. I. Lewis were unable to attend but sent word of their sympathetic interest in the objective of the meeting.

To this group, Professor Huntington read a letter from Professor Ducasse containing a suggestion that a journal of symbolic logic should bc established.

The record shows that Ducasse did much of the "leg-work" between the time of this Harvard meeting and the election of the first officers in 1935 by the organizing committee. Professor Ducasse became the first president of the American Association for Symbolic Logic, Inc., Publisher of the Journal.

The first meeting of the Association was held on Tuesday, September 1, 1936, in Cambridge, Massachusetts. It met jointly on this occasion with the American Mathematical Society.

Those acquainted with this Journal and Association today are well aware of the importance of the work of Ducasse and this early group of logicians.

CONTENTS

CURRENT PHILOSOPHICAL ISSUES

Essays in Honor of Curt John Ducasse

The following books have appeared thus far in this Series:

Causality in Natural Science—V. F. Lenzen
Emotions and Reason—V. J. McGill
A Good and Bad Government According to the New Testament—Jean Hering
The Phenomenological Approach to Psychiatry—J. H. Van den Berg
Operationism—A. C. Benjamin
Psychoanalysis and Ethics—Lewis S. Feuer
Culture, Psychiatry, and Human Values—Marvin K. Opler
The Origins of Marxian Thought—Auguste Cornu
Metascientific Queries—Mario Bunge
Anthropology and Ethics—May and Abraham Edel
Naturalism and Subjectivism—Marvin Farber
The Language of Education—Israel Scheffler
The Belief in a Life After Death—C. J. Ducasse
Philosophy, Science and the Sociology of Knowledge—Irving L. Horowitz
Philosophical Issues in Adult Education—Horace M. Kallen
Time and Modes of Being—Roman Ingarden
Methodology of the Behavioral Sciences—Rollo Handy
Principles of Empirical Realism—Donald Cary Williams
On the Human Subject—Nathan Rotenstreich

STANDPOINT COMMITMENTS AND THE FUNCTION OF PHILOSOPHY

MARVIN FARBER

> *When a question is to be investigated, one should not only ask oneself just which facts it is about, but also state them explicitly . . . the question should be stated as explicitly and unambiguously as possible. Thus, one will separate a complex question into the several questions making it up, and so clear away confusions.*
>
> C. J. DUCASSE [1]

I

From the Social-Historical Perspective

PHILOSOPHY MUST BE VIEWED as historically conditioned. That does not rule out freedom to construe the term "philosophy" in a novel manner, as contrasted with the realities of past usage and historical functioning. In this respect it is to be compared with poetry, music, and mathematics. A proposal to restrict usage narrowly would be as contrary to history as it would be to the spirit of creative inquiry.

The various conceptions of philosophy range all the way from mythology to philosophy as a science. One thinks of historical examples, from classical philosophy to rationalism, and Kant's challenge to metaphysics; and of such recent examples as Husserl, Whitehead, and others for whom philosophy had the dignity of scientific standing. That C. J. Ducasse is a member of this group is shown by some of his most characteristic writing.

In order to show the role played by philosophy historically, the

[1] "The Method of Knowledge in Philosophy," in *University of California Publications in Philosophy,* 1945, p. 146. Cf. also Ducasse, *Philosophy as a Science* (New York: Oskar Piest, 1941).

central problems and the motivation of representative philosophers should be recalled. Early in the modern period, the issue of Church versus State provided motivation, and that required a theory of reality and of man. Again, it was the status of the individual. Taking the concept of God seriously, in opposition to anthropomorphism, Spinoza extended the use of reason in philosophy. Kant felt impelled to defend science against "skepticism," and to safeguard religious values. Lotze was moved by the heart's desires and longings, once science has had its say. Spencer generalized the concept of evolution, and delimited the sphere of the knowable for the purposes of religion, as well as to insure noninterference with science. Kierkegaard was concerned with modes of religious experience, with subjectivism and existence. Despite his manysided scientific and philosophical interests, James was also conspicuously concerned with the will to believe, with the act of faith. Nietzsche, highly individual in his style of work, is nevertheless "philosophical." He represents what may be described as criticism unbounded. The emphasis is on the individual, although there is a goal for humanity, in vague terms.

It would not be possible to deny anyone of Nietzsche's or Kierkegaard's type membership in the world of philosophy, for one's definition could be challenged. Like the concept of art, the concept of philosophy is simply enlarged by new approaches or constructions. One thinks not only of generally recognized philosophers, or the major thinkers of the tradition; but also of near-philosophers, partial philosophers, and writers to be included by courtesy. It would be convenient to classify such writers as logical, illogical, or nonlogical. But even if the degree to which the standards of logic are observed or not observed were pointed out in each case, something would still be missed in the portrayal of philosophy. For external as well as internal considerations are relevant. Whether a writer is consistent with premises that have been accepted can be ascertained without touching the question of the historical functions of a philosopher, or the question of the sources of his premises. How would such a classification treat the Nazi "philosophy," for example? What if it were to be presented "logically" (in a narrow sense of the term, to be sure)? On the other hand, it may be noted that there was a frank rejection of the ideal of objective science on the part of the Nazi writers, in favor of a "political" or national science.

The conception of a *philosophia perennis* signifies a division of philosophers into the supposedly correct, eternal type, and the passing, inferior types.[2] Opposed to that view in the recent past is the conception of philosophy as a record of the reflections of a dominant class on life and the world at large. According to that conception, the very idea of a *philosophia perennis* must have a historical explanation, and must be referred to the social interests safeguarded by it.

Eternalism and temporalism are prominently represented through the centuries as conflicting types of philosophy, with different historical functions. An eternalist is likely to have an interest in the preservation of being, or of a mode of being; whereas a temporalist may be impelled by the unsatisfactoriness of present conditions of existence. Although it is true that every significant philosophy has served social-historical interests, it does not follow that there is falsification in every case. A rigorous, objective philosophy may be as sound logically as any scientific mode of inquiry, even though it may be committed to the service of human interests and their fulfillment. This indicates the way in which the limitations of a relativistic conception of philosophy may be overcome.

II

The Subject Matter of Philosophy

Despite extreme and varied examples of historical types of philosophy, some characteristics are sufficiently prevalent to warrant a definition of the domain for philosophic inquiry. All knowledge, and all experience, are generally regarded as falling within the province of philosophy—in a certain way. What is that way? Duplication of what is done in the special sciences or in ordinary experience cannot be meant. There must be a distinctively "philosophical" way of treating knowledge and experience.

Before attempting to answer this question, even partially, it

[2] Cf. Fritz-Joachim von Rintelen, editor, *Philosophia Perennis,* two volumes (Regensburg, 1930).

may be well to add to its scope. Does all existence also fall to philosophy, and in what sense? It is characteristic of one tradition to tie existence down to subjectivity. That is done by regarding existence as meaningful only in relationship to a knowing subject. As a result, all talk of existence is restricted, and in some notable cases, submerged. Carefully formulated definitions and assumptive usage may predetermine the range of the concept of existence. That is illustrated by the subjective version of existence, so prominent among recent and contemporary writers.

The way in which existence is restricted to subjectivity must be clarified if a domain for philosophy is to be secured. It is not enough to state that everything talked about in scientific inquiry is related to human knowledge and experience. The lines must be drawn carefully if the domain of philosophy is not to lapse into that of the sciences. It is not suggested that a calamity would result thereby. But it is necessary to ascertain whether anything would be left out if the sciences are taken to be all-inclusive in their scope. That scientific inquiry cannot be limited to physical existence is shown by the nature of mathematics. The practical objective of pure mathematics is application to the realm of existence. But there must be freedom for idealization and ideal constructions. Philosophy requires such freedom on the greatest possible scale. One of its functions is to provide clarification of the processes of idealization in all regions of experience. It also undertakes to formulate explanatory principles in consonance with the established body of knowledge.

The question of the autonomy of philosophy is raised therewith. It is sufficient at this point to recognize that a domain for inquiry need not be physical or cultural, and that it may be ideal in character, even though the point of departure and the ultimate objective must be the real world of existence.

Now what determines the nature and range of a "subject matter?" There is little difficulty, initially at least, in such cases as parasitology, economics, or formal science. Although there are questions of interrelationship, the areas of interest of arithmetic, geometry, set theory, and formal logic can be delimited for the process of inquiry. For Dewey, the subject matter of logic is inquiry in a broad sense. The range of logical analysis is coextensive with that of possible knowledge; and the range of intentional analysis (the method of descriptive phenomenology) extends as far as possible experience, subject to the special conditions that are imposed.

The question of the subject matter of philosophy depends upon the question "What is philosophy?" As has been indicated, there is no unique, unalterable answer to that question. Without becoming involved in a tenuous relativism, one can allow for different meanings of "philosophy," with resultant changes in the questions allowed in the universe of discourse.

If one could really begin with a clean slate, a formally determinate system might be possible. But that is not the case, in view of the types of question treated by so-called philosophers, at present as well as in the past. Some questions are traditionally rooted; others are of current motivation and reference. Some are meaningful in terms of one conception of philosophy, but are alien to other conceptions of philosophy.

III

Standpoint Questions and the "Meeting of Minds"

The different motives leading to philosophic discussion and the different functions served in its long history enable us to account for its changing subject matter. There are also the traditional "standpoint" differences, and diverse individual conceptions of philosophic inquiry, with some degree of creative freedom in combining features of the arts as well as the sciences. Philosophic utterances range all the way from incomprehensible poetry to intelligible, rigorous science.

If there is to be a "meeting of minds" and rational communication in philosophy, the divergent standpoints must be reckoned with. There are questions and statements that are meaningful in terms of one standpoint, but are not accepted as legitimate, real, or valid from another point of view. Assumed absolutes or special metaphysical principles and modes of experience provide ready illustrations. Such questions are to be construed on the basis of their own premises and in their own terms, in any case. That does not preclude appraisal of the premises and basic concepts from other points of view: and also in the light of the established knowledge and evidence. The problem is to avoid a relativism of points of view, while doing full justice to whatever merits there may be in standpoint-conditioned knowledge. In its best form, the latter appears as hypothetical knowledge, conditioned by special premises and definitions. The ideal of tolerance is observed if every point of view is considered with respect to its own premises. For the purposes of appraisal, logic and the principles of methodology must be applied.

There are always secondary or derived questions in a given philosophy, and they may be quite disturbing. Thus, the questions defined in terms of a traditional theological system may be modified by another theological system, or disallowed as meaningless by a nontheological system. How "secondary" questions have appeared to be vitally important can be seen in the case of the "great debate" in which Royce and other idealists engaged near the close of the last century. The fate of the "absolute" hung in the balance. Could it be said that humanity, or the world, would be affected by the outcome?

IV

Restrictive Principles and the Function of Philosophy

The manysided functions of philosophy in the past have had the merit of giving expression to new and unlimited lines of thought, resulting at times in the incubation of new special sciences. Such "pathfinding" activities were possible because the types of question were not restricted to a carefully delimited system. New problems and questions have arisen historically, and in the course of experience. There are also ever new types of question arising as a result of the constructive activities of the mind, especially when viewed in reflection. If problems and methods are not to be delimited at any one time; if methods are not to be outlined once and for all; and if questions arise which are not to be assigned to existing special systems of knowledge; then there is at least a tentative place for "philosophical" questions and procedures.

But the procedures of philosophy are not relieved of the burden of human error. Just as all scientific statements are subject on principle to possible future modification or cancellation, and just as a principle of fallibilism is not to be denied, quite generally, for any claims to scientific knowledge, so philosophical knowledge is unable to overcome these limitations. The attempts to do so occupy a considerable portion of the historical lore of philosophy, from the ancient Greeks to the present. But they have met with failure. Man must live with the consciousness of finitude and possible error, even though he manages to do very well in practice. Philosophical writers cannot disregard the limitations of experience and the possibility of error that may affect all inquiry. The recognition of this principle prevents any claim to philosophical exclusiveness, as involving so to speak a novel epistemological realm of apodictic knowledge. There is always the possibility of assimilating any significant philosophical proposition to existing or emerging special systems of knowledge. To "possible future modification" and "fallibilism" must be added the principle of nonexclusiveness, or of possible absorption in a special system of knowledge.

Within due limits, philosophical explanatory positions such as idealism (subjectivism) or naturalism (objectivism) may also be subject to the restriction of nonexclusiveness. A transcendent, supernatural level of being could not be expected to enter into total commerce with a naturalistic realm, if at all. Apart from such cases of ontological transcendence, there is always a possible analogue, or a linguistic equivalent, in alternative positions. But there is a far-reaching difference between the mere use of linguistic devices, or of logical structures, and the actual nature of existence, as reported by scientific knowledge and ordinary experience. The principle of possible linguistic intertranslation yields to the principle of the priority of physical existence as soon as the interest turns to ontology. There is no room in ontology for imaginative constructions. The constitutive activities of the mind, individual or social, often result in purely ideal objects. They belong to a different order than what is established as a matter of fact, with a locus in the realm of physical events.

V

The Autonomy of Philosophy

The autonomy of philosophy is not to be decreed or safeguarded by the vote of any group of scholars. A later vote could always rescind an earlier action.

Total difference and independence are not necessarily required for the purposes of autonomy. Philosophy could still be declared autonomous if it were construed as a discipline founded on the sciences, and hence as dependent upon the sciences. It is a curious fact that the charge of "dependence upon the sciences," or "following the sciences," may seem to be damaging to the ears of the very person who seeks to subordinate philosophy to religion, or to the prevailing ideas of his social system. More curious still is the avowal of a philosophy free from presuppositions supposedly with no antecedent or ulterior commitments, on the basis of a social order tacitly accepted as a finality, with all its vested interests and special privileges. The "pure ego" is already a fully sophisticated citizen; and the "good will" that is extolled is not likely to question property interests.

There will be philosophical inquiry so long as there are philosophical questions, which means questions exceeding or not fitting into the given special systems of knowledge. Whether such questions will always be handled by professional philosophers is another matter.

Perhaps the term "autonomy" suggests too much, or more than has to be said for the justification of philosophy. There should be no suggestion that philosophy as a whole may not be questioned critically; and no suggestion that only "initiates" within its field are to deal with its problems. It is hardly necessary to observe that the class of so-called initiates, whether official or self-styled, would constitute an unhappy totality.

The burden of an answer should be placed on the occurrence of questions peculiar to philosophy, and not to be answered by any of the existing special sciences or organized systems of knowledge. Whether there are to be professional scholars mainly devoted to such questions will depend upon (a) their legitimacy, and also (b) upon practical considerations.

(a) Questions meaningful in a logically organized system of knowledge, which are not constructible in terms of one of the special sciences or formal systems of knowledge, may be assigned to another discipline, and that could be philosophy. Philosophy need not be the name for a single system of knowledge, specialized in its turn. It is in fact the title for a group of systems, more or less incomplete, and comprising theoretical as well as valuational disciplines. All such systems must conform to logical requirements. They may be hypothetical, explanatory, or descriptive in character, with special conditions indicated that mark them off as distinctive. In this sense, philosophy is an extension of the sciences. This extended usage is highly desirable, for in its most general sense science means "logically organized knowledge," with the requirement that all the procedures for obtaining and establishing knowledge or answering questions be acceptable logically. There is thus no fateful line of cleavage between philosophy and *other* types of science. That there are differences is no more surprising than that there are differences among the special sciences, including formal systems. The question of legitimacy can thus be conveniently answered in one way. That still allows all the free play that may be needed for the framing of questions said to be distinctive—questions that do not happen to have been absorbed by special sciences in the past, although some of them at least might have been, by appropriate extension of the questions allowed.

(b) It is a practical matter, as to whether a separate group of specialists devote themselves largely to philosophical questions. The cultural system must decide whether that is feasible. Right now, there are educational functions best served thereby; and there are good scholarly reasons as well. But that need not always be the case, so that philosophical questions could be handled by special scientists, or by others, provided that they have the necessary knowledge and interest.

VI

Methods of Procedure and Assumptive Arguments

There are methods of procedure in philosophy, and not one method, in response to diverse problems. Methods have their proper regions of application; they should not be overextended in their use. While legitimate in one context, they may be nonpertinent or misleading in other contexts. This is seen, for example, when a subjective procedure is used for the purposes of a general philosophy, and especially to provide an ontology. There are questions that are "proper" to a mode of inquiry; and there are questions that are "strange" to it.

Methods are instituted to solve problems or to answer questions. Now problems or questions arise directly in the course of natural experience; or they arise because of the use of conceptual devices, including systems of knowledge and special procedures; or they are due to a standpoint that has been adopted, for which there is usually indebtedness to a long tradition. The diversity of methods is the response to the diversity of sources of problems.

It is only natural to become enamored of a procedure to which one has become accustomed and especially if it has proved to be fruitful in its context. A kind of intellectual inertia may be added to the cultural factors making for the preservation of a standpoint, and for vested procedures.

An important stage in philosophic inquiry must be the relentless search for assumptive elements in all the theses and issues with which it is concerned. It is not suggested that it would be possible to dispense with assumptions in all senses of the term, or that it would be desirable to do so. But apart from such cases as assumptions in formal science and explanatory principles in empirical science, assumptions may also involve the acceptance of authority, or of special entities and cognitive faculties. A certain analysis, definition, and scale of value may be assumed. Assumed elements enter into philosophical thought tacitly as well as explicitly. It is necessary to bring all such elements to light, and to consider their role and standing in experience.

On the other hand, the acknowledgment of an existing world, or of a pre-existing world, has been declared to be a matter of "assumption." That is questionable usage, however, inasmuch as the case for an independently existing or pre-existing world may rest on established matters of fact. It is misleading to regard such basic facts as "assumptions." That would be in itself an assumptive designation, if the real world of experience and of scientific inquiry is meant. To regard that world as an assumption could only appear meaningful on the basis of special beliefs or an artificial construction. The latter occurs if the field of existence is restricted to the objects of actual experience. From that point of view, all talk of independent existence or pre-existence (meaning existence antecedent to the actual process of experience) would involve special assumptions. This entire point is assumptive, however. It cannot be sustained in the face of the established knowledge provided by experience and the sciences.

In general, assumptive arguments, issues, and standpoints are prominent in philosophy, and are part and parcel of its tradition. The concept of the "given" rests upon assumptions that must be questioned—as though there were a realm of existence "given" to "the mind." For such an assumed construction as the Kantian theory of the mind and of existence, one may indeed speak of "the given." But another analysis may be considered, one that is carefully guided by the facts concerning man as a knower and his subordinate place in the physical world.

It would be illuminating and rewarding to unmask numerous "perennial" issues as maintained assumptively. They belong to the honorific order of insolubilia, well calculated to preserve work for countless philosophers in the future because the conditions laid down forbid a satisfactory solution.

The logical quest for examining assumptions is still far from the seemingly heroic aim to dispense with all assumptions or presuppositions. That seems to be the thoroughgoing approach that would eliminate all naiveté and dogmatism, or at least a precondition to the correct approach. It has been a prominent motive in modern and recent philosophy.

VII

The Aim of Freedom from Presuppositions

The ideal of complete emancipation from all presuppositions has had its historical significance. It has signified a means for avoiding cultural influences, whether political, social, or religious, or due to the philosophical tradition itself. The claim that the Hegelian philosophy was free from presuppositions was declared to be the greatest presupposition. The circumstances leading to Brentano's difficulties with the Church may well have been in Husserl's mind when he referred to the ideal of freedom from presuppositions in his *Logical Investigations.* That would seem to be a truly radical ideal, and would mean beginning without any prior acknowledgment of epistemological, metaphysical, or valuational principles. How is that to be understood?

In the course of everyday experience, and in all scientific

thinking, the existence of the natural world is acknowledged as a matter of basic fact. The ideal of freedom from presuppositions would involve the suspension of all ontological commitments. That would mean the refusal to assert existence or reality even in the apparently assured presence of a stimulus, because of the fallibility of experience and knowledge. It would also mean the refusal to assert the antecedent existence of nature and of cultural traditions, as well as the existence of areas contiguous to the immediate perceptual field.

It would seem that only a solipsism of the present moment would satisfy the demands of an extreme radicalism, in this sense. But this is really a reduction to non-significance of the ideal of radicalism.

In a positive, constructive sense, it is enough to "question" all epistemological, metaphysical, and valuational grounds or premises, with the aim to make clear their methodological function, as well as their standing in their respective systems of knowledge. If beliefs are placed in abeyance for the purposes of such critical inquiry, that does not mean the rejection of our knowledge of existence, or any other kind of knowledge. Emancipation from "absolutes" of all kinds—"necessary" being, apodictic truth, or value principles conferred by authority, whether external or internal—would well justify the ideal of freedom from presuppositions. Some of the very principles that yield to the procedure of the systematic suspension of beliefs may be reinstated in another properly qualified form, in a manner determined by the evidence. The ideal of freedom from presuppositions turns out to be a preparatory stage in the process of examining all beliefs and processes of knowledge for evidence, validity, or consequences. In an exaggerated form it may take the place of the very absolutes that are being dislodged. In that case, it turns out to be a negative procedure, sterile so far as the real world is concerned.

In short, one does not leave the natural world when questioning that world. Nor does one dispense with factual knowledge about existence when adopting an attitude of universal, "radical" inquiry. This quest is aimed at beliefs and assumptions regarded as underlying the experience and knowledge of existence. Whether existence is to be acknowledged as a basic fact, or regarded as the correlate of experience and belief, is of deciding importance. What the term "existence" is taken to mean may well predetermine the outcome of philosophic thought.

VIII

On the Meaning of Existence

The question of the meaning of existence has been and no doubt always will be a recurrent theme for philosophy, in keeping with its interest in the clarification of basic ideas. Existence is being understood progressively with each advance in knowledge, and in the normal course of experience. Whether the philosophical treatments of existence have added to that process, or have contributed new difficulties, must be considered carefully.

What does existence mean? More than that, perhaps: what does it really mean; and what does "really" mean? Vastly different answers have been given, from the common-sense or literal interpretation in terms of the science of a given period, to its interpretation in terms of a theory of experience. The Berkeleyan view, that *esse* is *percipi,* is made plausible with the aid of a simple confusion in usage and an unconscious fallacy, involving the term "idea." The term "idea" names a quality of an object, and is also assumed to be "in the mind," in a sense never clarified. For Kant, the question of existence is more complex, in view of his effort to do justice to the claims of science and realism, as well as to the claims of idealism. The status of existence as a category of the understanding is obscured by the doctrine of a thing in itself.

If care is not taken, the question of the "meaning" of existence may be stated in an unanswerable form. One could indeed say "Existence is existence," and not be wiser. The suggestion is then tempting, to treat existence as inaccessible, or to construe it in terms of the processes of experience. It is well to replace questions that are not being answered satisfactorily by questions that can be answered. Thus, special questions can be asked about the properties of existence, about existent events, and about selected features or regions of existence, with answers to be provided primarily by the sciences.

Of direct interest to philosophy, because its answer makes a difference in the discussion of important issues, is the *factual* question, as to whether there was a realm of existence before there were human knowers. The earth is now estimated to be billions of years old; and the origin of man is judged to be comparatively recent, with estimates ranging from 50,000 years to a million years. Hence human knowing is a recently emerging event in nature.

If this is granted in principle, so that only matters of detail are subject to change, some writers are bound to be hard pressed to justify their positions. Whether the earth is one half the indicated age, or twice as old, is of little importance to what is at issue. The indicated facts and the argument would indeed be altered by evidence that man "has always been" (a view treated sympathetically by Jaspers), although no positive thesis concerning the limitation of existence to experience would be established thereby. But the available evidence does not support that view. The literature of existentialism and phenomenology has continued the effort of past idealists to exploit the relatedness of existence as known to a knower. This quaint form of argumentation, which engaged philosophers early in the century in the controversy between realists and idealists, lives on in recent subjectivism, and at times appears in an explicit and recognizable form. The belief that the thesis of independent existence is outflanked thereby is simply based upon a *non sequitur*.

The affirmation or the acknowledgment of an antecedently existing realm of events is a primary condition for giving meaning to "existence." It is bigger than human knowers, and bigger than any actual relatedness to human knowers. To say that there is always a "possible" relationship to a knower is merely to introduce an infinitely pliable condition, which is not really effective in any way.

If prior existence with respect to human knowers is a matter of fact, then there are significant consequences concerning the concept of existence. The intricate web of epistemological arguments must be reconsidered in the light of the fact of independence. Other features of existence—spatial, temporal, structural, historical, and descriptive—may also be pointed out, as matters of fact. It then becomes clear that existence "means" all such things and infinitely more, and that it is not a "surd," or an ultimate concept incapable of clarification. Definition in a narrow, traditional sense is not always workable, or even desirable. That applies to the most fundamental concepts. Clarification, with the aid of factual propositions, will be sufficient in such cases.

IX
On the Subjective Treatment of Existence

The "subjective" mode of viewing existence is strongly established in the philosophy of the twentieth century. This historical line of approach derives from St. Augustine and Descartes, and in recent philosophy, from Kierkegaard and Husserl. It is also illustrated by numerous "covert" subjectivists.[3]

One motive leading to the subjective view of existence was sensitivity to the status of the individual. In the medieval period, the status of the individual was defended philosophically in opposition to the realistic conception of universals. The nominalists anticipated modern empiricism, for which the nature and rights of the individual constituted a prime motive. This line of development merged with the sciences, and was associated with cultural movements resulting from the commercial and industrial revolution. But Kierkegaard's interest in the individual was by no means connected with an interest in natural science. It is sufficient to cite his scornful reference to the scientific use of the microscope as distinguished from the dimension of spiritual interests with which he was concerned.[4] In this sense, he was not a continuator of the nominalist-empiricist tradition. More pertinent would be tracing his intellectual alignment to the mystics of the medieval period. The mystics in effect presented a challenge to the claim

[3] Cf. M. Farber, "Pervasive Subjectivism," *Philosophy and Phenomenological Research,* Vol. XXV, No. 4, June, 1965.

[4] Cf. S. Kierkegaard, *Diary,* translated by G. M. Anderson (New York: Philosophical Library, 1960), pp. 95 ff. Thus, "Of all sciences, physical science is decidedly the most insipid . . . The researcher . . . begins dissipating his brain on details: now someone is going . . . to the moon, . . . now the Devil knows where in the arse after an intestinal worm; now we must have a telescope, now a microscope: who in the name of Satan can stand it!" It was not "dialectically clear" to Kierkegaard, "*how* philosophy is to make use of natural science."

that the Church was the sole vehicle of mediation between the believing individual and the spiritual order. Different though Kierkegaard's views were from those of the mystics, they nevertheless shared crucial features of the privacy of experience and the appeal to subjective evidence.

The subjectivism of Kierkegaard is crude and undeveloped in comparison with the explicitly elaborated subjectivism of Husserl and those that derive from him. The methodological lines are drawn clearly by the latter, and a self-contained region for inquiry is outlined. This region is peculiarly philosophical, for it is attained only by means of a universal suspension of judgment, along with a restriction to essential relations and laws. Existence can only be meaningful for such a method through relatedness to activities of experience. The "noetic" activities of experience are meaningfully related to their "noematic" correlates, or to that which is meant as such. Philosophic inquiry is therewith limited to "pure" conscious experience and its correlates. The only possible version of existence for such a view would be an existence "constituted" by means of processes of experience, within the conditions of the method. As for natural existence, there is nothing that survives the "nullification" (or "destruction") of the world, through the "reduction" or restriction to pure conscious experience. It was not possible to restore existence to its natural status, once the "retirement to immanence" was effected. The acknowledgment of a "pregiven life-world" showed that Husserl was abundantly aware of this problem. Existence presented a "methogenic" problem for his subjectivism. The point was, to show how one could account for existence once the subjective turn has been completed. It is really an insoluble problem on that basis, for the subjective realm for inquiry is doubly removed from the order of real events. That the latter must be brought in "from outside" is attested to by formulations such as "pregiven" life-worlds.

It is only the overextended, universalized subjective procedure that is embarrassed by this problem. The subjective procedure is designed to assist in the analysis of meaning, and in the clarification of structures of experience. It cannot function as an ontological method, except in a secondary, auxiliary sense. In short, a monistic conception of method must yield to a pluralistic conception.

For the subjectivist, the meaning of transcendence, or its very possibility, is a crucial problem. Transcendent of an individual's subjective realm (that is to say, his reflective view of his conscious processes of experience) are other individuals, who must be shown to be equally real. Also transcendent is the entire realm of physical existence, including animal bodies and cultural activities. But "transcendence" also refers to higher levels of being, or to values not realized in our experience, such as "freedom" in a vacuous sense, or immortality in a sense different from everything in experience. "Transcendence" is really a group title for various methogenic problems, conferred by a subjective procedure in philosophy. The advantages deriving from the secure "here and now" of subjectively viewed experience, in its frozen eidetic form, are finally outweighed by the disadvantages incurred by having to proceed beyond inner experience ontologically or valuationally. Unless one begins with real existence as the basic fact, he can never provide it or account for it on subjective grounds. From subjectivity only subjectivity can be derived. It must be recognized that subjectivity is an artifice, a device of method for descriptive analysis. It is ancillary, instrumental. The whole man, like the whole world, requires a group of methodological devices and procedures, to meet the many types of problem, and to answer the highly diversified kinds of question that arise. The physical-organic world meets the cultural world in man. To restrict our philosophical method to subjectivism would be an error of one-sidedness as well as overextension, for which the just punishment is the insoluble problem of transcendence.

X

On Describing the World

The issue concerning the nature of existence and its status with respect to human knowers presents the problem of transcendence in its most crucial form. Discussion of that issue has been handicapped by the failure to recognize methogenic questions for what they are—i.e., as being due to the methods employed and the basic premises. It is possible for subjectivists and objectivists simply to philosophize past one another without touching.

The view that the subjectivist principle is a condition of the world of existence has a strong appeal, and is not easily dislodged by criticism. In its radical formulation, there is no world "by itself"; there can only be a human-related world. So the line of thought goes. The appeal is to description. But description can be selective; it can be subordinated to a dominant theory of man and the world; and it can be achieved by means of methods with their own merits or limitations. Do these considerations apply to the question of the relationship of existence and knowing?

When one perceives a mountain, and perceives it truly, it is a mountain that can endure apart from the perceptual process that is involved. The report about its various features—its height above sea level, its geographic location, etc.—provides a description of an objective mountain. If an observer's "interpretations" are misleading, or if he departs from the facts in any way, the description will be judged in error. One may include mention of his personal appreciation and feelings upon seeing the mountain, and that might aid in conveying an impression of the grandeur of the object viewed, in relationship to a relatively diminutive observer. In any case, it is always possible to distinguish between the features of the mountain, the set of appearances of the mountain as viewed from an observer's perspective, and the emotional or aesthetic reactions of the observer. If one is interested in deposits of metals, or in lumber, etc., his description of the resources of the mountain will surely be concerned with an objective formation of nature, with an independently existing world that endures, or as it may be termed, a relatively persistent event. For the mountain is an event, even if it "endures" longer or has greater temporal spread or thickness than, say, a thunderstorm.

Now let us suppose that the object for description is a bear in a forest. The same distinctions may be drawn as in the foregoing illustration. The object (or event) will not endure as long, *really,* and not merely because you or I observe it. We are in the picture to a certain extent. There are perspectives and aspects; there are meanings and interpretations; there are true observations and perhaps erroneous ones. But the bear, which pre-existed our present relationship to him, will again enjoy independent existence if our interest in him is purely cognitive.

The same applies to human beings, who are also independent of one another in at least one ontological (physical-existential) sense. There are, however, relations of dependence to be noted, with respect to man as a culturally conditioned being. So far as I am concerned, as a mere observer, there is no existential dependence on me. Not only can I think of the human being I am describing as independently existent; I must think of him in that way, or my conception of him is incorrect as a matter of fact.

The matter is simple enough if I consider the world and its parts in relationship to me as an observer. My more or less true description of the mountain, or of the bear, are accounts of parts of the independent world. I introduce elements that are in part my contribution—the color-aspect that I apprehend, the unity I discern, as a fusion of successive experiences, the awe or caution I may feel—these are among the complications to which I contribute. It is nevertheless easily possible to distinguish the subjective from the objective-subjective factors, and to speak with confidence of various features of the mountain by itself, or the bear by itself.

The private who describes his sergeant may make it more difficult to carry through an objective description. But even that may be done, with sufficient care. A group of observers, or various reports of witnesses, will enable us to have a description of the sergeant in relationship not only to privates under his command, but to his superior officers, to merchants, and to members of his family. The sergeant, like the mountain and the bear, is independent of the observer.

Now there is one cardinal objection to this line of thought that will certainly occur to subjectivists, overt or covert, declared or undeclared. It is too straightforward, and too clear. Those defects are sufficient to make the account unfit for some conspicuous philosophical purposes of the present.

The observer has been taken to be an individual, whose reports are to be tested in comparison with the reports of others. If the observer is a subjectivistic philosopher, he may well ask, "Who, then, are these so-called 'others'?" Following Husserl, Merleau-Ponty (in his *Phenomenology of Perception*) assigns a lower level of certitude to the status of other persons. Construed as a methodological device, a subjectivistic procedure has its limited usefulness. But to draw ontological consequences from its use would be naïve indeed. It would reduce the procedure to the level of a deceptive device.

Would the argument be altered by making the world of existence dependent upon a society of knowers? But if all knowers were to disappear, would there be no world? And would the same be true of the time when there were no knowers? If one replies that there would be no known worlds without knowers, that would merely have the force of a redundancy. Merleau-Ponty's convenient disposal of this question gives the impression of a defense of a lost cause. To shift from the fact of the recent emergence of knowers, which supports the thesis of natural independence, to the fact of man's relationship to the world, which is meaningful only because of man, is evidence of unclarified motives and rational processes. The procedure consists in defining meaningfulness in relationship to man, and in using the redundancy that results to imply ontological dependence (or necessary relatedness to human subjectivity).

In the case of outer perception, it is the world of existence, or more exactly, its parts, that are being described, unless one errs. One can also attend, in reflection, to the experiencing of the world or its parts. There is still a possibility of error, although it is greatly reduced through the specialization of the procedure.

What can be said to a person who denies that there is an independent world, and who insists that one is only concerned with the contents of his mind? In the spirit of Moore, one might appeal to him to grant the reality of one's hand, or of his own hand, as being in an external world. The point of the appeal would be to try to shake him out of a narrow, stubborn position that violates the lessons of experience, and utilizes a narrow, stubborn conception of the mind, the body, other minds and bodies, and the world. The argument for solipsism amounts to a game that almost no one takes seriously, probably not even the solipsist. The point that one grant the reality of a hand may be to arouse an awareness of the willful arbitrariness of the solipsist view. No position can be taken seriously that violates the facts established through experience and the methods of knowledge.

On the other hand, solipsism may amount to a methodological stage, as seen in pure phenomenology, where "transcendental egology" is the starting point. With the procedure explicitly outlined, that is admittedly a legitimate stage of method. It is a device for the clarification and understanding of the processes of experience. There need be no denial of an external world. There is merely a suspension of belief in it. This "methodological solipsism" is not the dogmatic doctrine so well suited for philosophical freshmen. That the elaboration of a "pure egology" proves to be too tempting to stand merely as a device of method, and that it becomes a means of instating idealism as a universal philosophy, is no argument against its legitimacy as a stage of inquiry. It does not have to be misused, or misplaced.

Dogmatic solipsism, as an extreme form of subjective idealism, faces the danger of being reduced to a solipsism of the present and hence passing moment; or of being rejected as untrue to experience and knowledge. Probably better than exhorting the self-styled genuine solipsist to grant the existence of his body, or someone else's body, would be to ask him to grant the independent reality of his parents, living or dead, or the germs that may destroy a living being. If he refuses, and allows his subjective processes to apply solely, probably all further appeals would be fruitless. The critique along the lines of experience and established knowledge would be the only method of reply, to release such a person from his self-imposed caricature of what experience tells him.

The only way open to a solipsist is to proceed to a universal idealism, operating with an absolute mind. To protect himself against the charge of inconsistency with experience, he may enter the more comfortable, larger system of an absolute subjectivity, with the existence of the world the prime problem.

The best way to treat solipsism is to recognize and appropriate its possible merits, and to subordinate it, as a specialized mode of inquiry, under the more general heading of methods of inquiry, comprising objective as well as subjective types. How individual solipsists are to be treated will depend upon their behavior.[5]

But solipsism is by no means a serious obstacle in the way of describing the world. It may well be the least important one, because it is almost never taken seriously. Far more important are those subjectivistic views of the world that manifest an antiscientific tendency. Added to them are the onesided, selective, and sometimes falsifying accounts of the natural and cultural world. The reasons may be purely intellectual, and due to well-intentioned errors, especially in the case of the external natural world. Or they may be due to considerations of faith, motivating a rejection of the scientific view of man and the world, either directly by a critique of naturalism, or indirectly on epistemological or moral grounds. In the case of the cultural world there are further factors, affecting even some social scientists themselves. The influence of private interests and of cultural traditions is so great that it is extremely difficult to avoid antecedent bias in what should be objective inquiry. That is why even a highly sophisticated philosopher may be heard on occasion to regard social class distinctions as finalities, and to repeat racist dogmas as though they were verities. Is there anything to guarantee that a subjective investigator will not be misled by such influences?

The most rapidly changing aspects of the real world are cultural in character. Resistance to change may be manifested in slanted, misleading accounts of social events and relations. But error can be exposed just as effectively as in the case of the natural world. Observers and their reports can be examined in the light of the relevant established knowledge, and with respect to other reports. The question of the apprehension of social reality has at least one great advantage over the apprehension of the natural world. There is less inclination to interpose the contributive activities of the mind, and to declare limits to what can be known. It seems that it is far easier to think of closing off, mutilating, or even

[5] Concerning solipsism, cf. G. Dawes Hicks, *Critical Realism* (London: Macmillan & Company, Ltd., 1938), pp. 262 ff., where Hicks tries to show that it is contradictory and logically untenable. Cf. also V. I. Lenin, *Materialism and Empiriocriticism* (New York: International Publishers, 1927), in which solipsism appears as the outcome of subjectivism.

annihilating the natural world, than to contemplate changing the social world in any significant respect.

XI

Beyond Standpoint Commitments

The traditional conflict between rival standpoints—idealism and realism, or spiritualism and materialism, etc.—has led some writers to seek to disqualify both of the contending sides. It is possible to define a pair of opposing standpoints in such a way that they are totally incompatible, or only partially incompatible. If they are so construed that they cannot be affected by knowledge provided by the sciences and ordinary experience, it would seem clear that they have the status of articles of faith. But not all representatives of such positions are to be regarded as disposed of therewith, for there are different degrees and manners of commitment. If the theses in question are rendered explicit and precise; and if all of them are considered in connection with our knowledge of the relevant facts; then it would be expected that a choice between them may be made in certain important respects. That would apply particularly to the concepts of time, space, and existence. It is not necessary to go so far as to pronounce "a plague on all those houses." Some of them may well succumb to criticism, but not necessarily all of them. One must be prepared to recognize the instances in which thinkers have achieved correct or promising insights, regardless of the standpoint.

A critical, reflective philosophy must also be self-critical and self-reflective. It must be prepared to consider all alternative views or positions in their full significance. The ideal of total reflection is a distinguishing mark of philosophy. That embraces a thoroughgoing radicalism in its method, so that there are no unexamined assumptions. Neutrality with respect to standpoint commitments can only be allowed in contexts not accessible to the methods of reason. There can be no "tolerance" of alternatives where the facts or the methods of reason can decide.

The entire procedure has its motivation. The ideal of unmotivated inquiry is as impossible as it is indefensible. The motivation should be made explicit, so that it can be appraised. It may be purely rational; or it may be concerned with human welfare. A complete philosophy must be both "pure" and "applied." That does not mean transcending the existing social conditions or the human realm. In important respects, philosophy will always be historically conditioned.

State University of New York at Buffalo

UNDERSTANDING PHILOSOPHY

MORRIS LAZEROWITZ

Philosophy is certainly an activity which needs constantly to be defended. Indeed, it is hardly conceivable at all except as a constant struggle against sophistry.
PETER WINCH, Review in *Mind,* Vol. LXXIII, 1964, p. 608.

Metaphysics has a long and distinguished history, and it is consequently unlikely that there are any new truths to be discovered in descriptive metaphysics. But this does not mean that the task of descriptive metaphysics has been, or can be, done once and for all. It has constantly to be done over again. If there are no new truths to be discovered, there are old truths to be rediscovered.
PETER STRAWSON, *Individuals,* Introduction (London: Methuen, 1959) .

Time and again I have emerged from a course of reading in philosophy with the conviction that the authors were really avoiding specific problems by converting them into tenuous sophistries that have very little real meaning.
ERNEST JONES, *Free Associations* (New York: Basic Books, 1959) , p. 60.

What is your aim in philosophy?—To shew the fly the way out of the fly-bottle.
LUDWIG WITTGENSTEIN, *Philosophical Investigations* (New York: The Macmillan Company, 1953) , p. 103.

PROFESSOR DUCASSE ONCE SAID that the ills of philosophy are chiefly due to the lack on the part of philosophers of "a clear realization of the nature of the problem to be solved on the one hand, and, on the other, knowledge of the sort of method appropriate to the solution of problems of the nature given." [1] He also pointed out that philosophical divergences of opinion are not occa-

[1] *Philosophy as a Science: Its Matter and Its Method* (New York: Oskar Piest, 1941) , p. xviii.

sioned by "inadequate observation or description." [2] And Wittgenstein, in a similar vein, has remarked: "[Philosophical problems] are, of course, not empirical problems; they are solved, rather, by looking into the workings of our language. . . ." [3] These are useful things to say about a field of intellectual endeavor which is highly prized and at the same time is characterized by continuous anarchy that resists scientific discipline. For they tend to sharpen our awareness of the condition of total drouth in philosophy; and they heighten the need to seek for an explanation of this condition. It will be the aim of this essay to improve our understanding of philosophy by looking at it through the eyes of an important thinker, Freud, who was interested in philosophy but turned away from it in disappointment.

Aristotle said in his *Metaphysics* that "All men by nature desire to know." As a generalization his statement appears to be an exaggeration of the actual state of affairs; but it cannot be doubted that those who enter into the sciences are motivated by a desire to know. It would seem that those who take up technical philosophy, or to use Freud's term "philosophy proper," are also moved by a wish to know, for philosophy looks like science, and has, indeed, been conceived of as the most fundamental of all the sciences. As is natural enough, Freud viewed it as a field of human endeavor from which important and useful things may be learned. In a letter he wrote in 1907 to a Viennese publisher he included Theodor Gomperz's *Griechische Denker* in his list of ten books, to which, as he said, "a man owes some of his knowledge of life and his *Weltanschauung;* books which one has enjoyed and gladly recommends to others, but do not evoke awe or dwarf one by their great stature." [4]

Freud's words seem to be a plain enough indication that he held philosophy in high esteem, that he looked on it as a subject whose cultivation would certainly be far from a waste of time. A number of years later, however, he underwent a change of mind

[2] *Ibid.,* p. 142.

[3] *Philosophical Investigations* (New York: The Macmillan Company, 1953), p. 47e.

[4] Quoted in Ernest Jones' *The Life and Work of Sigmund Freud* (New York: Basic Books, 1953), Vol. 3, p. 422.

about the worth of philosophy. In his *Autobiographical Study,* when touching on his later speculative works, he wrote: "I should not like to create the impression that during this period of my work I have turned my back on patient observation and have abandoned myself entirely to speculation. I have on the contrary always remained in the closest touch with the analytic material and have never ceased working at detailed points of clinical or technical importance. Even when I have moved away from observation, I have carefully avoided any contact with philosophy proper. The avoidance has been greatly facilitated by constitutional incapacity." [5]

The reason why Freud was concerned to avoid contact with philosophy while engaged in theoretical psychoanalytic work would appear to be that philosophy, as he conceived it, was a wholly speculative field and that contact with it might stimulate a tendency within him to abandon himself "entirely to speculation." His former warm recommendation of a well-known history of Greek philosophy as a "good friend" suggests that he felt an attraction of some strength to philosophy, and his later remark indicates that the needs of his professional work required resisting this attraction, even when (perhaps we should say, especially when) he "moved away from observation." I do not think, however, that we need take as more than a *façon de parler* his self-declared constitutional incapacity for philosophy. For if he had had such an incapacity, he could hardly have feared infection by philosophy or seriously felt a need to avoid it. More important than this, the weight of his continuous practice makes unrealistic the notion that Freud had anything to fear from highly speculative fields. No one who has read his theoretical writings, including his analytical studies of historical figures, could fail to be impressed by how much his conclusions were governed by observations made in his clinical practice. In view of this fact it might even be natural to think that his former recommendation was just an expression of good will towards a field which to him consisted of theories having only the value of an intellectual diversion.

[5] *An Autobiographical Study,* authorized translation by James Strachey, 2nd edition, edited by Ernest Jones, The International Psychoanalytical Library (London: The Hogarth Press and the Institute of Psychoanalysis, 1946), p. 109.

It can fairly be said that philosophy played only a negligible role in Freud's thinking, but not too negligible for him to record his discontent with it. And perhaps his change of mind came about not simply because philosophy seemed to consist of theories which are never brought down to earth by observation or experiment, but because he suspected that they are the kind of theories which cannot, *in principle,* be linked with scientific procedures. The overtones of his comments about the philosophical rejection of the possibility of unconscious mental processes point to such a suspicion. In his *Autobiographical Study* he wrote that

> the study of pathogenic repressions and of other phenomena which have still to be mentioned compelled psycho-analysis to take the concept of the 'unconscious' seriously. Psycho-analysis regarded everything mental as being in the first instance unconscious; the further quality of 'consciousness' might also be present, or again, it might be absent. This of course provoked a denial from the philosophers, for whom 'conscious' and 'mental' were identical, and who protested that they could not conceive of such a monstrosity as the 'unconscious mental.' There was no help for it, however, and this idiosyncrasy of the philosophers could only be disregarded with a shrug." [6]

He goes on to remark that "Experience (gained from pathological material, of which the philosophers were ignorant) . . ." compelled the acknowledgement of the existence of the unconscious. Being made acquainted with pathological material has not won from many philosophers the admission of the possibility of unconscious thoughts, which suggests that evidence does not now, as it did not then, count against the *philosophical* identification of the mental with the conscious.

To put the matter shortly here, a philosopher who says, "All thoughts are really conscious thoughts," or with Locke says, "Consciousness always accompanies thinking," can in all sincerity maintain his position in complete disregard of any sort of observational evidence. And the reason why he can do this is that his view is *philosophical,* which is to say that it is the kind of view

[6] *Ibid.,* pp. 55–56.

that is not linked to evidence. About a certain Aristotelian view, which has never been without its advocates, one commentator has said, "The modern reader cries out for evidence, not argument." [7] Unlike the modern reader (who is not without his own idiosyncrasies), the philosopher has what might be called a *defining* idiosyncrasy. This is that he can, and does, hold views in disregard of all evidence, and that he can, and does, rely on argument instead of observation. The philosopher is able to do this because his view is not the kind of view in whose acceptance or rejection observation plays a role. The philosophical words "No mental process is unaccompanied by consciousness" do not express a proposition which goes against Freud's empirical claim about the existence of unconscious mental processes, however much they may seem to do so. Some sort of awareness of the *verbal* nature of the philosophers' "identification" of *mental* and *conscious,* and the difference between what he was concerned with and what philosophers were concerned with, might have been responsible for his dismissing with a shrug the philosophical contention.

Sensing that a philosophical statement is the sort of statement which is supported by an argument rather than by observation is a step toward glimpsing the inner workings of philosophy. It brings us nearer to a clear perception of the verbal character of philosophical utterances, which makes disagreements between philosophers, as well as between philosophers and others, "degenerate into unfruitful disputes about words." [8] It is conjectural but not out of the question that Freud had a disconcerting perception of the way philosophy actually works, and that it was this which, underneath, prompted his disavowal. A letter he wrote about a book by the Russian philosopher, Chestov, lends plausibility to this idea. In it he said,

> Probably you cannot imagine how alien these philosophical convolutions seem to me. The only feeling of satisfaction they give me is that I take no part in this pitiable waste of intellectual powers. Philosophers no doubt believe that in such studies

[7] Benjamin Farrington, *Greek Science, Its Meaning for Us* (Penguin Books, 1944), p. 110.

[8] *An Autobiographical Study,* p. 57.

> they are contributing to the development of human thought, but every time there is a psychological or even a psychopathological problem behind them.[9]

Somewhere Freud says, "No, science is not illusion. But it would be an illusion to suppose that we could get anywhere else what it cannot give us." It goes without saying that philosophers have had, as indeed they continue to have, the idea that their subject is a kind of science and that it seeks to discover the truth about various matters, about space, causation, mind, beauty, goodness, etc. And they of course think that they can get from philosophy the kind of thing we expect from science. Like many others, Freud could not avoid the idea that philosophy endeavors to discover facts about reality but does not go about its task in a scientifically responsible way. A widespread impression of philosophy is that it is an armchair science. But there are features of philosophical theories, demonstrations, and disagreements that are out of joint with the idea that philosophy is a discipline in which truth is sought—features which, like Poe's purloined letter, are in plain view but arouse little or no curiosity. These features make it at least probable that any similarity between science and philosophy is delusive and that it is an error to think that we can get from philosophy the *kind* of thing we get from science, knowledge or reasonable hypotheses about the existence, nature, and causes of things. Freud may well have had a perception of the great difference between the two, may have seen through their superficial similarity; and what he referred to as his "constitutional incapacity" for philosophy might have been the feeling of antipathy, to which he gave expression in his letter, against "philosophical convolutions," the verbal twistings and turnings ("moves" is the current term) which are the stuff from which philosophy is made. Like many intellectuals, he turned away from philosophy, instead of bringing it under his scrutiny.

Freud has described the blows which astronomy, biology, and psycho-analysis have struck at the self-esteem of educated mankind, and if the hypothesis to be presented in these pages about

[9] Quoted by Ernest Jones, *op. cit.*, p. 140.

the nature of philosophy is, in essentials, correct, the narcissism of a special group of intellectuals will receive still another blow. For this hypothesis transforms a familiar and valued friend into a stranger who, moreover, is "repulsive," to use an adjective applied by one philosopher [10] to the hypothesis. If correct, it places a class of thinkers with a long and respected tradition into the unwelcome position of being the dupes of an intellectual activity in which they constantly engage but whose true nature has remained effectively veiled from their understanding. It should be said at once that it is desirable to link an assumption which has destructive import with something positive and constructive, something which will replace what is destroyed. But when this turns out not to be possible, the improvement of our understanding of a human creation has, nevertheless, a value of its own which it does not lose when achieved at the cost of a sacrifice. Perhaps this is part of the underlying meaning of the tale that Odin was permitted to look into the well of wisdom only by paying for it with one of his eyes.

The hypothesis to be developed here is that the philosopher does not use language for the expression of conscious thoughts; unwittingly he uses language only to give expression to unconscious thoughts. The philosopher does special kinds of things to language, without being aware of what he is doing, and at the same time he uses the language to express forbidden thoughts which are hidden from him. In a metaphor, language is the philosopher's plasticene which he molds in various ways and into which he impresses his deepest phantasies. Freud has remarked that there is an underlying psychological identity between poetry, religion, and philosophy. He wrote:

> . . . the delusions of paranoics have an unpalatable external similarity and an internal kinship to the systems of our philosophers. It is impossible to escape the conclusion that these patients are, in an *asocial* fashion, making the very attempts at solving their conflicts and appeasing their primary needs which, when these attempts are carried out in a fashion that is accept-

[10] *Psychoanalysis, Scientific Method and Philosophy, A Symposium,* ed. by Sidney Hook (Washington Square: New York University Press, 1959), p. 178.

> able to the majority, are known as poetry, religion and philosophy.[11]

Nowadays it will come as a surprise only to very few to be informed that the underlying purpose of poetry, religion, and philosophy, the psychological role they play for us, is the same. Here, however, it is necessary to remark on a difference between poetry and religion on the one hand and philosophy on the other. By and large, and without going into exceptions, it may be said that lines of poetry and religious utterances have a descriptive use, i.e., a use to describe occurrences, states of affairs, things, etc. For the most part, poets and prophets employ language for the expression of conscious thoughts, independently of the unconscious thoughts that may be associated with them. Philosophical utterances, however akin they may be to poetic and religious statements in psychological respects, are a different sort of linguistic breed. Philosophical statements do not have the descriptive use they appear to have. They are not about occurrences, states of affairs or things. For example, Zeno's implied claim that time is self-contradictory and does not exist and Hobbes' *philosophical* proposition that all desires are really selfish are not about the existence of time and the nature of desire. But they are not, as some philosophers might be inclined to hold, senseless. A philosophical statement, apart from the unconscious thoughts of which it is the bearer, does not have the kind of job to perform that it is natural to attribute to it, and which if not performed renders it literally unintelligible. Its job at the upper level of our minds is not to express thoughts; the work it performs is linguistic, not descriptive. Whatever descriptive import it has is confined to the unconscious phantasies it expresses. To put the matter incautiously, but in a way which brings out a point of dissimilarity as well as a point of similarity between poetry, religion, and philosophy, the *descriptive sense* of a philosophical sentence is nothing in addition to the unconscious thoughts it is made to express.

It is difficult to come to terms with the idea that, for example,

[11] *The Standard Edition of the Complete Psychological Works of Sigmund Freud*, translated from the German under the general editorship of James Strachey (London: The Hogarth Press and the Institute of Psychoanalysis, 1955), p. 261.

Hobbes' or Zeno's words are not to be taken at face value, as being about time and about desire, but instead, like dreams, stand in need of interpretation. That philosophical utterances have been constantly misconstrued and that in order to understand them we require an explanation of their linguistic structure and their unconscious purport is attested to by the strange fact that in its twenty-four hundred years of existence technical philosophy has not produced a single uncontroverted proposition.[12] Only a weakened sense of reality, produced by a powerful need, could make it possible for anyone to dismiss this fact as of little significance and as having an obvious explanation. Two common explanations may be noted in passing. One is that philosophy is not a demonstrative science and that we cannot expect from it what we expect from a demonstrative science; but this explanation leaves us puzzled as to why philosophers give arguments in demonstration of their views. The other is that philosophical problems are so complex and difficult that they have resisted solution and have therefore left room for debate; but this leaves us in the dark as to why philosophers have for so long been able to advance their solutions with the greatest assurance, as indeed they continue to do. Philosophers who give these reasons forget them the moment they begin doing philosophy: they argue as if they thought that philosophy is a demonstrative science, and they advance their views as if they did *not* think that the complexity of philosophical problems rendered proposed solutions uncertain. It is evident that the explanations are thin rationalizations, sops to the feeble demands of a weakened sense of reality. One well-known philosopher wrote in a recent review of a book: "The book leaves us with two cheering impressions, first, that there is progress in philosophy, second, that there is no shortage of problems for philosophy to make progress in."[13] It is hard to imagine anyone being made hopeful about a field which in its history of twenty-four hundred years has produced only

[12] This is true despite the remarkable claim that in philosophy there are "old truths" which need to be rediscovered. If we substitute "views" for "truths" in Strawson's statement quoted at the beginning of this paper, we have a description of what actually goes on in philosophy.

[13] *Philosophical Books* (Leicester, England: Leicester University Press, 1964), Vol. IV, No. 3, p. 6.

flourishing anarchy. If the sense of reality this philosopher shows does not recommend itself to us, we can at least admire his patience and sustained optimism.

The unfruitful history of philosophy is sufficient reason for assuming that it is the nature of the subject which permits its propositions to be permanently debatable and its arguments permanently open to assured acceptance as well as to assured rejection. The historical fact, which philosophers have managed so far to keep at a safe distance from themselves, strongly indicates that a philosophical theory is not the kind of theory which has a truth-value and that a philosophical disagreement is not the kind of disagreement that can in principle be resolved by evidence of some sort. It certainly makes permissible the inference that we have all along been looking at philosophy through the wrong kind of spectacles. This is only an inference, of course, and, as might be expected, has been rejected by those who are intrenched in the subject and seek by every means to protect their investment in it. After all, which philosopher can tolerate the thought that he has been deluded about his subject, which has become his intellectual home, and has been mistaken in believing that the aim of his investigation is to discover truth. Few will be able to bring themselves to make the unwelcome inference; but in any case, it can be replaced by considerations which show, without reference to the history of the subject, that a philosophical view is not what it has always looked to us to be. It can be shown that a philosophical disagreement exists under a condition which, in the normal case where the truth-value of a proposition is at issue, would rule out its continuation, if not its existence from the very beginning. For it can be shown that a philosophical dispute is carried on with all the parties knowing everything that is required for knowing who is right and who is wrong, if there is a right and a wrong.[14] To put it in other words, the dispute is maintained while there is no piece of relevant evidence missing, no incompleteness of data, to leave room for divergence of opinion. The remarkable conclusion from this is that if one party to the dispute is mistaken he knows that he is mistaken but nevertheless thinks

[14] See M. Lazerowitz, *The Structure of Metaphysics* (London: Routledge and Kegan Paul, 1955), especially Chapter IX.

he is not, and also thinks to be wrong the position he knows to be right.[15] This conclusion presents us with an absurdity. But with its rejection must also go the notions that a philosophical view is either true or false, and that the work of a philosophical argument is to establish the truth-value of a proposition. If we reflect with detachment on the matter, we can see that these notions must be incorrect. We can see that a dispute which is carried on with all the relevant facts known is not about the facts, however vivid the appearances to the contrary may be. The lady who before our very eyes is sawed in half by the magician but comes out whole was just not sawed in half. What might be called the "illusion of philosophy" is the idea, which has the strength of an *idée fixe,* that philosophical utterances have truth-values.

Consider a typical, and current, philosophical dispute, one which lends itself to a relatively brief examination. This dispute can be conveniently examined in relation to a non-philosophical statement that no one, either philosopher or non-philosopher, would dream of denying or doubting or arguing about in any usual circumstance. In his *The Great Mathematicians* H. W. Turnbull makes the following statement: "There are the well-known propositions that a circle is bisected by any diameter, or that the angles at the base of an isosceles triangle are equal, or that the angle in a semicircle is a right angle, or that the sides about equal angles in similar triangles are proportional. These and other like propositions have been ascribed to Thales." [16] It is hard to think that anyone could find anything in the form of words Turnbull uses to which to take exception; but as is well known, some able philosophical thinkers have been able to do so in certain

[15] Philosophers by a kind of inadvertence admit this when, as happens frequently, they characterize each other's "mistakes" as obvious. In this connection the words of one philosopher are worth quoting: "The philosophical positions that Moore opposes can, therefore, be seen to be false *in advance* of an examination of the arguments adduced in support of them. We can know that something is wrong with Prichard's reasoning before we study it." [Norman Malcolm, *Knowledge and Certainty* (Englewood Cliffs, N. J.: Prentice-Hall, 1963), p. 181]. The "we" cannot fail to include Prichard, the implication being that Prichard must have held his view while knowing it to be false. The writer offers the remarkable explanation that "philosophical reasoning has a peculiar power to blind us to the obvious." (P. 180)

[16] P. 5.

circumstances. They have denied that there are such things as propositions. Other able philosophical thinkers have, of course, maintained that there are propositions. The disagreement has the air of centering on a question of existence, comparable to the question regarding the existence of the Loch Ness monster, which continues to excite disagreement. Its likeness to the question about the Loch Ness monster vanishes, however, when we attempt to identify what it is that the philosophical question asks and what the disagreement is about. For on the assumption that the question and disagreement are about the facts, every possible identification yields the paradox of a disagreement going on with everyone knowing who is right and who is wrong.

It is quite clear that philosophers who would not dispute that there is, for example, the theorem that a diameter of a circle bisects it, may, and in fact do, divide over whether there are propositions. Now if the *philosophical* view that there are no propositions implies that there is no such theorem as that a diameter bisects its circle, then the paradox obtains. For the disputing philosophers would all know a given theorem, i.e., a certain proposition, while disagreeing over whether there are any propositions. However the debate is in the end to be construed, it is evident that it cannot be over the existence of theorems, axioms, assertions, etc. A new attempt to identify the subject of debate has to be made.

The term "proposition" has, as it is used in philosophy, a number of senses. Without going into qualifications and refinements, we may say that the special sense involved in the dispute is given by the phrase "literal meaning of a declarative sentence." Thus, the word "proposition" is used to refer to the meaning of a declarative sentence, or to what it says. One argument that has been given for the view that there are propositions, as distinct from sentences which express them, is that we can be aware of a sentence without knowing its meaning, so that in learning what it means we are made aware of something over and above and in addition to the sentence itself. Another argument, used against those who deny that there are propositions, is that different indicative sentences, in the same language or in different languages, have the same meaning, which again is taken to show that the literal meaning of a sentence, the proposition it expresses, is something distinct from the sentence. The picture that these arguments conjure up of what is involved in understanding a sentence is that two processes are involved, seeing and thinking, each process having its own proper object: by sight we are made aware of a sentence and by thought we are made aware of a proposition.

We may now seem to have identified what it is the existence of which philosophers are debating; but to suppose this is a mistake. They cannot, in arguing about whether propositions exist, be disagreeing about the existence of theorems, assertions, and the like—although we may remain mystified about what makes it possible to disagree over the former without at the same time disagreeing over the latter. But the puzzle as to what the dispute is about remains, if we take it to center on the question whether indicative sentences have literal meanings. Construing the dispute to be over the correct answer to this question does not enable us to circumvent the paradox of people disagreeing about the answer to a question while knowing what the answer is. For a philosopher who maintains that there are no propositions, equally with a philosopher who maintains that there are, knows perfectly well that there are indicative sentences which have literal meanings, and so knows that there are propositions. The philosopher who insists that there are propositions knows that his opponent is aware of the fact that many indicative sentences have literal meaning and so knows that his opponent in debate is aware of the fact that there are propositions, but continues to argue with him, as if trying to correct his lack of knowledge. The situation we are confronted with is baffling, to say the least. And indeed we can make no sense of it so long as we take the dispute about the existence of propositions to be over whether in fact indicative sentences have literal meaning. If the paradox is to be avoided, the only recourse is to suppose that the existence of literally meaningful indicative sentences is not involved in the dispute about whether there are propositions.

A further interpretation of the dispute, construed as a factual disagreement of some sort, suggests itself at this point. This is that it is about whether the meanings of indicative sentences are *entities,* or objects. There are features of the dispute, such as choice of terminology and the way certain arguments are framed, which make plausible this interpretation. Some philosophers who advocate the view that there are propositions go so far as to maintain that indicative sentences are *names,* which suggests that propositions are being thought of as objects or entities that are named by sentences, objects for which the sentences "stand." On this construction, a philosopher who maintains that there are propositions is really asserting that propositions are entities; and a philosopher who says that there are no propositions is not denying the existence of propositions but instead is maintaining that propositions are not entities, that they are not a kind of thing. But avoiding one difficulty, as this interpretation enables us to do, lands us in another. For there is no process of examining a proposition to determine whether it is an entity or is not an entity. This is not to say that a procedure is lacking at present which might in the future be discovered. Rather, it makes no literal sense to speak of a process of examining the meaning of a sentence in order to determine whether it is an entity: the phrase "examines the meaning of a sentence in order to ascertain whether it is a thing" describes nothing. By drawing closer we can determine whether what we see is a shadow or a thing, but there is no drawing closer to determine whether a shadow is a thing. In the same way there is no drawing nearer to and scrutinizing more carefully the meaning of a sentence: the words "Plato examined the literal meanings of indicative sentences and found that their meanings are really entities," and also the words "Roscelin examined their meanings and came to the opposite conclusion," do not describe any sort of process. There is nothing to be done in addition to understanding a sentence in order to know whether its literal import is a thing or not, so that if it is a thing, all parties to the dispute know this, and if it is not a thing, all parties to the dispute know this. An anecdote is to the point in this connection. On one occasion when Bertrand Russell was present I ventured to say that two things could not occupy the same place at once. Russell's immediate rejoinder was: "That is not true. A color and a shape can be in the same place at once." The next day I related the intellectual skirmish to several learned colleagues. Their unhesitating reply was that colors and shapes are not things. It is evident that no sort of examination of colors and shapes could resolve the disagreement over whether they are or are not things. However unnatural it may strike one, the conclusion that forces itself on us is that the difference of opinion is not over whether a shape is a thing. And it is the same with the disagreement over whether what an indicative sentence says, the proposition it expresses, is an object.

There is a further possible construction to be considered: the dispute might be construed as being verbal in nature. Many intellectuals have voiced the suspicion that philosophical questions and theories are in some way verbal, and some philosophers have given a kind of recognition to this suspicion in a technique they have developed, linguistic analysis. Looked on as verbal, about the conventional use of terminology, the dispute regarding the existence of propositions is to be interpreted as a dispute, when conducted in the English language, about the use of the *word* "proposition." A philosopher who holds that there are no propositions is to be taken as maintaining, in the non-verbal form of speech, that the word "proposition" has no use in the language; and a philosopher who holds that there are propositions is to be understood as implying that the word "proposition" does have a use in the language. This may now seem to have brought us nearer to the true nature of the dispute; but it requires only little reflection to see that the paradox we have been seeking to avoid reappears. For it goes without saying that everyone knows perfectly well that the word "proposition" does have a use in the language: no philosopher engaged in the dispute would think of saying that Turnbull's use of "proposition" is improper, or, to use Hume's expression, "wrong apply'd."

It can be seen that no matter which way we turn and no matter what we identify as the subject under debate among philosophers, the paradox is not avoided so long as we retain the idea that the dispute is one about fact and that the claim and counterclaim have truth-values. That is, so long as the question "Are there such things as propositions?" is construed as a request for factual information, either linguistic or non-linguistic, we are confronted by the paradox of people advancing different answers and arguing about which is true and which false while in possession of the answer. If, now, we can bring ourselves to give up the notion that the question is a request for factual information, i.e., that it is the kind of question that has true and false answers, and that the dispute is about fact of one kind or another, we avoid the paradox and also reach a promising vantage point. Plainly, we then have to reconsider the words of the philosophers and try to understand them anew, in a metaphor, remove old spectacles and try out new ones. The two sentences, "There are propositions" and "There are no propositions," have to be understood in terms of their relevance to each other; and if the second is not to be construed as denying that there are propositions, the first is not to be construed as declaring the existence of propositions. The first sentence conceals its metaphysics behind the language in everyday use, and an understanding of it can best be reached by first considering the second sentence, which appears to be in conflict with the language in everyday use. To put it briefly, the sentence "There are no propositions," not construed as expressing a factual claim about propositions nor yet as making an obviously false claim about ordinary terminology, is open to the interpretation that it is a statement embodying a terminological decision, the decision to cast out of the language the word "proposition." On this interpretation, the philosophical sentence is related in a special way to the verbal sentence, "The word 'proposition' has no use." If the terminological decision it introduces were accepted and put into general practice, the verbal sentence would then say what is true. But as things are, the verbal sentence says what is false, whereas the philosophical sentence which introduces the terminological decision expresses what is neither true nor false. So to speak, the content of the philosophical sentence is a verbal innovation; but its form, its linguistic dress, is taken from the mode of speech in which statements of fact are made. It is in the form of words used to make a true or false claim about the existence and nature of things, and this creates the idea that the existence of propositions is being denied. Wittgenstein in one place describes the philosopher as someone who objects to a language convention under the impression that he is putting forward a factual claim. The philosopher, he said,

> objects to using this word ["pain"] in the particular way in which it is commonly used. On the other hand, he is not aware that he is objecting to a convention. He sees a way of dividing the country different from the one used on the ordinary map. He feels tempted, say, to use the name 'Devonshire' not for the county with its conventional boundary, but for a region differently bounded. He could express this by saying: 'Isn't it absurd to make *this* a county, to draw the boundaries *here*?' But what he says is: 'The *real* Devonshire is this.' [17]

Compare "There really are no propositions."

The question which now arises is why a philosopher rebels against the conventional use of the word "proposition," what determines his reading out the word (with bell, book, and candle) from the language. For the word does its assigned work well enough, and for that matter the philosopher does not carry the decision he makes in his "philosophic moment" into his non-philosophic talk. The question has answers at different levels of our mind; but superficially the philosophical decision to exorcise the word must link up with the counter-sentence, "There are propositions," or "There are such things as propositions." This sentence cannot be viewed as declaring the fact that the word "proposition" has a use in the language; i.e., the philosophical sentence which expresses a position entering into the debate cannot be understood as expressing a fact which everyone knows and which is not at issue in the debate. Like its companion sentence it has to be understood as giving concealed expression to a linguistic decision, at least part of which is the decision to retain the word "proposition" in the language. This construction would explain what makes it possible for the dispute to be carried on in the presence of all the facts. But the decision to retain the word is not the whole decision. This can readily be gathered from the curious fact that some philosophers have held the "view" that indicative sentences are *names*. Thus Professor Alonzo Church has said that "(declarative) *sentences,* in particular, are taken as a kind of names, the denotation being the *truth-value* of the sentence, *truth* or *falsehood,* and the sense being the *proposition*

[17] *The Blue and Brown Books* (Oxford: Basil Blackwell, 1958), p. 57.

which the sentence expresses."[18] These philosophers are as aware as anyone of the grammatical fact that an indicative sentence does not count as a part of speech and is not classified as a noun. Attributing an odd mistake to them succeeds only in presenting us with a situation which flouts the intelligence.

The assumption that is forced upon us is that some philosophers have decided to classify indicative sentences with nouns, and this assumption throws light on the dispute we are considering. A philosopher who says, "There are propositions," or better, says, "There are such entities as propositions," has decided not only to retain the noun "proposition," but has also decided to classify the word with a special group of nouns, nouns which are general names of *things*. Thus, one philosopher who has rejected the view expressed by the words "There are such entities as propositions" characterized it, typically, in the form of speech employed in talk of things, as "the metaphysical doctrine that propositions are real entities."[19] And another philosopher, who came out for a "reduced ontology,"[20] urged that "meanings themselves, as obscure intermediate entities, may well be abandoned."[21] Wittgenstein has observed that we tend to look for a substance whenever we find a substantive; and though it is not altogether acceptable as it stands, his formula is suggestive. In philosophy it is by no means rare to find a noun which is not the general name of a thing, e.g., the word "nothing," being turned into a noun which is such a name, this, to be sure, only by an artificial stretching of categories, not by actually turning it into a general name of a thing. This would seem to be what has happened in the case of the term "proposition." The word is a noun which, like the nouns "today" and "existence," is not used in the language to name things, and what the philosopher of the Reality of the Proposition has done is to stretch the word "thing" or "entity" or "object" so that it applies to what is referred to by the phrase "literal meaning of an

[18] "The Need for Abstract Entities in Semantic Analysis," *Amer. Acad. of Arts and Sciences Proceedings,* Vol. 80–81, p. 101.

[19] A. J. Ayer, *Language, Truth and Logic,* second edition (London: V. Gollancz, Ltd., 1949), p. 88.

[20] W. V. Quine, "Semantics and Abstract Objects," *Amer. Acad. of Arts and Sciences Proceedings,* Vol. 80–81, p. 96.

[21] *Ibid.,* p. 91.

indicative sentence." In this way he artificially assimilates the term "proposition" into the class of object-naming substantives, and this leads some philosophers to the further artificial assimilation of indicative sentences into the category of proper names. In the grammar book of some philosophers an indicative sentence is the proper name of its literal meaning.[22] A philosopher who is opposed to these reclassifications, which according to his lights conceal important differences between the use of "proposition" and substantives that denote objects and between nouns and indicative sentences, will eliminate them by exorcising the offending word "proposition" from the language.

All this maneuvering with grammar and terminology when carried on in the mode of speech in which things and occurrences are described creates the lively illusion that the existence of an elusive, occult entity is being debated. This illusion is apparently so important to philosophers, to those who are hostile to propositions as well as to those who embrace them, as to prevent their penetrating it and seeing the maneuverings for the linguistic gossamer that they are. Wittgenstein's observation that we may be "irresistibly attracted or repelled by a notation" [23] is undoubtedly true. But in itself the shifting of terminology and classifications this way and that can hardly be a fascinating enough game to account for the philosopher's preoccupation with it. Nor can the illusion, created by the non-verbal form in which philosophers present their re-editings of language, account for the continued absorbed interest of the philosopher. Something else must be involved to account both for the illusion having the strength of a delusion and for the philosopher's interest being held captive for so long. Behind the "entity" which is being debated must hide ideas which are very much alive in the unconscious of philosophers. The linguistic reclassification and also the exorcism of the term "proposition," which are done at the preconscious level of our thinking and which brings into existence an intellectual illusion at the conscious level of our thinking, must express

[22] Thus Quine has said, "Statements have frequently been treated as names of propositions, these latter being construed as entities of a sort better described as *meanings* of statements." *Op. cit.*, p. 90.

[23] *The Blue and Brown Books*, p. 57.

important material in the deeper strata of the mind. In connection with what he calls a "pure transcendental idea" Kant makes an observation which might be applied to the illusions engendered by the controversy about propositions: "Even the wisest of men cannot free himself from them. After long effort he perhaps succeeds in guarding himself against actual error; but he will never be able to free himself from the illusion, which unceasingly mocks and torments him." [24] We may well think that he cannot free himself from the illusion because of a need for it. In lectures Wittgenstein gave in 1934–35 he described a philosophical problem as "the product of an obsession—a linguistic obsession that is not recognized." [25] And in his *Philosophical Investigations* he says, "The Philosopher's treatment of a question [undoubtedly referring to his own procedure] is like the treatment of an illness." [26] His remarks would seem to have their source in a perception into the nature of philosophy and its deeper roots in the mind.

The unconscious purport of the sentence, "There are such entities as propositions," and its denial, "There are no propositions," is a matter of speculation, speculation which need not, however, be devoid of plausibility. About metaphysics, the part of philosophy which investigates supersensible realities, those lying beyond the range of possible sense experience, Freud has the following to say:

> I believe in fact that a great part of the mythological view of the world, which reaches far into the most modern religions, is *nothing other than psychological processes projected into the outer world.* The obscure apprehending of the psychical factors and relationships of the unconscious is mirrored—it is hard to put it otherwise; one has to use here the analogy with paranoia —in the construction of *a supersensible reality,* which science has to retranslate into the *psychology of the unconscious.* One could venture in this manner to resolve the myths of Paradise, the Fall of Man, of God, of Good and Evil, of Immortality and so on, thus transforming Metaphysics into Metapsychology.[27]

[24] *The Critique of Pure Reason,* trans. by Norman Kemp Smith (London: Macmillan and Co., Limited, 1933), pp. 327–328.

[25] From notes taken by Alice Ambrose.

[26] P. 91.

[27] Quoted in Ernest Jones' *The Life and Work of Sigmund Freud* (New York: Basic Books, 1953–57), Vol. III, pp. 352–353.

As is well known, following the suggestion made here, enlightening analytical studies have been written which have interpreted the myths of Paradise, the Fall, God, and so on in terms of the psychology of the unconscious. It would not be surprising if it turned out that behind the metaphysical talk of the supersensible —behind the illusion that it makes pronouncements about a kind of reality—were to be found the familiar primitive myths of Paradise and the Fall, etc. And these myths can have their soporific effect on the critical powers of so many intellectuals only because of the ideas which hide behind them. The Platonic "theory" of universals, which is only the verbal imitation of a theory about entities,[28] harks back to the religious Orphic-Pythagorean conception of the Isles of the Blessed. For many thinkers philosophy, and particularly metaphysical philosophy, is a highly intellectualized substitute for religion; and it may well be that behind the façade of philosophical talk about the supersensible a philosopher experiences a highly attenuated form of the state of "passionate sympathetic contemplation" [29] in which he "is identified with the suffering God, dies in his death, and arises again in his birth." [30] In any event, no more is needed than to be attentive to the choice of language which philosophers use in the expression of their theories and to take into account some of their adjacent comments to see that the religious myths of Paradise (in which there is no place for a harsh super-ego), the Fall, God, immortality are very much alive in their minds. When, in the *Phaedrus,* Plato poetically speaks of the realm of universals as "the heaven above the heavens . . . [where] abides . . . the colourless, formless, intangible essence, visible only to the mind, the pilot of the soul," [31] his words are only a picturesque way of calling attention to the differences between the proper names of ordinary language and the artificially reclassified proper names in the Platonic grammar book. Only in appearance do his words describe a reality, but unquestionably they provoke in us thoughts of

[28] Created by the unannounced, academic reclassification of general words with proper names. See "The Existence of Universals" in *The Structure of Metaphysics.*

[29] F. M. Cornford's interpretation of the Greek word for "theory," *From Religion to Philosophy* (New York: Harper, 1957).

[30] *Ibid.*

[31] *The Dialogues of Plato,* Jowett translation (New York: Random House, 1937), Vol. I, Sec. 247.

Paradise, whether conscious or not. And God, immortality, and even the Fall, can be discerned in the verbal theatre of the Platonic Forms, God and immortality quite clearly, the Fall perhaps less clearly. The latter emerges in Socrates' "favorite doctrine," the reminiscence theory that knowledge is the remembering of universals which the soul knew in its prior residence above the physical heaven, to use St. Paul's description, "the invisible kingdom of God." The question which leaps to mind is what happened to make the soul leave the supersensible realm of the forms to inhabit a physical body, which is its prison and from which it longs to escape. One of the things Socrates is represented as saying in the *Phaedrus* makes it plain enough that the departure was an Expulsion: ". . . intelligence of universals . . . is the recollection of those things which our soul once saw while following God." [32] The soul is a fallen angel whose wings have "wasted and fallen away" [33] because they were "fed upon evil and foulness and the opposite of good." [34] Psychoanalysis has been able to extract the secret of the nature of the "evil and foulness," the original sin, that brought about the Fall of man.

For many philosophers, for those who deny the existence of the supersensible as well as for those who construct systems of supersensible realities, metaphysics is a linguistic sanctuary which provides them with possibilities for resolving their conflicts about religion.[35] It is also a linguistic battlefield. On it are waged shadow wars over terminology and grammar; and behind these wars others can be seen in which religion is the bone of contention. Contests about religion and its renunciation that once could not be carried on without violent physical eruptions could, on the whole, be carried on with relative security under the cover of philosophical positions and counterpositions—Platonism, Aristotelianism, Nominalism, Conceptualism, and so on. Some philoso-

[32] *Ibid.*, sec. 249.

[33] *Ibid.*, sec. 247.

[34] *Ibid.*

[35] Hegel is worth quoting in this connection: "The objects of philosophy, it is true, are upon the whole the same as those of religion. In both the object is Truth, in that supreme sense in which God and God only is the Truth." *The Logic of Hegel,* translated by William Wallace (Oxford: Oxford University Press, 1931) , p. 3.

phers still prefer this concealed mode of religious warfare, for a variety of reasons, one perhaps being that philosophy in their eyes confers on it an intellectual dignity which it does not have by itself. The following words which introduce a contemporary attempt at a nominalistic reformulation of language, make plain one determinant which underlies the rejection of the metaphysical view that there are abstract entities. Professors Goodman and Quine write: "1. *Renunciation of abstract entities.* We do not believe in abstract entities. No one supposes that abstract entities —classes, relations, properties, etc.—exist in space-time; but we mean more than this. We renounce them altogether." [36]

To come back to the view that there are such entities as propositions, which, as will be recalled, represents the decision to look on the word "proposition" *as if* it is the general name of a kind of object. The "entity" that is named by the word is said to be *abstract*—which is an oblique way of saying that "proposition" is an abstract noun that is not used to denote objects.[37] Unlike things that we see and feel, it is intangible to the senses and can be apprehended only in thought. Philosophers who are or who become hostile to the view and support their rejection by declaring that "proposition" is a word which "can be construed as syncategorematic: significant in context but naming nothing" [38] are evidently impressed by the difference between the actual use of the term "proposition" and terms which are names of "real entities." This is a difference which they do not wish to see "hushed up," [39] and they therefore resist the philosophical classification which does this. But their rejection goes deeper than opposition to an idle enlargement of a grammatical category. A philosopher who takes the stand that propositions are abstract

[36] "Steps Toward a Constructive Nominalism," *The Journal of Symbolic Logic,* Vol. 12, 1947, p. 105.

[37] The following comment from Wittgenstein is of particular interest in this connection: " 'The symbol *"a"* stands for an ideal object' is evidently supposed to assert something about the meaning, and so about the use, of *'a'*. And it means of course that this use is in a certain respect similar to that of a sign that has an object, and that it does not stand for any object." *Remarks on the Foundations of Mathematics,* ed. by G. H. von Wright, R. Rhees and G. E. Anscombe (New York: Macmillan, 1956) , p. 136.

[38] See footnote No. 36.

[39] Wittgenstein's expression.

entities is giving covert expression to a religious belief, a belief which his sophistication may not permit him to have consciously; and a philosopher who opposes this stand has decided to take the path of heresy. One observation may be quoted here: "The theory of meaning, even with the elimination of the mysterious meant entities, strikes me as in a comparable state to theology—but with the difference that its notions are blithely used in the supposedly most scientific and hard-headed brands of philosophy." [40]

There are, quite certainly, other determinants than the one mentioned which enter into the acceptance and rejection of the metaphysical view about propositions. That is to say, there are further ideas which the sentence "Propositions are abstract entities" is unconsciously made to denote. Two of them are easily guessed and may be mentioned briefly. These concern death and dirt. These two ideas are probably closely linked in the unconscious, for the dead body soon becomes foul dirt in the process of mingling its substance with nature. The scandal created by the odors which came from the holy Father Zossimov's body may have had as one of its determinants the unconscious equation, dead body=feces. Be this as it may, in the *Parmenides,* in which various Platonic theories about the nature of the abstract entities denoted by general words are examined, Socrates embraces the view that there are "absolute ideas of the just and the beautiful and the good, and of all that class." [41] But he resists the notion that there could be "absolute ideas" corresponding to such things as "hair, mud, dirt, or anything else which is vile and paltry." [42] It is clear that the "heaven above the heavens" is a world free from dirt; it houses non-material entities which are the objects of "pure" thought. Midas changed food (which becomes dirt) into gold which he could not eat; Plato sought to escape from dirt by creating a world which could not be seen or touched, a world (brought about by the magic of philosophical grammar) where reside the impalpable essences.

According to Kant, the three great problems of metaphysics

[40] W. V. Quine, "Semantics and Abstract Objects," *op. cit.,* p. 92.

[41] *Plato, op. cit.,* Vol. II, Sec. 130.

[42] *Ibid.,* Vol. II, Sec. 130.

revolve around the notions of God, freedom, and immortality, and one of these, which is connected with the idea of death, would seem to play a predominant role in the psychology of philosophers. For in the *Phaedo* Socrates tells us that true philosophers are "always occupied in the practice of dying, wherefore . . . to them least of all men is death terrible." [43] Philosophy itself seems to have been a kind of halfway house to death for Socrates, and so it may be for philosophers in general. Ernest Jones has called death "the King of Terrors," and Freud thought it important to try to come to terms with it. How philosophers have been able to divest death of its dread is thus of special interest. If one only looks, one can easily find their solutions buried in many theories, each the presentation of a piece of altered language. An easily recognized instance is the academic extirpation from language of the word "time," presented in the form of a statement of fact, i.e., the "theory" that time is unreal. The metaphysical view that there are abstract entities which exist timelessly can be seen to be an important and poetically appealing attempt by linguistic means to come to terms with the emotional problem posed by the ultimate fate from which "His Majesty, the Ego" [44] can find no real escape. The poetry and metaphors with which Plato surrounds his theories about the nature of the temporal world and the world of the everlasting essences make plain the psychological mechanism used to come to terms with death: the mechanism of reversal. By means of the device of turning a thing into its opposite a philosopher is able to rob death of its terror. In the *Republic,* the world is described as a cave where only the shadows of people are to be seen. This description is reminiscent of the Homeric account of Ulysses' visit to the mythological underworld of the Greeks, and the Platonic description may well have been written under the influence of the Homeric description. In any case, the presence of the mechanism of reversal is unmistakable. This world, the world of colors and odors and sounds, the world of sense experience, is changed into its opposite, into the shadowy world of death; and the final nothingness, wherein is "the colorless, formless, intangible essence," is psychologically trans-

[43] *Ibid,* Vol. II, Sec. 67.

[44] Freud's expression.

formed into the ultimately desirable. This world is rejected, and "the undiscovered country from whose bourne no traveller returns" [45] is transfigured into Paradise. The transformations are of course inner transformations and these are effected with the help of linguistic creations which are presented in the ontological form of speech. So to speak, an *abstract* entity is nothing, which has been verbally transmuted into *something*.

The philosophical view that there are abstract entities, and the special view that propositions are abstract entities, may be characterized as a contrived linguistic structure, intended as a medium for inner contemplation. It is constituted by the introduction, in the fact-stating idiom, of a hidden language change, which at one level of our mind presents us with an intellectual mirage and at other levels of our mind works to express needed phantasies. To the uppermost level the words "Propositions are abstract entities" present the delusive appearance of making a factual claim about the existence of things of a special kind, comparable to the claim that there are such creatures as leprechauns. For deeper levels of the mind, the words say that there are objects which cannot soil and also that there are refined and wondrous objects which we shall be privileged to perceive. But the "objects" are nothing more than inner states projected into the outer world, the externalization of emotions. It is interesting to note that some philosophers have, in a way, begun to realize the linguistic character of the activity that is philosophy. Thus one philosopher has described himself as "playing a report-writing game for a revised universe." The "revised universe" is revised language and the game of report-writing is a way of giving expression to unconscious contents of the psyche—which makes the game one that a philosopher cannot easily give up.

It is permissible to guess that Freud had an intuitive perception into the game-aspect of what philosophers do with words, the nature of their "convolutions," which made him decide to avoid contact with philosophy. But it was a perception which he never attempted to clarify or pursue. Instead of arousing curiosity about a subject which has attracted very great thinkers over an enor-

[45] Hamlet.

mous period of time, his perception seems to have provoked only rejection. But what is rejected without improved understanding has a way of not being left behind. Thus, Freud attempted to bolster his claim regarding the existence of an unconscious part of the mind by unwittingly producing one of the standard philosophical theories about our knowledge of other minds. Any philosopher will recognize the so-called "argument from analogy" in Freud's words. In his *Autobiographical Study* he argued that giving recognition to the unconscious was "only treating one's own mental life as one had always treated other people's. One did not hesitate to ascribe mental processes to other people, although one had no immediate consciousness of them and could only infer them from their words and actions. But what held good for other people must be applicable to oneself." [46]

Smith College

[46] P. 56.

METAMORPHOSES OF THE PRINCIPLE OF VERIFIABILITY

ALICE AMBROSE

> *"All false art, all vain wisdom, lasts its time, but finally destroys itself, and its highest culture is also the epoch of its decay. That this time is come for metaphysics appears from the state into which it has fallen among all learned nations, despite of all the zeal with which other sciences of every kind are prosecuted."* KANT, *Prolegomena to Any Future Metaphysics* (Chicago: The Open Court Publishing Co., 1933), p. 141.
>
> *"There is no single book to which you can point as you do to Euclid, and say: This is Metaphysics, here you may find the noblest objects of this science. . . . proved from principles of pure reason . . . in all ages one Metaphysics has contradicted another, either in its assertions or their proofs, and thus has itself destroyed its own claim to lasting assent."*
>
> *Ibid.*, p. 20.

BUT FOR THE STYLE OF THIS PASSAGE, the complaint it expresses might well have been made by members of the Vienna Circle. As is well known, metaphysics as a science fell under the critical scrutiny of both Kant and the positivists: "If [metaphysics] be a science, how comes it that it cannot, like other sciences, obtain universal and permanent recognition?" [1] Both Kant and logical positivists were in agreement that the "assertions [of metaphysics] must be either science or are worth nothing at all." [2] And undoubtedly the suspicion that these assertions were worth nothing at all was what prompted Kant's question "whether such a thing as metaphysics be at all possible?" and also led to the

[1] *Prolegomena to Any Future Metaphysics*, p. 2.

[2] *Ibid.*, p. 29.

positivist attempt to eliminate metaphysics. What the positivists found disquieting was the presence, in a subject with scientific pretensions, of statements for which "we can not specify any respect in which our experience . . . would . . . be different if the statement were false and if it were true." [3] A. J. Ayer states that "it is characteristic of such rival philosophical theses as realism and idealism that each is consistent with all the appearances . . ." [4] and that "it is just this that condemns them." [5] Professor C. J. Ducasse has summed up the situation as follows: "It seems to me . . . that many of the statements found in books on metaphysics, epistemology, and other parts of philosophy [are such that] we do not know of any test of them, which, if applied, would either prove, or disprove them, or show them either less or more probable than their alternatives. Therefore, for the purposes of anyone seeking knowledge, such statements are wholly negligible." [6] But I think a just account of the position of logical positivism must represent its conclusion from this state of affairs as much more drastic than that indicated by Professor Ducasse's comment on it: that the statements of metaphysics are "wholly negligible" is "substantially what Carnap means when he describes them as 'nonsense' or 'meaningless.' " [7]

As is well known, logical positivists claimed that the statements of metaphysics are quite literally nonsense. Kant thought he had shown that metaphysics can never have the status of a science. But to eliminate metaphysics from the field of fruitful investigation is not to eliminate it from intelligible discourse; and the latter was the program the positivists proclaimed. "Our charge against the metaphysician," Ayer declared, "is not that he attempts to employ the understanding in a field where it cannot possibly venture, but that he produces sentences which fail to conform to the conditions under which alone a sentence can be literally significant." [8] The logical positivist turned his attention away from the supposed

[3] C. J. Ducasse, *Philosophy as a Science* (New York: Oskar Piest, 1941), p. 88.

[4] A. J. Ayer, *Logical Positivism* (Glencoe, Ill.: The Free Press, 1959), p. 15.

[5] *Ibid.*, p. 15.

[6] *Op. cit.*, p. 88.

[7] *Ibid.*, pp. 88–89.

[8] A. J. Ayer, *Language, Truth and Logic*, 2nd edition (London: V. Gollancz, Ltd., 1949), p. 35.

realities to which theology and metaphysics refer and investigated their language. His conclusion was that however significant metaphysical talk may be emotionally, it fails to do what it purports to do, express something true or false. Logical empiricism, or logical positivism, took on the aspect of an intellectual crusade, a crusade with the joint mission of eliminating metaphysics from discourse and of unifying the sciences through the medium of a common language. The elimination of metaphysics was the motive force behind the positive program of unifying the sciences. Its intellectual underpinning was a thesis about factual statements, the thesis, namely, that intelligible talk about the world is constituted by statements amenable to testing by the methods of the natural sciences.

In 1936, Carnap wrote in "Testability and Meaning"[9]: ". . . among empiricists there seems to be full agreement that at least some more or less close relation exists between the meaning of a sentence and the way in which we come to a verification or at least a confirmation of it. The requirement of verifiability was first stated by Wittgenstein, and its meaning and consequences were exhibited in the earlier publications of our *Vienna Circle* . . . The thesis needs both explanation and modification. What is meant by 'verifiability' must be said more clearly. And then the thesis must be modified and transformed in a certain direction."

In this essay I wish to trace the metamorphoses of the verifiability requirement through the final stage in which its use is supplanted by a special kind of examination of language by Wittgenstein. I shall argue that there is no modification of the principle of verifiability which can escape a crucial objection, and that what the positivists should have done is what Wittgenstein did in work subsequent to the *Tractatus*. In his *Philosophical Investigations* Wittgenstein said that "The results of philosophy [as he does it] are the uncovering of one or another piece of plain nonsense and of bumps that the understanding has got by running its head up against the limits of language,"[10] and "My aim is: to teach you to pass from a piece of disguised nonsense to

[9] *Philosophy of Science,* Vol. 33, 1936, p. 422.

[10] L. Wittgenstein, *Philosophical Investigations* (New York: The Macmillan Company, 1953), p. 48e.

something that is patent nonsense." [11] It is as though he never entirely gave up the thesis of the logical positivists. But unlike the positivists he did not use the unverifiability of metaphysical statements to dismiss them. I shall in this essay try to make clear how his critique of philosophical language connects with the positivists' critique and yet how unlike their application of a general criterion his procedure is.

According to positivists there are two classes of statements to which any criterion of significance should guarantee meaning: *a priori* statements and empirical statements. And the criterion should preserve the distinction between them.[12] As a point of departure for our examination of the transformations which criticism has necessitated in the positivist criterion let us consider a general characterization of meaning which bears on this initial distinction: that the meaning of a statement is its method of verification. In the Lent term lectures of 1932, Wittgenstein said: In what way a proposition makes sense depends on how you can verify it and what you can do with it.[13] And as late as the *Investigations* he wrote: "Asking whether and how a proposition can be verified is only a particular way of asking 'How d'you mean?' [14] The answer is a contribution to the grammar of the proposition." [15] Suppose one asks concerning a decimal expansion "Is there a period?" The answer, said Wittgenstein, will have the sense which the method of finding one gives it.[16] It is clear that to this question, or to "Are there odd perfect numbers?" or "Is '$p \supset q . \supset . r : \supset : p \supset r . \supset . r$' true?" only *a priori* demonstrations are relevant. No matter of fact has any bearing on the truth or falsity of a given answer. By contrast, any answer to the question, "Are there specks of dust on the window?", will be testable by observation. To these radically different methods of establishing

[11] *Ibid.*, p. 133e.

[12] As is well known, whether such a distinction can be maintained has been challenged. (F. Waismann in a series of articles entitled "Analytic-Synthetic" appearing in *Analysis*, Vols. 10–13, 1949–1953; also W. V. Quine, "Two Dogmas of Empiricism," *The Philosophical Review*, XL, No. 1, January, 1951).

[13] From lecture notes taken by Alice Ambrose.

[14] The German is: "Wie Meinst du das?", pp. 112 and 112e.

[15] *Ibid.*

[16] From lecture notes taken by Alice Ambrose.

truth or falsity correspond, according to positivists, a difference in kind of meaning. Kant classified some statements as both synthetic, i.e., about the world, and *a priori,* i.e., capable of establishment by reason alone. The positivist holds that no statement to which observation is irrelevant can make any factual assertion. As Ayer has put it, they are "devoid of factual content"; [17] their truth "follows simply from the definition of the terms contained in [them]." [18] On the other hand, for the remaining class of meaningful statements, those expressing empirical propositions, there is no possibility of perceiving "in the symbol alone that they are true." [19] That sense-observation is relevant to verifying or falsifying them is a mark of their radical difference from *a priori* statements. This feature of empirical statements positivists embodied in a general criterion for their meaningfulness. We shall take as our starting point here the original formulation of the criterion: a non-*a priori* statement is meaningful if and only if it can be verified or falsified in sense-experience.

Before turning to the difficulties which positivists themselves recognized in this formulation it is worth noting that metaphysical statements appear to straddle both of the classes of meaningful statements described above. They seem to assert something factual; as Kant said, "Metaphysical judgments . . . are all synthetical." [20] At the same time, demonstrations adduced for them make no use of observation or experiment. For example, Bradley's claim that the Absolute is one and Berkeley's claim that physical objects exist only when perceived are reached by a chain of reasoning in which no observational evidence whatever is appealed to. Both claims appear to assert something factual, but this appearance, according to the positivists, is spurious. For not only is there no possibility of carrying out a verification or falsification but there is *no describing* a means to either one. That is, metaphysical statements are "in principle" untestable. Philosophy has been characterized as the catch-all of insoluble problems. But

[17] *Language, Truth and Logic,* p. 79.

[18] *Ibid.,* p. 82.

[19] L. Wittgenstein, *Tractatus Logico-Philosophicus* (London: Routledge & Kegan Paul, Ltd., 1955), 6.113.

[20] *Op. cit.,* p. 22.

it comes seriously in question whether they are real problems if the proposed solutions cannot in theory be checked. The test of verifiability relegates these problems to the limbo of pseudo-problems.

What the positivists found, however, was that the principle as first formulated did both too much and too little. The aim was to eliminate metaphysics and thereby rid the language used in science of a kind of infection. But the principle also eliminated as meaningless statements whose factual significance is undeniable, for example, all universal statements, for whose conclusive establishment an infinity of confirmatory observations is required. In the case of these, verification could not in principle be carried out, so that they would have to count as meaningless (and by a curious anomaly, their negations meaningful). On the other hand, the principle would allow some meaningless statements to count as meaningful, for example, those of the form S v N, where S meets the requirement of verifiability but N does not. Prof. K. Popper's attempt to circumvent the difficulty which the requirement of conclusive verifiability created for universal statements carried a parallel difficulty for existential statements. His new formulation of the criterion for meaningfulness, that a non-*a priori* statement count as meaningful if it is falsifiable, would rule out as meaningless such an existential statement as "Unicorns exist," since no finite set of observations would falsify it. And the negation of this meaningless statement would on this criterion be meaningful. Further, if a statement S satisfied this criterion then so would any conjunction S.N, since $\sim$ S implies $\sim$ (S.N) : "S and the Absolute is perfect" would be meaningful. It is not possible to escape the difficulty presented by universal and existential statements by applying one criterion of meaningfulness to the one sort and the other criterion to the other sort, for no criterion remains which covers statements involving both universal and existential quantifiers, such as "For any substance there exists some solvent."

These difficulties led to a modification of the criterion. A non-*a priori* statement was declared meaningful if it was capable in principle of being *confirmed,* that is, if evidence which would render it probable could be described. Although this weakened principle of verifiability ruled out such statements as "Underlying the qualities apprehended by our senses there is an unknowable substance in which the qualities inhere," a difficulty different from those canvassed followed in its train. This difficulty is brought out by the consideration that what can be rendered probable can, in principle, be established conclusively and thus known to be true. A statement's probability ranges between 0 and 1, inclusive, and the possibility of rendering a statement probable entails the possibility of attaining the goal of certainty, i.e., the possibility of achieving the goal of which the available evidence falls short. Ayer, in common with many logical empiricists, held that "all empirical propositions are hypotheses which are continually subject to the test of further experience; and from this it would follow not merely that the truth of any such proposition never was conclusively established but that it never could be; for however strong the evidence in its favour, there would never be a point at which it was impossible for further experience to go against it." [21] He goes on to admit, in connection with M. Lazerowitz' criticism, that "this would mean that my 'strong' sense of the term 'verifiable' had no possible application . . ." [22] But if the only sense in which a proposition could conceivably be verified is the weak sense specified in the amended version of the criterion, then "weakly verified," or "rendered probable," would no longer have a use to distinguish statements from those to which "conclusively verified," or "rendered certain," applies. And this is as much as to say the weakened criterion has no longer a clear meaning, if any meaning at all.

One further attempt by Ayer to formulate a criterion free from objections fell before his own criticism. His new formulation was that a statement S is meaningful if S in conjunction with suitable subsidiary hypotheses yields observation statements not derivable from the subsidiary hypotheses alone. Thus S is meaningful when an observation statement O follows from the conjunction of statements, S and S $\supset$ O—no matter what S is, "provided only that it [has] the grammatical form of an indicative sentence." [23] If O is "This is white" and S "The Absolute is lazy," S would on this

[21] *Language, Truth and Logic,* pp. 9–10.
[22] *Ibid.*
[23] *Ibid.,* p. 12.

account be meaningful. And even if it were required that $S \supset O$ should be independently testable in the sense specified by the criterion, the criterion would still allow sense to S.N, where S satisfies the criterion but N does not. For the subsidiary hypothesis $S.N. \supset .O$ when combined with S.N will yield O, and thus guarantee meaning to S.N.

The consequence of these failures to free the criterion from the difficulties cited was the abandonment of the attempt to specify the meaningfulness of a statement by reference to testability. We have seen that if S and N are sentences conforming to the rules of a natural language the criterion and its modifications allow literal import to certain truth-function combinations of S and N. This situation could not occur in a language whose vocabulary precluded the formation of statements which the criterion was intended to exclude. Accordingly, logical positivists took a different approach to the problem of specifying conditions of literal significance. This was suggested by the possibility of constructing an artificial language free from metaphysical terminology, a language into which only statements of a natural language which are amenable to testing by the methods of science could be translated. Positivists then addressed themselves to a painstaking construction of an "empiricist" language. Properly devised it would keep metaphysical expressions out of the scientist's workshop language, reduce or eliminate vagueness in the criteria for the use of expressions, and in philosophy would prevent the formation of pseudo-statements, particularly those referring to transcendent "realities." The new principle of literal significance can be put as follows: A non-*a priori* statement has cognitive import if it is translatable into a statement that can be formulated in the empiricist language. Rules of sentence-formation in such a language presented no special problem—the syntax agreed on was that of some such system as *Principia Mathematica.* The crucial question concerned the choice of non-logical vocabulary, which came down to a choice between kinds of observation-terms. With the limitation of the non-logical vocabulary to observation-terms metaphysical expressions could find no place in the language. To imitate Wittgenstein's language in his Aristotelian Society paper,[24]

[24] "Some Remarks on Logical Form," Suppl. Vol. IX, 1929.

they were crowded out of linguistic space. The possibility of forming such sentences as "The Absolute is perfect" was precluded; and difficulties with various versions of the verifiability principle which arose from the possibility of constructing sentences of the form S v N and S.N were avoided. Further, since "all" and "some" figured in the empiricist language they created no special difficulties, as they had done for the verifiability, or falsifiability, principle. For one thing, if S was cognitively meaningful, so was $\sim$ S.

Certain of the difficulties which emerged in the translatability criterion of meaningfulness derived from the kinds of observation-terms initially chosen. These difficulties are of a different order from what one might call workshop difficulties. I need not detail the latter since the extant work of the positivists themselves deals with them clearly and exhaustively.[25] Suffice it to comment that they are difficulties of translating scientific statements of the natural language into statements involving only observation-terms. A word was held to be significant only if sentences in which it occurred were reducible to the basic observation sentences. The program of reduction was hampered by the fact that some words are not capable of elimination from a sentence by simply replacing them by their definiens, as "triangle" can be replaced by "three-sided figure." Three classes of terms presented special difficulties: dispositional terms, such as "magnetic," metrical terms, such as "length," and terms for theoretical constructs, such as "electron." These difficulties, however, did not have the kind of recalcitrance possessed by those following on the different attempts to specify the basic observation-terms of the empiricist language. Against each attempt at specification the charge was made that positivists committed themselves to an unverifiable philosophical position. In the beginnings of the Vienna Circle observation-terms were made to designate "the given," i.e., items in the scientist's immediate experience, and the basic language

[25] Especially Carnap's "Logical Foundations of the Unity of Science," *International Encyclopedia of Unified Science,* Vol. 1, No. 1, 1938, and "Foundations of Logic and Mathematics," *Ibid.,* No. 3, 1939; also C. G. Hempel's "Fundamentals of Concept Formation in Empirical Science," *Ibid.,* Vol. II, No. 7, 1952, and "Problems and Changes in the Empiricist Criterion of Meaning," *Revue Internationale de Philosophie,* 1950.

was "phenomenalistic." Later positivists made the observation-terms denote observable characteristics of physical objects, so that the basic language was a "thing-language." Whichever language is chosen as the one into which only intelligible statements translate, one problem was felt to be inescapable. This was the problem of connecting inferentially the statements recording the scientist's experience with thing-statements, i.e., those which go beyond a "sense content" and refer to physical objects or events.

Consider the statement, "I see a criss-cross of lines in the spectroscope." This record of sense-experience a scientist takes to be (a) in support of or in refutation of a hypothesis about some physical state of affairs, and (b) capable of being checked against similar records of other scientists. According as the observation-terms of the basic language denote the "contents of consciousness" or publicly observable qualities and things, (a) and (b) presented special problems. These problems are aggravated when coupled with the thesis that all intelligible fact-claiming statements are expressible in a single language, which means that ultimately all states of affairs are of one kind, and all objects are of one kind—the data of our minds, physical bodies, minds themselves, social groups. If the basic observation-statements are reports of immediate experience ("protocol" statements), then the twin problem exists of connecting such statements with thing-statements, and the non-overlapping protocol languages of scientists with each other. It is clear that no statement about one's immediate experience entails a thing-statement, else the possibility of recording an hallucinatory experience would be precluded. Further, if the protocol and physical languages refer to different facts then there is no explaining how physical descriptions are verified. One attempt to solve this problem was the reductionist program of showing that a statement about physical things is equivalent to a series of conditional statements about sense-contents. Thus "*x* is a table" was taken to mean "if condition A is fulfilled, S will have sense-experience *a*," etc. *ad infinitum*. This, of course, is the philosophical position of phenomenalism. I shall not canvass its difficulties here. The second difficulty a phenomenalist language faced was that there seemed no escape from solipsism. In *The Unity of Science* Carnap pointed out that if the words of S_1's protocol language, e.g., "thirst," named sensations of S_1, whereas the same word of S_2 referred to sensations of S_2, then each protocol language would be used only solipsistically. No protocol statement of S_1's language could express the fact that S_2 was thirsty. In fact S_1's statement to this effect would be unverifiable by him if "thirst of S_2" meant a (private) sensation of S_2. Thus there would be no common language among scientists and therefore no check on each other's records, nor would there be any reason for taking the totality of them to be evidence for some one proposition.

One "intersubjective" language, i.e., a language common to all who use it, rather than a number of egocentric languages, was the desideratum. By taking observation-terms to stand for observable characteristics of physical bodies the end seemed to be attained. Statements recording the sense-evidence by which a scientist confirms or refutes a hypothesis in question, if expressible in physical terms, would present no solipsistic problem revolving around "the privacy of experience." It was Carnap's thesis in *The Unity of Science* that every statement of perceived fact can be so expressed. Singular statements attributing sense-qualities to physical objects were held to be translatable into statements about "a quantitatively determined property of a definite position at a definite time." [26] And the scientist's own protocol statements were held to be deducible from statements about bodily states: "Red is being seen by S now" was taken to entail and be entailed by "The body S is seeing red now." This was the thesis of physicalism. All objects, all qualities, all states of affairs were held to be of one kind, whence intelligible statements in every science, including biology, psychology, and sociology, could be formulated in a single language, the "physical" language. Critics have of course pointed out that the price of an intersubjective language of this sort is philosophical materialism, that the thesis that every empirical statement is expressible in a physical language is no more than the materialistic thesis that all facts are physical. The issue of materialism versus dualism or idealism is merely transferred to a linguistic level.

[26] Pp. 52–53.

The criticism that logical positivists committed themselves to unverifiable philosophical positions was one which, on their own program, they were concerned to meet. There is a tendency, in assessing their attempts to state the conditions of literal significance, to become preoccupied with this sort of criticism, and also with criticisms showing the need to reformulate the verification principle or to remove obstacles to the program of reducing intelligible statements of the language of science to those of a single empiricist language. But underlying all these criticisms is the assumption that positivists are simply attempting to describe what the conditions of meaningfulness actually are. As Ayer put it, "They were propounding a definition of meaning which accorded with common usage in the sense that it set out the conditions that are in fact satisfied by statements which are regarded as empirically informative." [27] But it seems quite clear that both the verification principle and the translatability criterion state, not what the conditions of meaningfulness in fact are, but what they have to be *if* metaphysics is to be eliminated and *if* metaphysical expressions are to be kept out of the scientist's language. The criteria had to be rigged to secure the desired end. Positivists have made a show of demonstrating the impossibility of metaphysics while assuming it in their criteria of meaningfulness. The "conclusion" that metaphysics is meaningless rests on custom-tailored criteria; it commits a *petitio principii.*

The claim that the various formulations of the verifiability criterion beg the question is developed in detail by M. Lazerowitz.[28] The failure of the verification principle to escape this crucial objection can be seen if one looks at the difficulties in the formulations of it which I have so far slurred over in presenting the positivist position. When, in the original formulation, positivists said a statement is meaningful if and only if it can be verified or falsified, the referent of the term "it" is ambiguous. In the sense in which a statement can be said to be meaningful or meaningless, the word "statement" means *sentence.* In the sense in which a statement can be said to be verifiable or falsifiable, "statement" means *proposition.* And "sentence" and "proposi-

[27] *Logical Positivism,* p. 15.

[28] *The Structure of Metaphysics* (London: Routledge and Paul, 1955), pp. 55–56.

tion" do not mean the same. As Moore points out in his *Commonplace Book,* "Every proposition which is true, except propositions about sentences, *could* have been true, even if there had been no sentences: from the fact that it is true that the sun is shining it doesn't follow that there are any sentences." [29] "Sentence" and "proposition" are not interchangeable terms, as indicated by the fact that a sentence may sensibly be said to be meaningful, or written in red ink, but cannot sensibly be said to be verified or to be true, or to be deducible from another sentence. As Moore said, "To talk of *deducing* one sentence from another is not English." [30] We might, then, reframe the criterion so as to conform to English usage as follows: A declarative sentence which does not express an *a priori* proposition is meaningful if and only if the proposition it expresses can be verified or falsified in sense-experience. But the criterion so formulated involves a contradiction: A sentence cannot express a proposition and at the same time be meaningless. To say that a sentence expressing a proposition is meaningless because it expresses an unverifiable proposition therefore will not do. However, the criterion can be so restated as to avoid this objection, viz.: A sentence which does not express an analytic proposition is meaningful only if it expresses a proposition verifiable in sense-experience. But then a fresh difficulty breaks out, namely, that it is custom-cut to exclude as meaningless any sentence failing to express a proposition open to sense testing. It does succeed in eliminating such sentences as "A transcedent God exists" and "There are abstract objects, denoted by numerals, which are apprehended only in thought." But it does so only by linguistic fiat, and can hardly be expected to influence the metaphysician or the theologian. One can imagine a traditional metaphysician pointing out that one might as well condemn a sentence as meaningless because it does not express a proposition verifiable visually, or that *he* could make the equally arbitrary stipulation that a sentence be meaningful only if it expresses a proposition open to supersensible verification. Certainly a metaphysician like Bradley, who wrote, ". . . we seem to touch and have communion

[29] P. 375.
[30] *Ibid.,* p. 258.

with what is beyond the visible world,"[31] would object to a criterion tailored with an eye to eliminating this sentence from intelligible discourse.

I think it is clear that the same objection, of begging the question, applies to the criterion which makes the meaningfulness of a non-*a priori* sentence depend on its translatability into an empiricist language. In fact the translatability condition recommended itself in consequence of the failure of the variants of the verification principle to exclude certain truth-function combinations of S and N. It is interesting to note that Ayer in his Introduction to *Logical Positivism* admitted that meaninglessness is achieved by decree: "The most that has been proved is that metaphysical statements do not fall into the same category as the laws of logic, or as scientific hypotheses . . . or any other common sense descriptions of the 'natural' world. Surely it does not follow that they are neither true nor false, still less that they are nonsensical? No, it does not follow. Or rather, it does not follow unless one makes it follow. The question is whether one thinks the difference between metaphysical and common sense or scientific statements to be sufficiently sharp for it to be useful to underline it in this way."[32]

Now there is a very great difference between "meaningless by decree" and "meaningless according to current linguistic conventions." One does not increase one's riches by calling one's pennies dollars. Nor does arbitrarily stretching the use of the term "meaningless" so that it applies to a new class of sentences constitute the discovery that the sentences *are* meaningless. Considerations directed to showing that certain sentences ought to be forcibly turned out of language do not show that they in fact are meaningless. But neither does the failure to show they are meaningless justify the conclusion that they are meaningful. There can be no doubt that they are different from commonsense or scientific statements, and that if we are to come to a correct perception of this difference it must be underlined. Supposing for the moment that metaphysical sentences are meaningful, the

[31] F. H. Bradley, *Appearance and Reality* (Oxford: at the Clarendon Press, 1930), p. 5.

[32] Pp. 15–16.

positivists have done a service in making perspicuous the unique position occupied by the propositions they express. Metaphysical propositions are not *a priori,* else examination of the words expressing them should show that they are. But if they are empirical, i.e., are such that their actual truth-values are not their only possible truth-values, then they fall into a category distinct from all other empirical propositions in that neither observation nor experiment is relevant to establishing which truth-value they have. Classifying propositions by reference to "the modes of verification proper to [them]" [33] proved to be an important preliminary to a linguistic investigation, namely, of the *sentences* used to assert them and of the key-words figuring in them. At the same time, focussing attention on verifiability tended to crowd out attention to the features of metaphysical sentences which account for the fact that the propositions they express are unverifiable in sense-experience. It was this kind of scrutiny of the use of words occurring *in* metaphysical sentences which enabled Wittgenstein to specify at least one use of words in "a typically metaphysical way" [34] and to make questionable whether sentences in such cases express unverifiable propositions or no propositions at all.

Wittgenstein's transition from concern with verifiability to concern with usage is reflected in his lectures and writings. In lectures of 1932–33 one finds the same statement of the verifiability criterion of meaning, with the same ambiguous play on the word "proposition," as in the case of the positivists:

> In the verification of a proposition lies its sense.
> A proposition gets its sense from the verification.
> In what way a proposition makes sense depends on how you can verify it and what you can do with it.
> If there is no possible evidence for or against "The world sprang into existence five minutes ago" then it is meaningless.
> If we do away with all means of verification we destroy the meaning.

[33] John Wisdom's phrase, Introduction to M. Lazerowitz' *The Structure of Metaphysics,* p. xi.

[34] *The Blue and Brown Books* (Oxford: Basil Blackwell, 1958), p. 46.

However, in the Lent and Easter terms of the same year verification is regarded as a means of effecting connections between propositions, e.g., entailments. The sentences figuring in the expression of these connections are said to get their meaning from their uses in relation to each other: "The meaning of a symbol is its place in the calculus—the way it is used is its meaning." One exhibits the meaning of a "proposition" by showing its relations to other propositions—what it follows from and what follows from it. So the question "How can one know that . . . ?," a question about verification, is not irrelevant to the question "What is the meaning?" The answer to the former, as surely as to the latter, "gives the grammar of the proposition": verification shows the relations of a proposition to others. Of course it is not being claimed that giving the meaning in this way is like producing a translation. Wittgenstein distinguishes between "being the meaning of" and "determining the meaning of." "It rained yesterday" may be verified in different ways, and each type of verifying proposition he says helps to determine the meaning of the sentence without *being* its meaning. For example, "I remember that it rained yesterday" helps to determine the meaning of "it rained yesterday" without being the meaning of it. Similarly, reading that Cambridge won the boat race, which verifies that Cambridge won, is not part of the meaning "Cambridge won," although it is connected with it. If we consider how we would explain the meaning of a sentence, Wittgenstein said, the connection between meaning and verification becomes clear. The system of sentences of which a given sentence forms a part, where such relations as confirmation, entailment, refutation are displayed as holding between what they express, shows something about the meanings of the sentences, i.e., their *use*. He said, "The sense of a proposition is its use. If you want to know the sense of a proposition, find how it is used. What is its verification?" [35]

These observations by Wittgenstein indicate that a shift is already underway to examination of the uses of sentences as a

[35] From notes of lectures of the Lent term, 1932. A similar comment appears in the *Investigations* (p. 112e) when he remarks that the answer to the question concerning the sort and possibility of verification of a proposition is "a contribution to the grammar of the proposition."

means of determining their meanings, with considerations about verifiability directed to connecting verifiability with use. We see this shift reflected in the change from the question, "How is it verified?" to the question, "What would it be like?" For there is a ready transition from this latter question to "What use does it (a sentence) have?" Consider the following example from his 1932 lectures: "There is a white rabbit between the two chairs whenever no observations are being made." This sentence does not have a use in language to assert any state of affairs which could be shown either to exist or not to exist. He characterizes it as otiose, the way wheels unconnected with the movement in a watch would be otiose. It is out of connection with any other sentences of the language, e.g., with such sentences as "Fact p would refute (or fact q be evidence for) the existence of such a rabbit." Another way of putting the point is to say that we have fixed no application for "unobservable rabbit." The question, "What would it be like for there to be such a rabbit?" is a way of asking, "Does it make sense to say there is one?" and "What use does 'unobservable rabbit' have?" In subsequent lectures, 1934–35, the transition from questions about propositions to questions about sentences emerged clearly in the juxtaposition, within the same paragraph, of (1) and (2): (1) To ask what it would be like for p to be true is to ask for a grammatical connection between p and other propositions, and (2) to ask "Can you give me the grammar of a sentence?" is to ask "Can you give me the sentences with which this one hangs together and say in what way they are connected?".

The question now arises as to what specific linguistic features some philosophical statements have which make them similar to "There is an unobservable rabbit between the two chairs." Is there a characteristic use of words occurring within these sentences which is responsible for the failure of the sentences to "connect" with other sentences in ordinary language? Wittgenstein made an important observation in *The Blue Book* concerning one such use. It suggests a method for singling out in philosophical statements a use of language which might well condemn them as nonsense. I do not wish to imply that this is *the* method for conducting a critique of the philosopher's language.

As Wittgenstein remarks, "There is not *a* philosophical method, though there are indeed methods, like different therapies." [36] Nevertheless there is a number of philosophical statements which have in common a special use of words, and this use has to be held up and compared with ordinary uses in order to determine whether they function in the language to convey information about fact. He wrote: "When philosophers use a word—'knowledge,' 'being,' 'object,' 'I,' 'proposition,' 'name'— . . . one must always ask oneself: is the word ever actually used in this way in the language-game which is its original home?—What *we* do is to bring words back from their metaphysical to their everyday use." [37] One such metaphysical usage is described in the following: ". . . in stating our puzzles about the *general vagueness* of sense-experience, and about the flux of all phenomena, we are using the words 'flux' and 'vagueness' wrongly, in a typically metaphysical way, namely without an antithesis; whereas in their correct and everyday use vagueness is opposed to clearness, flux to stability, inaccuracy to accuracy, and *problem* to *solution.*" [38]

By pointing out that a given word is used in a philosophical context in such a way that its antithesis is left without any conceivable application Wittgenstein exhibited one great difference between philosophical and everyday usage. The words of the philosopher, e.g., "Everything steadfastly flows," have the air of making factual assertions; their point seems to be that of conveying information about the state of things. And usually only the philosopher's surrounding talk hints that some word has been deprived of its ordinary use. It should be clear that when Wittgenstein shows how some specific philosophical statement fails to make a factual claim because the use of language precludes its making one he is doing something very different from the positivist, who by his verifiability principle legislates the failure. What Wittgenstein does in certain cases, though connecting up with their criterion via the question "What would it be like?," cannot be charged with begging the question. I shall now illustrate his procedure by considering several philosophical

[36] *Philosophical Investigations,* p. 51e.

[37] *Ibid.,* p. 48e.

[38] *The Blue and Brown Books,* p. 46.

statements in which words are used "in a typically metaphysical way, namely, without an antithesis." [39]

Take first what looks like a complaint against our senses[W]: "We can never see an accurate circle." This, says Wittgenstein, is no complaint, or if you like, it is a pseudo-complaint, because there is no accuracy to compare the inaccuracy with, no imaginable accurate circle with which to compare the inaccurate circles presented to our senses. Show me what an accurate circle is like, he challenges, and perhaps I'll see one tomorrow. I think it is obvious that if the senses never *can,* in principle, reveal an accurate, perfectly round circle then "circle observed to be accurate" will not describe any theoretically observable figure, whereas in everyday use—in their "original home"—"accurate" and "inaccurate" both have a descriptive use. The philosopher who asserts the inaccuracy of the senses has deprived the term "inaccurate" of its antithesis and in doing so might seem to have given the word a new use, one in which it applies to all possible observed circles. But in fact what applies to all *possible* circles will not describe any if it does not serve to distinguish between possible circles: the application of "accurate circle" would not be different from that of "circle," and "accurate" would not serve to modify "circle." To put the matter differently, if "accurate" does not have a use to describe circles, neither does "not-accurate." To say that all sense-given circles are inaccurate circles is equivalent to saying that all sense-given circles are circles—whence what looked to be a factual report on the inadequacy of our senses reduces, in point of factual content, to a tautology.

Two alternative conclusions can be drawn concerning the status of the *philosophical* sentence here discussed (in contrast to the non-philosophical sentence, "All circles drawn freehand have turned out so far to be inaccurate"). Each of these conclusions has support in various things Wittgenstein has said. Each relates to the construction placed on the philosophical sentence, "We can never see an accurate circle." If this sentence is construed as

[39] The examples having superscript W are taken from *The Blue Book* and from informal discussion in the intervals between dictation of *The Blue Book* (as reported in notes taken by Margaret Masterman and Alice Ambrose), and the remaining ones from historical sources where the parallel is obvious.

expressing a matter of fact, then the conclusion to be inferred is that it is nonsensical; it fails to do what it purports to do because "accurate" no longer has its ordinary, descriptive use, and the philosopher has provided no other use. If, on the other hand, the sentence is construed as expressing a necessary truth in the language in actual use—English, in the present case—then one of two conclusions is forced upon us: either (a) the philosopher is making a false claim about English usage, or (b) he is by fiat using the sentence to express a necessary truth in *his* special language. Conclusion (a) seems unacceptable, since "accurate circle," unlike "square circle" in "We can never see a square circle," does function descriptively in ordinary language; and the philosopher is not unaware of this fact about usage. Conclusion (b) then remains: that he is so using language as to *make* the sentence express a necessary proposition. In support of the conclusion that the sentence is nonsensical I call attention to Wittgenstein's remark, "My aim is: to teach you to pass from a piece of disguised nonsense to something that is patent nonsense." [40] In support of conclusion (b) I cite his description of the metaphysician's assertions as expressing "discontent with our grammar." [41] What the metaphysician wants, he says, "is only a new notation . . . [but] . . . he is not aware that he is objecting to a convention." [42] So interpreted, the metaphysician's statement does not have as its point the communication of fact at all, however much the contrary appears to be the case: "He [does] not tell us a new truth and [does] not show us that what we said before was false." [43] This kind of conclusion I take to be one of Wittgenstein's most important contributions to understanding the nature of the assertions a philosopher puts forward. It is supported by the fact that the philosopher refuses to accept any evidence against his claim—which is to say that the use of a philosophical sentence is not to express a fact but to express, in the philosopher's language, a necessary truth.

Wittgenstein said in *The Blue Book* ". . . what we always do

[40] *Philosophical Investigations,* p. 133e.

[41] *The Blue and Brown Books,* p. 57.

[42] *Ibid.,* p. 57.

[43] *Ibid.,* p. 60.

when we meet the word 'can' in a metaphysical proposition . . . [is to] show that this proposition hides a grammatical rule. That is to say, we destroy the outward similarity between a metaphysical proposition and an experiential one . . ." [44] In my opinion what Wittgenstein says about the use of words in putative factual sentences represents a transition to his viewing the sentences of philosophers as "grammatical." We can discern how the transition is made by examining the connection between the application of the verifiability principle when words are used without their antitheses and the metaphysician's introduction of a new notation which precludes such words from descriptive use. For this purpose the example just discussed is instructive. Wittgenstein's challenge to the philosopher who declares the inaccuracy of sense-experience suggests that one could not say "what it would be like" to observe an accurate circle.[45] His challenge, though formulated in the non-verbal idiom, contains a verbal point. The reason we do not know what it would be like to observe an accurate circle is that "observed accurate circle" has been deprived of descriptive use.[46] And the reason we cannot refute the philosopher's claim by producing an accurate circle is that, *in advance,* "accurate" is deprived of its application to any possible circle. Thus the sentence (P) "There are no sense-given accurate circles" is cut off from its relations to empirical sentences: for one thing, the empirical sentence (E) "I see a perfect circle" is not so related to $\sim$ (P) as to allow us to assert of propositions e and $\sim p$ that e entails $\sim p$. For "There are no sense-given accurate circles" is now in a position like that of "There are no square circles," the truth-value of which is not affected by what exists or doesn't exist. That is, the philosopher's use of it is to express a necessary proposition (it "hides a grammatical rule"), though clearly its ordinary use is not this.

Once the consequences of using a word so that it is not coupled with its antithesis becomes clear from this example, a flood of

[44] *Ibid.,* p. 55.

[45] As some positivists have put it: "We do not know what it is like for this to be true."

[46] In general, when Wittgenstein says that we do not know what ϕ would be like it is his way of calling attention to the fact that the expression "ϕ" has no descriptive use.

similar examples rushes to mind. Consider, for instance, the following:

> Our senses can only disclose how things seem, not how they are.
> Change is unreal, no more than mere appearance.
> Motion is impossible.
> All desires are selfish.
> Empirical propositions are all hypotheses.

Take the words "seems" and "apparent." In English, these have as their antitheses "is," and "real," and the members of each pair can be applied to the same things: what in fact only seems to be could be, and what is apparent might be real. Expressed in the verbal idiom: "seems to be, and actually is," "thought to be real but turned out to be apparent," have a use to describe situations. But when the philosopher says, "A thing as it really is apart from its appearances cannot be apprehended by the senses," "thing as it really is" is deprived of its application to anything apprehended by the senses, and "thing as it appears" is made to apply to all observable things. Hence the second phrase will fail to describe even the appearances, since it will no longer distinguish amongst possible sense-disclosures. "What is revealed to the senses are only appearances" in point of factual content says no more than "What is revealed to the senses is revealed to the senses." Similarly with "Nothing ever changes," or "Change is unreal." F. H. Bradley in *Appearance and Reality* gives the impression that he is using the words "change" and "real" in their usual senses and by his argument proving something about the things the words refer to: proving, for example, that only in appearance do trees grow, that they really remain the same. But in fact he is so using "real" and "change" and "apparent" that "real change" has no descriptive function, and "apparent change" applies to whatever "change" applies to. Thus, the metaphysician's sentence "All change is apparent change" expresses only the uninteresting tautology "All change is change." By depriving "real change" of its use, the philosopher unwittingly also deprives "apparent change" of its use.

The two ways of construing metaphysical statements, (1) as nonsensical, (2) as "grammatical rules," and the connection between them, now becomes apparent. On the first interpretation, to pursue the present example, it can be said that by casting "real change" out of language the metaphysician makes "apparent change" senseless, so that although he presents "All change is apparent change" as a deep pronouncement about reality, he is giving us "a piece of disguised nonsense" through misapprehension of the workings of our language. By pointing out that an expression severed from its usual antithesis has only the semblance of conveying any fact, Wittgenstein may be thought of as exposing disguised nonsense as "patent nonsense"—and this in a more enlightening way than does the use of the verifiability principle. But although explicit statements by Wittgenstein make prominent this treatment of metaphysical assertions, a second and different treatment is also apparent. This is that the metaphysician turns a sentence which does not express a necessary truth into one which does, because he wants "a new notation." A sentence such as "There are no square circles," which according to present conventions expresses a necessary proposition (a "rule of grammar"), functions so as to preclude "square circle" from descriptive use. A sentence such as "There is no real change" functions, by the philosopher's unconscious decision, to effect a similar end for "real change."

There is a possible if not easy transition from "metaphysics is nonsense" to "metaphysics is reconstituted language": the transition from viewing the philosopher as taking one of a pair of opposites to have in fact no descriptive use to viewing him as *suppressing* one of that pair without being aware that he is "objecting to a convention" and changing usage. The philosopher's behavior does not suggest either that he takes "there is no real change" to express a matter of fact or, in our language, to express a necessity. It is possible that Wittgenstein began to think that such a sentence neither was nonsensical (through failing to do what it purports to do—express a fact) nor a misdescription of current usage, and that in consequence he went on to think of it as introducing a non-conventional rule of grammar.

In conclusion I shall cite briefly a few further examples in philosophy with regard to which similar observations can be made. Motion has been held to be impossible because the concept *motion* is self-contradictory. "Stationary" thus loses its antithesis, which is to say it loses its everyday use. And as no new moorings with other words of the language have been provided for it by the philosopher it ceases to have a place in the language. The same is true for "All desires are selfish" and "All empirical propositions are hypotheses." A philosopher who makes these statements precludes his being able to say what it would be like for a desire not to be selfish or for an empirical proposition not to be just a hypothesis, i.e., to be certain. Another interesting example is the positivist "reduction" of statements about sense-experience to statements about bodily states ("S is seeing red now" to "The body S is seeing red now").[47] In a "typically metaphysical way" no provision is made for the use of "non-physical."

A final example, which at the same time provides a good illustration of Wittgenstein's conception of his task of "bringing words back from their metaphysical to their everyday use" is to be found in his treatment of solipsism[w]. In *The Blue Book* he writes:

> Now the man whom we call a solipsist and who says that only his own experiences are real, does not thereby disagree with us about any practical question of fact, he does not say that we are simulating when we complain of pains, he pities us as much as anyone else, and at the same time he wishes to restrict the use of the epithet "real" to what we should call his experiences; and perhaps he doesn't want to call our experiences "experiences" at all (again without disagreeing with us about any question of fact). For he would say that it was *inconceivable* that experiences other than his own were real.[48] . . . The solipsist's 'Only this is really seen' reminds us of a tautology.[49]

Wittgenstein's comments [50] on the solipsist's use of language were in substance as follows:

> If it is logically impossible for me to say that another person has toothache, it is equally so for me to say I have. To the per-

[47] R. Carnap, *The Unity of Science*, p. 87.

[48] P. 59.

[49] P. 71.

[50] At roughly the time of the dictation of the above passage.

> son who says "Only I have real toothache," the reply should be, "If only you can have real toothache there is no sense in saying, 'Only I have real toothache.' Either you don't need 'I' or you don't need 'real' . . . 'I' is no longer opposed to anything. You had much better say, 'There is toothache.' [51] "Only I have real toothache" either has a common sense meaning, or, if it is a grammatical proposition, it is meant to be a statement of a rule; it wishes to say, "I should like to put, instead of the notation 'I have real toothache' 'There is toothache' . . ." What the solipsist wants is not a notation in which the ego has a monopoly, but one in which the ego vanishes.

It is quite clear that the solipsist's statement of his position has turned "I" out of its original home, where its use is linked with other-person pronouns. When Wittgenstein describes his task as bringing words back from their metaphysical to their everyday use he may be interpreted as saying that he is bringing words back into the language. For the metaphysician, in suppressing one of a pair of correlated terms, eliminates them both.

Smith College

[51] Similarly in *The Blue Book:* "[The solipsist] ought therefore to use a notation in which such a phrase as 'A has real toothache' (where A is not he) is meaningless, a notation whose rules exclude this phrase as the rules of chess exclude a pawn's making a knight's move. The solipsist's suggestion comes to using such a phrase as 'there is real toothache' instead of 'Smith (the solipsist) has toothache.'" P. 59.

PERCEPTION AND SENSATION AS PRESENTATIONAL

CHARLES A. BAYLIS

IN THE EARLY TWENTIES, when I was one of Professor Ducasse's students at the University of Washington, he would usually return the papers I submitted to him covered with his comments, queries and criticisms. I evidently looked dismayed at all the writing on one typescript he returned to me, for he kindly explained that "All those critical remarks represent a compliment, not a condemnation. I wouldn't spend that much time on a worthless paper." This answer made good sense and helped me to learn much from Ducasse. Now I am happy to have this opportunity to return his compliment by offering a radical alternative to his views on perception.

I know nearly all of Ducasse's earlier writings in this field, but, unfortunately, I have not as yet seen his latest ones, even in typescript. But I did talk with him about them last December at the Boston meeting of the Eastern Division of the American Philosophical Association. If I understood him correctly he told me that on his view what we are directly acquainted with in perception or sensation is always something that is mental in nature and is never identical with a physical object or with any characteristic of such an object. This type of view, I know, has tough roots in the writings of Descartes and Locke, and perhaps other sources in the works of Berkeley and Hume. What I hope to do here is not to make detailed criticisms of Ducasse's accounts but to propose a defensible presentative view of both perception and sensation. My account entails the consequence that ordinarily we perceive correctly physical objects themselves and/or sense their sensible qualities without error.

Indeed, by far the most remarkable fact about perception and sensation is that in the vast majority of cases we perceive physical objects as they are and/or sense without error the sensible qualities they exhibit. Moreover we normally do this without conscious inference from mental data to objects and with no apparent evidence of unconscious inference of that sort either. The *prima facie* case for this is that were such inferential processes necessary it would be extremely difficult to explain, for example, how millions of us can drive safely through the congested streets of our big cities or the speedways of our countryside. Such feats would be *prima facie* impossible were inference, conscious or unconscious, required for every perception and sensation. For presumably even unconscious inference, if it occurs, requires neural processes which are relatively slow and time consuming.

Misperceptions do indeed occur, and occasionally illusions, and very rarely hallucinations. The process of perceiving is temporal and complex, very much more complex indeed, psychologists tell us, than we had formerly believed. At many crucial points in it a breakdown or malfunction will cause perceptual or sensory error. But the often neglected point of these facts is that when no such malfunctioning of the perceptual process occurs there is no error and we perceive and/or sense correctly. This is the normal case, the paradigm type of perceptual or sensory occurrence. Errors are always, we assume, due to something having gone wrong in the associated physical, physiological or psychological processes. When such errors occur we can often detect their sources ourselves, but if not we properly turn to scientific experts for help. In the absence of malfunction in the perceptual process we perceive correctly. Indeed we often learn to perceive correctly even in cases where we know of some abnormality in the perceptual process. Thus, for example, experienced spear fishermen have learned enough to bring home the fish they at first mislocated.

In contrast with such a presentative account, which holds normal perception to be *direct*—i.e., without conscious inference —and *correct,* yielding perceptual knowledge of physical objects and their properties and sensory knowledge of their sense qualities, what Lovejoy seems to have done, and Ducasse also, is to take cases of misperception or of mis-sensing as their models. They then try to explain veridical cases in terms of the kind of private mental data which they find or postulate in these instances of perceptual or sensory error. This approach leads Lovejoy at least to conclude that we never perceive physical objects themselves, or sensible qualities of these objects, directly but at best infer them, consciously or unconsciously from our private mental data, which in the case of veridical perception or sensation happily correspond to characteristics, i.e., qualities, properties, or relations, of physical objects.

This conclusion appears explicitly in Lovejoy's argument based on the time required for any perceptual or sensory process to take place.[1] He takes as a striking example our perception of a distant star, say a thousand light years away.

> The doctrine of the finite velocity of light meant that the sense from which most of our information about the world beyond our epidermal surfaces is derived never discloses anything which . . . 'really exists' in that world, at the instant at which it indubitably exists in perception. . . . Never, in short, if both the physiologists and physicists are right, can the datum or character-complex presented in the perception of a given moment be regarded as anything but the report of a messenger, more or less tardy and more or less open to suspicion, from the original object which we are said to know by virtue of that perception.[2]

He concludes that perceptual errors of the usual kinds result from identifying erroneously "the end-term with the initial term of the physico-physiological causal series" [3] involved in the perceptual process.

But surely no one uncontaminated by a representational theory would ever commit such a mistake. He has too good evidence for believing that the star is a physical object of very large size and of very high temperature to confuse it with a mental datum or image which is private to his mind and has neither volume nor tempera-

[1] *The Revolt Against Dualism* (La Salle, Ill.: The Open Court Publishing Company, 1930). This is one of five arguments, regarded as coercive by Lovejoy, presented in Chapter One of these Carus Lectures. For a criticism of them see C. A. Baylis, "A Criticism of Lovejoy's Case for Epistemological Dualism," *Philosophy and Phenomenological Research,* Vol. XXIII, No. 4, June, 1963, pp. 527–537.

[2] *Ibid.,* pp. 19–20.

[3] *Ibid,* p. 22.

ture. Nor would one who reflects a moment be willing to assert that he sees the star as it exists today—for it may well have been destroyed—or that it is today located in the heavens at the place where he sees it. Rather he would say that he sees the star that existed a thousand years ago at a place somewhere near where it was a thousand years ago. He no more makes this kind of mistake in vision than he does the corresponding one in hearing. He knows full well that the sound of a pile-driver's weight hitting the piling is the sound of the last blow of that weight, not a sound it is now making when it is about to be released for its next drop. Because we know that sound travels relatively slowly we seldom claim that a sound heard now began its existence now. Similarly, though light travels very rapidly, we know enough to agree that we are seeing the distant star as and where it was when the light now reaching us departed from it rather than where it is now, supposing that it still exists. The process of perception always takes time and what we perceive is always something temporally earlier than the concluding moment of that process.

Representationalists in perceptual theory have sometimes asserted that what we are aware of in perception is always a mental object rather than a physical thing, perhaps an image of some sort. Others, more wildly I fear, have suggested that in vision we see the images on our retinas. But it would take a rather elaborate arrangement of lights and mirrors and lenses for us to perceive our own retinal images. A more basic answer to the view that in vision we are always aware of a visual image of ours is that many people claim to have little or no visual imagery. Yet such people, as shown by their behavior, do seem to perceive physical objects and their sizes and shapes and locations quite accurately. For those who do have visual imagery the tests proposed by Berkeley and Hume for distinguishing images from percepts, namely, vividness, coherence, and controlability, are usually sufficient. Where they are not, as in the case of hallucination as contrasted with voluntary image formation, physiological tests are possible. If a visual datum is aroused by the stimulation of the eyes by light rays reflected from an object, we regard the datum as a sensory or perceptual one. If it is aroused centrally rather than peripherally in the nervous system we regard it as an image and classify the experience as a hallucination. In veridical perceptual or sensory experiences, as contrasted with hallucinatory ones, it seems eminently reasonable to hold that we perceive physical objects or aspects of them or sense qualities which not only seem to characterize the surface of a physical object but in fact do.

The second principal type of objection which Lovejoy raises against presentational theories of perception and sensation is that different people frequently report the secondary qualities of a physical object, e.g., the color of a traffic light quite differently. Some see it as red, others as chocolate colored, others as having still different shades. But surely, Lovejoy argues—and Ducasse, I believe, would concur—since these colors are incompatible it cannot be the case that the object possesses all of them and it may be the case that it possesses none of them. Consider for example the curtain of a theater on which differently colored lights are played by a projector. It seems to take on successively quite a number of different hues, red, blue, gray, green, purple, etc. It cannot have all these different colors, it is assumed, and may have none of them. What color shall we say it has? Shall we say that it has the color which is sensed by people with standard eyes, i.e., those who can meet certain selected test criteria, under standard lighting conditions, i.e., those which approximate to full daylight? But both of these standards have been set up by human beings who might just as well have chosen other conditions as standard. Or shall we say that an object simultaneously has many colors, all those that different people then see it to have? But this seems repugnant, even logically impossible to many people. Such puzzles seem to drive people like Lovejoy, and perhaps Ducasse also, to conclude that physical objects have no color at all. The different colors sensed, they tend to say, are not characteristics of an object but mental qualities of the different observers who err in attributing these hues to objects.

Fortunately this kind of a conceptual problem can be tidied up quickly if we make use of a distinction which some writers, including Ducasse, have urged, namely that between qualities and properties. A color property is a dispositional characteristic possessed by a physical object which enables persons of a certain type under certain lighting conditions to sense certain color qualities.

An object has *color property* 1, let us say, if and only if it has the capacity to enable all and only persons of type A (say those capable of sorting colored yarns in a specified way) under specified conditions of lighting X (say those approximating to sunlight) to become sensorily aware of color quality 1 over that object's surface. Well and good. But of course any uniformly colored object possesses many other color properties and manifests many other color qualities. It will have color property 2 because it will enable persons of type B under lighting conditions of type Y to become aware of color quality 2. And it will have color property 3, because it will enable a person of type C under lighting conditions of type Z to become aware of color quality 3. And so on. Since there are three variables here: the type of person, the type of lighting condition, and the type of color quality seen, we already have quite a number of possible color properties and color qualities for every object. And the list can be extended indefinitely. There seem to be no good grounds for denying that a given physical object has all of these color properties, and that all that is needed for the corresponding color qualities to be manifest is that the object be seen by observers of the appropriate sort under lighting conditions of the appropriate sort. To stipulate only one set of conditions as the standard ones limits not at all the color properties a given object has nor the color qualities that can be seen to suffuse its surface. The blackboard that we ordinarily call green also has the quality and property of being black because it is so observable in a dim light, and also the property and quality of being chocolate colored because it is so observable by people we call red-green color blind. It seems to me that I have sometimes heard Ducasse talk in this way, and I quite agree with him. But my conclusion is that these facts offer no sound basis for the view that color qualities are either private or mental. Rather they make it reasonable to conclude that any color an object can be seen to have it does have. And to manifest that quality for seeing it must have the corresponding property or power of being thus seeable under these circumstances by people with the appropriate visual powers.

The type of perceptual and sensory theory I have here been proposing to Ducasse is clearly a presentational one. According to it, in the vast majority of cases our complex perceptual apparatus functions normally and by means of its errorless performance enables us to perceive physical objects and their properties as they in fact are. In the course of such a perceptual process our sense organs are appropriately stimulated, afferent nerve impulses are carried to our brain, and efferent nerves set off appropriate responses. When all this physiological apparatus functions correctly we perceive physical objects without error, discern physical properties correctly, and respond to them suitably. Although in such perceptual activity our sense organs are suitably stimulated we may or may not be aware of the various sensory qualities the perceived object manifests. Thus in driving through heavy traffic, our attention may well be focussed on the size and shape, direction of motion and speed of approaching vehicles and not, usually, on their color. The color quality seeable by us under the given lighting conditions is presumably there, but because our attention is on more important features we do not notice it. Only some quite wild color could divert our attention from the mass and speed of the passing cars. Similarly, at a reception, we may note various characteristics of the people we meet and yet fail to note their hair color, unless, perhaps, we are hair fetichists or someone has hair of a striking hue. Ordinarily we notice and respond to only a few of the vast number of sense qualities, objective properties and even physical objects before us.

When we do notice something observable we normally are aware of it without conscious inference; we are aware of it in this sense directly. Sometimes, of course, as for example when we wonder whether an unusual shape on the horizon marks a peculiar rock formation or a man made edifice we may well look for clues which will enable us to infer which it is. But usually such inference is unneeded. Fortunately we do not need to infer the speed of approaching cars; we perceive it.

The choice I offer to Ducasse is a choice between rival perceptual schemata, one representational, the other presentational. I have attempted to point out some of the difficulties into which representationalists are led by the set of interpretive concepts they use. And I have attempted to show how a presentational account can readily escape the difficulties which representationalists have thought unavoidable under a presentational view. My own conclusion is clear: Most human perception is veridical. The errors that occur are due to some fault in the perceptual process, physical, physiological, neural, or psychiatric. In the absence of such sources of error, we both perceive and sense directly and correctly.

Duke University

THE PRINCIPLES OF EPISTEMIC APPRAISAL

RODERICK M. CHISHOLM

I

APPRAISAL, according to C. J. Ducasse, constitutes the ultimate subject-matter of philosophy. To appraise a thing is "to judge its merits or worth"; generically, therefore, "appraising is nothing more and nothing less than 'yea-ing' or 'nay-ing.'"[1] Ducasse notes further that there are three fundamental types of appraisal: emotional, as is evidenced in liking and disliking; volitional, as is evidenced in causing and preventing; and epistemic, as is evidenced in believing and disbelieving.[2] The present paper is concerned with epistemic appraisal.

I shall take as my text an important observation that Ducasse has made about such appraisal. For this observation, I think, provides us with a clue that will enable us to understand and answer a number of philosophical questions that have been raised about epistemic appraisal. It suggests, moreover, a way of systematizing the terms of our epistemic vocabulary; for example, "know," "evident," "reasonable," "acceptable," "indifferent," "possible," "doubtful," "gratuitous." And it suggests a way in which we might formulate an epistemic logic, or logic of epistemic appraisal.

II

Ducasse's observation is this: "In the large majority of cases, when we declare an opinion to have the status of knowledge, a part at least of what we mean by this is that it is better than—

[1] C. J. Ducasse, *Philosophy as a Science* (New York: Oskar Piest, 1941), p. 138.
[2] *Ibid.*

superior to—certain others (which we might appraise more specifically as erroneous, or as possibly sound but unproved, etc.) and better also than absence of opinion, or of opinion having the status of knowledge, on the same subject." [3]

Ducasse speaks here of the relation of being *better than,* or of being *superior to,* which he construes as a relation that holds, not among propositions, but among *opinions,* or, as we may also put it, among *believings;* it may also hold between instances of believing and instances of refraining from believing. Thus, to use an older terminology, it is a relation that holds, not among *objects* of belief, but among *acts* of belief. Believing a given proposition may be, for a particular man at a particular time, better than or superior to believing another; it may also be better than or superior to "mere absence of opinion . . . on the same subject."

The relation in question is an epistemic relation; thus Ducasse uses "superior" as well as "better." If we say that it is better, in this sense, for a man to believe one proposition than to believe another, we may not mean that believing the one is *morally,* or *ethically,* better than believing the other. Hence an alternative to saying that one epistemic attitude is "better than" another would be to say that the one is epistemically "preferable" to the other. Or we might say that the one is "more reasonable" than the other. The latter term is perhaps the most natural and so let us use it in what follows. But let us use it in such a way that we may say that one attitude is *more* reasonable than another without thereby committing ourselves to saying that the attitude *is* reasonable. (In the same way, we allow ourselves to say that the lesser of two evils is the one that is better, without committing ourselves to saying that it is good.)

There are three basic epistemic attitudes that one may take toward a given proposition at any particular time: (1) one may believe or accept the proposition; (2) one may disbelieve the proposition, and this is the same thing as believing its negation; or (3) one may withhold or suspend belief—that is to say, one may refrain from believing and refrain from disbelieving. Philo-

[3] *Op. cit.,* p. 194.

sophical language, as well as ordinary language, frequently obscures the distinction between disbelieving and withholding. If a philosopher tells us that we should "reject" a certain proposition, he may mean that we should disbelieve it—that we should believe its negation. Or he may mean that we should withhold the proposition. And if the man in the street tells us that he "does not believe" a given proposition, he is likely to mean that he believes its negation, but he may mean that he is withholding the proposition.

And so we should emend, in one respect, the observation that "appraising is nothing more and nothing less than 'yea-ing' and 'nay-ing.'" We may vote "Yea" or we may vote "Nay," but we may also abstain from voting. We may abstain in the case of emotional appraisal (there are some things we neither like nor dislike), in the case of volitional appraisal (there are some things we strive neither to cause nor to prevent), and also in the case of epistemic appraisal. And in many cases, epistemic abstinence is more reasonable than believing and more reasonable than disbelieving.

We may ask, then, for any given proposition and any given subject at any given time, which is the more reasonable course: believing the proposition, disbelieving the proposition, or withholding the proposition. In considering such a question, we may refer to any of the following possibilities: (a) believing the proposition is more reasonable than withholding it; (b) believing it is more reasonable than disbelieving it; (c) withholding it is more reasonable than believing it; (d) withholding it is more reasonable than disbelieving it; (e) disbelieving it is more reasonable than believing it; and (f) disbelieving it is more reasonable than withholding it. And then there are the six additional possibilities that we obtain by negating each of these.

III

Let us now consider what is suggested by each of these possibilities.

(a) A proposition falling within our first category is one such that (for a given subject at a given time) believing it is more reasonable than withholding it. Any such proposition could be said to be one that is *reasonable* (for that subject at that time). "Reasonable," in this sense, may be said to be a term of high epistemic praise. If we use it we are "yea"-saying, for of the twelve possibilities that our categories provide, this one puts the proposition in the best possible light.

The propositions that fall within the negation of this first category—those propositions which are such that it is *not* more reasonable to believe them than it is to withhold them—may be said to be epistemically *gratuitous*. They are gratuitous for there is no need, epistemically, to accept them.

(b) The second category comprises those propositions which are such that believing them is more reasonable than disbelieving them. If we say of a proposition that it falls within this category, we are expressing only faint epistemic praise. For believing may be more reasonable than disbelieving only in virtue of the fact that of the two possibilities believing is the lesser evil, epistemically. Consider, for example, the proposition that the Pope will be in Rome on the third Tuesday in October, five years from now. Believing it, given the information that we now have, is more reasonable than *disbelieving* it; i.e., it is more reasonable to believe that the Pope will be in Rome at that time than it is to believe that he will *not* be there. But *withholding* the proposition, surely, is more reasonable still.

The negation of this second category yields a class of propositions having somewhat questionable epistemic status. The propositions belonging to this class are those which are such that believing them is *not* more reasonable than disbelieving them. Any proposition which is such that withholding it is more reasonable than believing it should fall within this category.

(c) If we say of a proposition that it falls within our third category, we are expressing epistemic dispraise or condemnation, for we are saying of it that withholding is more reasonable than believing. We are saying "Nay"—but in the sense of "Do not believe" and not in the sense of "Believe that not." Let us say that any proposition falling within this category is epistemically *unacceptable*.

Among the propositions that are thus unacceptable are, of

course, those propositions such that their negations are reasonable, in the sense defined above. But the class of unacceptable propositions would seem to be considerably wider than the class of propositions that have reasonable negations. Sextus Empiricus tells us that, according to Agrippa, "it is necessary to suspend judgement altogether with regard to *everything* that is brought before us."[4] Other, more moderate sceptics would have us suspend judgment with respect merely to those propositions that refer "beyond the appearances." But according to both types of sceptic, there are unacceptable propositions that have unacceptable negations; for example, the proposition that there are many things "beyond the appearances" is unacceptable and so is its negation. The older positivistic philosophers would say of metaphysical propositions that both they and their negations are unacceptable. Perhaps we can all agree that paradoxical propositions—for example, Russell's "The class of all those classes that are not members of themselves is a member of itself"—fall within this category. And if what we shall say below is correct, there are still other unacceptable propositions that have unacceptable negations. Hence, although we can say that all reasonable propositions have unacceptable negations, we cannot say that all unacceptable propositions have reasonable negations.

If a proposition falls under the negation of this third category, it will be one such that withholding it is not more reasonable than believing it; hence we may say of it that it is epistemically *acceptable.* All propositions that are reasonable will be, of course, acceptable, but there are many acceptable propositions that cannot be said to be reasonable. An adequate theory of memory,

[4] Sextus Empiricus, *Outlines of Pyrrhonism,* Book I, Ch. 15, p. 177. Epictetus, however, reminds us that believing is often more reasonable than withholding and says of this type of sceptic: "He has sensation and pretends that he has not; he is worse than dead. One man does not see the battle; he is ill off. The other sees it but stirs not, nor advances; his state is still more wretched. His sense of shame and self-respect is cut out of him, and his reasoning faculty, though not cut away, is brutalized. Am I to call this 'strength'? Heaven forbid, unless I call it 'strength' in those who sin against nature, that makes them do and say in public whatever occurs to their fancy." *Discourses,* Book I, Ch. 6 ("Against Followers of the Academy"); quoted from Whitney J. Oates, ed., *The Stoic and Epicurean Philosophers* (New York: Random House, 1940), p. 233.

for example, might require us to say this: if I have that experience which might naturally be expressed by saying that I "seem to remember" a certain proposition to be true ("I seem to remember having seen that man before") then the proposition that I thus seem to remember (the proposition that I have seen that man before) is one that is, for me, *ipso facto,* acceptable. It may be, however, that although the proposition is acceptable it is not reasonable; i.e., although withholding it is not more reasonable than believing it, believing it cannot be said to be more reasonable than withholding it. "Acceptable," then, expresses less praise than does "reasonable." But it expresses more praise than does the doubtful compliment, "Believing is more reasonable than disbelieving."

(d) Where the third formula says that withholding is more reasonable than believing, the fourth says that withholding is more reasonable than disbelieving. If a proposition falling within the third category is one that is unacceptable, then one falling within the fourth is one that has an unacceptable negation. Hence a proposition falling within the negation of this fourth category—a proposition such that withholding it is *not* more reasonable than disbelieving it—will be a proposition that has an acceptable negation.

(e) If we say of a proposition that disbelieving it is more reasonable than believing it, we are expressing faint praise for the negation of the proposition. This faint praise is also expressed by *one* use of the ambiguous epistemic term "doubtful" (or "dubious"). To say that a proposition is doubtful in this sense of the term is to say that one can make out a better case for the negation of the proposition than one can for the proposition itself. (But in another, and more proper, use of the term, we may call a proposition "doubtful" without in any way expressing praise for the negation of the proposition; in this case we will be saying merely that the proposition is itself unacceptable. And "unacceptable," as we have just seen, though it implies dispraise for the proposition in question, need not imply any praise for the negation of that proposition. Any proposition that is doubtful in the first sense of the term will also be doubtful in the second; but those propositions that ought to be withheld will be doubtful in the second sense of the term but not in the first.[5] When the Pyrrhonist finds us dogmatizing and wishes to show us that a given proposition is doubtful, in the second of these two senses, he will apply the maxim of "opposing every argument with an equal argument," and in so doing he may seem to be concerned with showing us that the proposition is also doubtful in the first. This fact may be one source of the present ambiguity of the term.)

The negation of this fifth category—viz., the class of propositions which are such that disbelieving them is *not* more reasonable than believing them—yields a set of propositions having questionable negations. Any proposition having an unacceptable negation will fall within this class. And so, too, will any proposition that ought to be withheld.

(f) If a proposition falling within our first category is one that is reasonable, then a proposition falling within our fifth category will be one that has a reasonable negation. It will be a proposition such that disbelieving it—i.e., believing its negation—is more reasonable than withholding it. When we say of a proposition that it is unacceptable, we are saying "Nay" only in the sense of "Do not believe." But when we say the proposition has a reasonable negation, we are saying "Nay," not only in the sense of "Do not believe," but also in the sense of "Believe that not."

A proposition falling within the negation of this sixth category will be one that has a gratuitous negation.

IV

We have, then, definitions for at least four epistemic terms. A proposition is *reasonable* or "beyond reasonable doubt" (for a given subject at a given time) if (for that subject at that time) believing it is more reasonable than withholding it; it is *gratuitous* if it is not reasonable; it is *unacceptable* if withholding it is more reasonable than believing it; and it is *acceptable* if it is

[5] Ducasse notes an analogous ambiguity in the term "doubt." He suggests that when we say "I am in doubt as to whether S is P" we are expressing the fact that we are withholding the proposition, but when we say "I doubt that S is P" we are expressing the fact that we are disbelieving it. Taking the term in the first of these two senses, he describes withholding as a state of *dubitancy*. C. J. Ducasse, "Propositions, Opinions, Sentences, and Facts," *Journal of Philosophy*, Vol. XXXVII, No. 26, Dec. 19, 1940, p. 702.

not unacceptable. Whatever is reasonable is acceptable, but not conversely; and whatever is unacceptable is gratuitous, but not conversely.

Other epistemic terms may be defined merely by combining certain of the categories we have discussed.

Thus, we may say of a proposition that it *ought to be withheld* if both it and its negation are unacceptable: withholding the proposition is more reasonable than believing it and also more reasonable than disbelieving it.

Propositions may also be said to be epistemically *indifferent*. But here there is an ambiguity and we will do well to guard against possible confusion. "Indifferent" could be used in analogy with its use in moral philosophy. An act is said to be morally indifferent if it is one such that performance of it is permitted and non-performance of it is also permitted. Some philosophers have said, similarly, that a proposition is indifferent if it is one such that both it and its negation are acceptable.

But the expression "judgment of indifference" is used in writings on the theory of knowledge and on probability theory in a rather different way. A "judgment of indifference" about a pair of propositions is a judgment to the effect that there is no ground for choice between those propositions—neither proposition is more reasonable than the other. If we follow this use, we may be tempted to say that an indifferent proposition is one such that believing it is not more reasonable than disbelieving it and disbelieving it is not more reasonable than believing it. A proposition that is indifferent in this second sense need not be one that is indifferent in the first sense.

Discussing the second concept of indifference, J. M. Keynes quotes the following conversation:

> Absolute. "Sure, Sir, this is not very reasonable, to summon my affection for a lady I know nothing of."
>
> Sir Anthony. "I am sure, Sir, 'tis more unreasonable in you to object to a lady you know nothing of." [6]

[6] J. M. Keynes, *A Treatise of Probability* (London: Macmillan, 1921), p. 41; Keynes says that the passage is quoted somewhere by Bernard Bosanquet. It appears at the heading of Keynes' chapter entitled "The Principle of Indifference," in which the term "indifference" is used in the second of the two senses just distinguished.

To be sure, if nothing is known of the lady, then an unfavorable attitude is no more justified than a favorable one. But surely the reasonable thing, moral considerations aside, is to withhold both favor and disfavor until something more is known.

And similarly for our epistemic attitudes: if a proposition is such that believing it is no more nor less reasonable than disbelieving it, then withholding it is more reasonable than either believing it or disbelieving it. Hence a proposition that is indifferent in the second sense, may not—and indeed will not—be one that is indifferent in the first.

V

Let us now consider in more detail the logical properties of *more reasonable than*. I suggest that the following three principles are true and could thus be taken as axioms in an epistemic logic, or logic of epistemic appraisal.

(1) *More reasonable than* is a transitive relation: if one thing is more reasonable than another and the other more reasonable than a third, then the first thing is more reasonable than the third. Thus if for a given subject at a given time believing a certain proposition *h* is more reasonable than disbelieving a certain other proposition *i*, and if disbelieving *i* is more reasonable than withholding still another proposition *j*, then believing *h* is more reasonable than withholding *j*.

(2) *More reasonable than* is also asymmetrical: if one thing is more reasonable than another, then the other is not more reasonable than the one. Thus if withholding a proposition is more reasonable than believing it, then believing it is not more reasonable than withholding it.

(3) And, finally, if withholding is not more reasonable than believing, then believing is more reasonable than disbelieving. Or, more exactly: for any proposition *h*, any subject S, and any time *t*, if at *t* it is not more reasonable for S to withhold *h* than it is for him to believe *h*, then at *t* it is more reasonable for him to believe *h* than it is for him to disbelieve *h*. An instance of this principle would be: if agnosticism is not more reasonable than theism, then theism is more reasonable than atheism.

Let us now note some of the epistemic principles that are

yielded by our three axioms. We may assume that reference to a given subject, time, and proposition is constant throughout.

Three principles follow immediately from the second axiom, according to which *more reasonable than* is asymmetrical.

(4) If believing is more reasonable than withholding, then withholding is not more reasonable than believing.

(5) If believing is more reasonable than disbelieving, then disbelieving is not more reasonable than believing.

(6) If disbelieving is more reasonable than withholding, then withholding is not more reasonable than disbelieving.

Our third axiom tells us that, if withholding is not more reasonable than believing, then believing is more reasonable than disbelieving. Reminding ourselves that believing a proposition is the same thing as disbelieving its negation, and that withholding a proposition is the same thing as withholding its negation (for to withhold a proposition is to refrain from believing it and to refrain from disbelieving it), we may derive the following consequence from our third axiom.

(7) If withholding is not more reasonable than disbelieving, then disbelieving is more reasonable than withholding.

By applying the first axiom, which affirms the transitivity of *more reasonable than,* and contraposing conditionals, we obtain additional results. I shall summarize these by noting, with respect to each of the twelve categories that have been distinguished, what is implied by saying of a proposition that it falls within that category.

(8) If believing is more reasonable than withholding, then: believing is more reasonable than disbelieving; disbelieving is not more reasonable than believing; disbelieving is not more reasonable than withholding; withholding is more reasonable than disbelieving; and (as already noted) withholding is not more reasonable than believing.

(9) If believing is more reasonable than disbelieving, then: disbelieving is not more reasonable than withholding; withholding is more reasonable than disbelieving; and (as already noted) disbelieving is not more reasonable than believing.

(10) If withholding is more reasonable than believing, then believing is not more reasonable than withholding.

(11) If withholding is more reasonable than disbelieving, then disbelieving is not more reasonable than withholding.

(12) If disbelieving is more reasonable than believing, then: believing is not more reasonable than disbelieving; believing is not more reasonable than withholding; and withholding is more reasonable than believing.

(13) If disbelieving is more reasonable than withholding, then: disbelieving is more reasonable than believing; believing is not more reasonable than disbelieving; believing is not more reasonable than withholding; withholding is more reasonable than believing; and (as already noted) withholding is not more reasonable than disbelieving.

(14) If believing is not more reasonable than disbelieving, then: withholding is more reasonable than believing; and believing is not more reasonable than withholding.

(15) If withholding is not more reasonable than believing, then: believing is more reasonable than disbelieving; withholding is more reasonable than disbelieving; disbelieving is not more reasonable than withholding; and disbelieving is not more reasonable than believing.

(16) If withholding is not more reasonable than disbelieving, then: disbelieving is more reasonable than believing; withholding is more reasonable than believing; believing is not more reasonable than withholding; and believing is not more reasonable than disbelieving.

(17) If disbelieving is not more reasonable than believing, then: withholding is more reasonable than disbelieving; and disbelieving is not more reasonable than withholding.

Our three axioms do not enable us to derive any significant consequences from the hypothesis that a given proposition is such that believing it is not more reasonable than withholding it, or from the hypothesis that a given proposition is such that disbelieving it is not more reasonable than believing it.

VI

Recalling our epistemic definitions, we may now reformulate some of these results. A proposition is one that is *reasonable,* we said, if believing it is more reasonable than withholding it. A proposition is *gratuitous* if it is not one that is reasonable. A proposition is *unacceptable* if withholding it is more reasonable than believing it; it is *acceptable* if it is not unacceptable. And a proposition is one that *ought to be withheld* if it is itself unacceptable and also has an unacceptable negation.

Thus, principle (8) tells us that if a proposition is one that is reasonable, then it is acceptable and it has a negation that is both gratuitous and unacceptable. Principle (10) tells us that if a proposition is unacceptable, then it is gratuitous. And principle (15) tells us that if a proposition is acceptable, then it has an unacceptable—and therefore gratuitous—negation.

What, then, of *indifference?* In one sense of the term, we said, a proposition may be called "indifferent" if it is itself acceptable and if it also has an acceptable negation. A proposition is indifferent in this sense, therefore, if withholding it is not more reasonable than believing it and if withholding it is not more reasonable than disbelieving it. But principle (15) tells us that if withholding is *not* more reasonable than believing, then withholding *is* more reasonable than disbelieving; and principle (16) tells us that if withholding is not more reasonable than disbelieving, then withholding is more reasonable than believing. Our axioms have the consequence, therefore, that it would be contradictory to say of any proposition that it is epistemically indifferent in the sense defined. Hence no proposition is thus indifferent.

This consequence is as it should be. If we wonder whether it is so, we have only to ask ourselves: What proposition might conceivably be said to be epistemically indifferent? What proposition could be such that withholding it is not more reasonable than believing it and not more reasonable than disbelieving it?

Some moral philosophers affirm a "principle of permission": every possible act is one such that either performance of the act is permitted or non-performance of the act is permitted.[7] The

[7] For example, G. H. von Wright, *An Essay in Modal Logic* (Amsterdam: North-Holland Publishing Company, 1951), p. 38. In Chapter 1 of *Perceiving: A Philosophical Study* (Ithaca: Cornell University Press, 1957), I affirmed an analogous principle for epistemology: every proposition is such that either it is acceptable or its negation is acceptable. The principles set forth in my work were excessively latitudinarian; they had the consequence, for example, that if a proposition is unacceptable its negation is evident, and therefore that there is no proposition that ought to be withheld.

principle may be widened to say: for every possible state of affairs, either realizing that state of affairs is permitted or realizing the negation of that state of affairs is permitted. A corollary of the principle is that there are some acts that are morally indifferent—some acts which are such that both performance and non-performance are permitted.[8] But in epistemology—in the theory of epistemic appraisal—it would seem that we should have a "principle of non-permission": every proposition is such that either it is unacceptable or its negation is unacceptable. Or, in other words, every proposition is such that, either withholding it is more reasonable than believing it or withholding it is more reasonable than disbelieving it. And this is a consequence of our principle (15).

But let us remind ourselves that we have distinguished two senses of "indifference": (1) in the one sense, a proposition is indifferent if it is acceptable and has an acceptable negation; and (2) in the other sense, a proposition is indifferent if it is not more reasonable than its negation and if its negation is not more reasonable than it. According to what we have said, there are no propositions that are indifferent in the first sense of the term. But there are many propositions that are indifferent in the second sense of the term.

If, for example, there is a proposition that has a probability of .5 in relation to the totality of what a given subject knows, then that proposition is, for him, one such that there is no choice between it and its negation: believing it is no more reasonable than disbelieving it, and disbelieving it is no more reasonable than believing it.

But surely any proposition that is indifferent in this second sense is one that ought to be withheld. Indeed, one way of showing that a proposition ought to be withheld is to show that it

[8] But compare Kant: "It is, however, of great consequence to ethics in general to avoid admitting, so long as it is possible, of anything morally intermediate, whether in actions (*adiophora*) or in human characters; for with such ambiguity all maxims are in danger of forfeiting their precision and stability. Those who are partial to this strict mode of thinking are usually called *rigorists* (a name which is intended to carry reproach, but which actually praises); their opposites may be called *latitudinarians*. These latter, again, are either latitudinarians of neutrality, whom we may call *indifferentists*, or latitudinarians of coalition, whom we may call *syncretists*." *Religion within the Limits of Reason Alone*, Book One; quoted from Harper Torchbooks edition (New York: Harper & Brothers, 1960), p. 18.

is indifferent in this sense—that the proposition is no more nor less reasonable than its negation. Thus Sextus tells us that "the main basic principle of the Sceptic system is that of opposing to every proposition an equal proposition." The various sceptics sought to apply the maxim "To every argument an equal argument is opposed"; the point in so doing was to establish "equality in respect of probability and improbability," indicating thereby that judgment ought to be suspended.[9] And it is a consequence of our principles that any proposition that is thus indifferent ought to be withheld. According to principle (14), if believing is not more reasonable than disbelieving, then the proposition is unacceptable; according to principle (17), if disbelieving is not more reasonable than believing, then the proposition has an unacceptable negation; and according to our definition, if an unacceptable proposition has an unacceptable negation then it ought to be withheld.[10]

VII

There are, of course, alternative ways of developing a logic of epistemic appraisal. Axiom (3), in particular, might be replaced by one that is more liberal. According to axiom (3), if withholding is not more reasonable than believing, then believing is more reasonable than disbelieving; in other words, if a proposition is acceptable, then it is more reasonable to believe the proposition than to believe its negation. One might consider replacing (3) by this: if believing is more reasonable than withholding, then withholding is more reasonable than disbelieving.

The resulting system would differ from the one that I have expounded in essentially the following respects: (a) we could no longer assert that if believing is more reasonable than disbeliev-

[9] Sextus Empiricus, *Outlines of Pyrrhonism,* Book I, chapters 4, 6, 22, and 24. See the Loeb Library edition of *Sextus Empiricus* (Cambridge: Harvard University Press, 1933), Vol. I, pp. 7, 9, 115.

[10] Perhaps we can say that Sextus defined "ought to withhold" in terms of the second sense of "indifference." For he writes in Chapter 22 of Book I of the *Outlines of Pyrrhonism:* "The phrase 'I suspend judgment' we adopt in place of 'I am unable to say which of the objects presented I ought to believe and which I ought to disbelieve,' indicating that the objects appear to us equal as regards credibility and incredibility." Quoted from Loeb Library edition of *Sextus Empiricus,* Volume I, p. 115.

ing, then withholding is more reasonable than disbelieving; (b) we could no longer assert that if disbelieving is more reasonable than believing, then withholding is more reasonable than believing; (c) the only significant consequence we could draw from the hypothesis that believing is not more reasonable than disbelieving, and from the hypothesis that withholding is not more reasonable than disbelieving, would be that believing is not more reasonable than withholding; and (d) the only significant consequence wc could draw from the hypothesis that disbelieving is not more reasonable than believing, and from the hypothesis that withholding is not more reasonable than believing, would be that disbelieving is not more reasonable than withholding.[11]

These axioms do not allow us to assert that, if withholding is not more reasonable than believing, then withholding is more reasonable than disbelieving. They do not yield the "principle of non-permission," but allow instead for the possibility that some acceptable propositions have acceptable negations and are therefore "indifferent" in the first of the two senses we have distinguished. In view of what we have said, therefore, such a system would seem to be excessively latitudinarian.

VIII

With these concepts—or, more exactly, with the concept of *more reasonable than* as applied to believing, disbelieving, and withholding—we would seem to have what is essential for our basic vocabulary of epistemic appraisal.

"Reasonable" is a term of high epistemic praise; it is the highest praise that is provided by the twelve possibilities we have distinguished. But a proposition may attain to greater heights. A proposition is reasonable, we said, if believing it is more reasona-

[11] The system could be made even more liberal by adding the axiom: if believing is more reasonable than disbelieving, then withholding is not more reasonable than believing. But such an axiom is not plausible (despite the popular belief that from "Theism is more reasonable than atheism" we may deduce "Agnosticism is not more reasonable than theism"). Suppose we know that there are 100 balls in the urn, that 51 of them are red and 49 of them are not red, and that a ball is to be drawn at random. It is more reasonable for us to believe that the ball to be drawn is red than to believe that it is not (i.e., to disbelieve). But in this case, clearly withholding is more reasonable than believing.

ble than withholding it. Consider, then, those propositions that are reasonable and, in addition, are such that there are no propositions that are more reasonable than they are. Let us say that such propositions are *evident*. That is to say, a proposition *h* is evident to a given subject S at a given time *t* provided that: it is more reasonable at *t* for S to believe *h* than to withhold *h*, and there is no proposition *i* which is such that it is more reasonable for S at *t* to believe *i* than to believe *h*. Hence, we can say that whatever is evident is reasonable, but not conversely; just as we can say that whatever is reasonable is acceptable, but not conversely. (And, we may have a solution to one of the problems that troubled Meinong. Put in his terms: does "evident" apply to the *act* or to the *content* of judgment; does it apply to the *judging* or to that which is *judged?* [12] The answer would seem to be that "evident" applies to the *content* in virtue of what would be the reasonable nature of the *act*.)

We may say that a man *knows* a given proposition to be true, provided that the proposition is one that is believed or accepted by him, is true, and is evident.

Given the logical concept of probability, we can define a weaker sense of "know." [13] Thus a man could be said to *know, for all practical purposes,* that a given proposition *h* is true, provided that *h* is more probable than not in relation to everything that he knows, in the first sense of "know," to be true. (Or, if we wish to eliminate the reference to "everything he knows," we may say instead that S knows, for all practical purposes, that *h* is true, provided: there is a conjunction *e* of propositions that S knows, in the strict sense, to be true; *h* is more probable than not in relation to *e;* and there is no proposition *i* such that (a) S knows *i* to be true and (b) *h* is not more probable than not in relation to

[12] See A. Meinong, *Über Annahmen,* Second Edition (Leipzig: Johann Ambrosius Barth, 1910), p. 82 ff., and *Über Möglichkeit und Wahrscheinlichkeit* (Leipzig: Johann Ambrosius Barth), p. 440 ff.

[13] ". . . . to say that inference of a conclusion *C* from premise *P* has probability of degree *D* means that *P* validates degree *D* of *inclination to believe* the proposition which is content of C." C. J. Ducasse, "Some Observations Concerning the Nature of Probability," *Journal of Philosophy,* Vol. XXXVIII, No. 15, July 17, 1941, p. 400.

the conjunction of *e* and *i*.) As Hume remarked, "one would appear ridiculous who would say that it is only probable that the sun will rise tomorrow, or that all men must die; though it is plain we have no further assurance of these facts than what experience affords us." [14] We *may* say that we know that the sun will rise tomorrow, or that all men must die, despite the fact that these are not propositions that are evident. We can say we know them "for all practical purposes," because they are propositions that are highly probable in relation to what *is* evident. The propositions that we know in this weak sense, then, are propositions that are more probable than not to the totality of what we know in the strong sense.

Given, finally, the concept of logical entailment, we can define various senses of epistemic possibility—various senses of the expression, "It is possible, for all he knows, that. . . ." (i) In a basic sense of the term "possible," a proposition *h* may be said to be epistemically possible, for a given subject S, provided that not-*h* is not entailed by the set of all of the propositions that S knows, in the first sense of "know" just defined.[15] It is possible, for all that I know, that there is life on Venus, for nothing that I know, or no conjunction of things that I know, entails that there is *not* life on Venus. An unacceptable proposition may be epistemically possible, in this sense. And (ii), an even weaker sense of epistemic possibility is obtained if we say this: *h* is possible, for all S knows, provided that S *does not know h* to be entailed by any set of things that he knows. In this weak sense of the term, we may say, "It was possible, for all that Thomas Hobbes knew, that someday he would square the circle." Thus, if we say of a proposition only that it is possible, we are not expressing any epistemic praise at all. For, as Sextus observes, the person who restricts himself to saying "Perhaps it is" is "implicitly affirming also the seemingly

[14] *Treatise of Human Nature,* Book I, Part III, Section xi.

[15] On this sense of epistemic possibility, see: C. I. Lewis and C. H. Langford, *Symbolic Logic* (New York: The Century Company, 1932), p. 161 ff.; G. H. von Wright, *op. cit.*, pp. 31–2; Jaakko Hintikka, *Knowledge and Belief* (Ithaca: Cornell University Press, 1962); and Roderick M. Chisholm, "The Logic of Knowing," *Journal of Philosophy,* Vol. LX, No. 25, Dec. 5, 1963, pp. 775–95.

contradictory phrase 'Perhaps it is not' by his refusal to make the positive assertion that 'It is.' "[16]

Brown University

[16] *Oulines of Pyrrhonism,* Book I, Chapter 21; Loeb Library translation, pp. 113–115. If it is necessary to countenance the possibility that some evident propositions are false, the definition of "know" should be qualified. I have discussed the need for countenancing this possibility and have proposed a qualification in *Theory of Knowledge* (Englewood Cliffs: Prentice-Hall, 1966); cf. pp. 23, 48–9, 111–3.

A VERDICT ON EPIPHENOMENALISM *

BRAND BLANSHARD

DUCASSE HOLDS A VIEW about the relation of mind and body that seems to me in the main sound, and I want to offer a few considerations that may serve to support it. But in a volume dedicated to him and his work, I hope it will not be thought wholly irrelevant if I pause for a moment before plunging into my topic and indulge in the pleasure of reminiscence.

It has been my privilege—and a valued one—to know Ducasse fairly well. Some twenty-five years ago, the Philosophical Association appointed a commission to report on the place of philosophy in American education. Ducasse was a member of this commission, and so was I. The members travelled round the country together, consulting with their colleagues, holding more or less public hearings, and in the end reporting their conclusions in a book published in the forties. On long overland journeys by train and in the later discussions through which we hewed out our report, I saw a good deal of Ducasse.

He was, and remains, a striking figure. An ascetically frail and slender appearance belies the toughness that has carried him through eighty-odd strenuous years. He is something of an aesthete as well as an aesthetician, and one would never guess that the fastidiously dressed gentleman poring over his papers, with a green eyeshade to protect his oversensitive eyes, had been in his early days an adventurous jack-of-all-trades in Mexico and on our western frontier. But so it was. His work as a philosopher began late, and his exposure in youth to the harsh realities of earning a

* This paper is for the most part a revision of one written for the International Congress of Philosophy in Mexico in 1963. The material taken from this earlier paper is used with permission.

living under almost pioneer conditions helped, I suspect, to keep his philosophy in touch with fact and sense, and to sharpen the administrative judgment which he showed later as department chairman and dean.

It is symbolic that Ducasse should have never quite lost the traces of his French accent. He became long ago a dedicated and deeply involved American, but in his passion for logic and lucidity he remains refreshingly French. Though he has had a great deal to say about values in his books on aesthetics and religion, he deals with them in the French manner, with the stress always on clearness of analysis and with a firm avoidance of sentimentality. Indeed, he has managed to strike a happy balance between two impulses in present-day philosophy that are tending to tear it apart. One is the analytic impulse that has carried some minds of considerable power into dry sands of triviality. The other is the existentialist impulse that has driven many into brooding darkly over abysses of being and nothingness. The trouble with the first group is that they squander their acuteness on problems that are hardly worth solving. The trouble with the second group is that, though dealing with problems of importance, they lack the discipline to deal with them effectively. Ducasse, with his gift for analysis and his aversion to obscurity, is clearly nearer to the first group than to the second. But through combining catholic interests in the theory of criticism and the theory of knowledge, in the problems of metaphysics, psychology and religion, with an insistence on carrying precision of thought into all these fields alike, he has set an admirable example to the younger philosophers whom he has trained. There is a danger today that between the din of knife-whetting on the one side and of Delphic pontifications on the other, the voice of natural philosophy should be drowned out. We could do with more voices like that of Ducasse.

Philosophers who are mere philosophers are bad philosophers, and it is pleasant to recall how much more Ducasse was than a "dealer in notions." His sense of comedy was keen, and he was surprisingly ready to engage in pranks, to tell humorous and even Rabelaisian tales, and to serve as the butt of fun himself. Arthur Murphy, who was the chairman of our commission and who had served as a junior to Ducasse at Brown, used to take peculiar pleasure in rallying his senior, whom he called Jack Oakie—from John, his middle name and the cask supposed to lie in "Ducasse"; and the banter that flew between these two was worth hearing. Of course the substance of it has all drifted away now down the years. But there is still in existence, I think, a startling photograph of Ducasse and his fellow commissioners in prison uniforms, taken by a sidewalk photographer in New Orleans who supplied the background for the not very convincingly criminal faces. And should one pass over in silence, I wonder, the touching reciprocal affection that linked Ducasse with his celebrated Siamese cat, who used to sit on his shoulder serenely and contemplate his master while his master, with equal serenity, contemplated the universe?

There is another characteristic of Ducasse as a person that I am moved to mention—his intellectual courage. Early in his life, he became interested in psychical research, which he thinks has revealed evidence of philosophic importance about the relation between mind and body. Most American philosophers and scientists will not touch psychical research with a full-length fishing pole; and even if they are privately interested, they hesitate to admit it publicly for fear of a smirch on their scholarly escutcheon. The atmosphere is different in England, where many men of unimpeachable standing have taken an active part in such research—Sidgwick and Balfour, Oliver Lodge and Gilbert Murray, C. D. Broad and H. H. Price. But in this country Ducasse and William James are perhaps the only considerable philosophers who have been willing to plunge boldly into these dangerous waters. Though I do not go all the way with Ducasse in his conclusions in this field, I must admire the independence, the patience and the coolness that he has brought to it. His most recent book, *A Critical Examination of the Belief in a Life after Death,* is a good example of what philosophic reflection can do in defining the issues and ordering the data in a confused and controversial field.

Enough now of reminiscence and impression; I must turn to the subject of this paper. I want to contribute some ammunition to

Ducasse's attack on epiphenomenalism, however damp some of it will certainly seem to him. As a theory of the relation of body to mind, epiphenomenalism is important, if only because of the breadth of its popularity; among natural scientists it seems to be the theory most generally held, though not under its own forbidding name, or perhaps with any explicit formulation. I assume that most scientists would reject behaviorism and say with Ducasse that to ascribe the same denotation to "a sensation of pain" and "a motion of particles in a dental nerve" is rather worse than untrue; it is muddled to the point of absurdity. Unfortunately they would probably reject interactionism too. In spite of the fact that this is by all odds the theory most convincing to common sense, natural scientists have shown a stubborn reluctance to accept it. This seems to have two chief grounds.

First, to include in the explanation of a physical movement a mere volition or resolve is to introduce something from outside the public observable order that is the accepted domain of natural science. One cannot get rid of these mental events by the ostrich policy of behaviorism, but since they can be assigned no definite place in the physical order, and possess no mass or motion, they are a kind of event that is a continued embarrassment to the physical scientist.

Secondly, many scientists "feel in their bones" that productive power belongs to matter alone. Of course if causation is only uniform accompaniment, as philosophers of science so commonly say, there should be no difficulty in accepting interaction in both directions; but I doubt if practicing scientists really believe this view of causation. They are ready enough to believe that consciousness is the by-product of physical change, but they are not at all ready to believe that what, from the point of view of physics, are "airy nothings" can push particles about in one's brain. If there is any pushing or pulling in nature, any dynamic agency, any exercise of power or force, it is the work of matter alone. Ideas, therefore, are never causes or agents in the full sense; their place is that of vestal virgins, who were of course born themselves, but who never give birth to anything further.

The metaphor is that of Santayana, who is the most eloquent spokesman of this doctrine. Consciousness is for him merely "a lyric cry in the midst of business." He admits that it seems to be more, far more; that to the plain man and even to the philosopher when off duty, it is plain beyond question that their decisions make a difference to their behavior. But this is an illusion nevertheless. What is exclusively at work is "the dark engine of nature." Even upon the course of inference no idea ever exerts the slightest constraint. "Dialectic, then, while ostensibly following ideal implications . . . secretly expresses a material life." [1] "The controlling force in reasoning is not reason, but instinct and circumstance" [2] "the continuity is physical, not logical." [3]

In spite of the widespread implicit acceptance of this view, I believe it to be mistaken. It has indeed become a serious obstacle in the way of a theory of human nature which would give due importance to the function of mind. This paper is designed to help clear the way to such a theory. But first let us hear a little more precisely what the current theory is telling us. It tells us that the successive states of mind are by-products of a succession of events in the cortex. These cortical events are neural impulses that travel along the sheaths of the nerve fibers. They are apparently electrical in character, and last about 1/10,000 of a second each. The passage of these impulses down an axone, across a synapse, and up a dendrite is governed by imperfectly known laws. Though they govern events taking place in organic tissues, these laws are assumed to be in the end laws of physics; the statement that a nervous impulse has passed along a fiber is a statement that a vast army of particles—or "wavicles"—has behaved in a certain way, and it is assumed that this behavior takes place in strict accordance with those laws of motion, gravitation, attraction, reflection, acceleration, and transformation of energy, which hold of bodies generally. The laws are statistical in the sense that they describe the behavior, not of single particles, but of aggregates. This hardly affects their stability, however, since whatever may be true of individual particles, the behavior of large aggregates of them is for practical purposes invariable.

[1] George Santayana, *The Realm of Essence* (New York: Charles Scribner's Sons, 1928), p. 99.

[2] *Ibid.*, p. 104.

[3] *Ibid.*, p. 103.

Regarding these laws two further theses are commonly accepted. First, they are not necessary; they are all empirical generalizations, even when, like the laws of motion, they are supposed to hold everywhere and always; they are synthetic statements of *de facto* conjunction, not *a priori* statements of entailment; there is no logical must about them. Secondly, they are purely mechanical laws, in the sense that nothing in the way of teleology, no striving for an end, no purpose, is implied. One may say, of course, that even the flow of a river is teleological in the sense that it behaves in all its workings in such a way as to achieve the consummation of falling into the sea; but in that sense all behavior is teleological. The river does not wind or descend *in order* to reach the ocean; the iron filings do not *strive* to reach the magnet; the neural impulse is not an effort toward a goal. It is as free of purposive direction as the river winding toward the sea.

Now, on the theory before us, there are two series of changes, one physical, the other mental; and for each state, P_1, P_2, etc., in the physical series, there is a state M_1, M_2, etc., in the mental series that is caused by it and in some sense corresponds to it. But corresponds in what sense? Some writers have answered: in the sense that there is an isomorphism or resemblance in structure between the two states. This seems to mean that each ultimate unit of the brain state, such as an electron or a short segment of its movement, may be correlated point for point with an ultimate unit of the conscious state—say a momentary sensation, memory or emotion—and the patterns of relation exhibited in the two complexes may be the same. The search for such isomorphism seems to me hopeless. Not only is it impracticable to break a state of mind into some billions of distinguishable units, but even if it could be done, there is no reason to believe that their pattern would resemble the spatial pattern of protons and electrons. The best that could be hoped for would be a one-many correlation, in which a relatively simple event, like a sensation of red lasting a tenth of a second, might be correlated with the set of changes as a whole induced in the optical nerve by the impingements through that period of an immense number of waves. But even if this could be carried out for each unit of consciousness—whatever exactly such a unit might mean—there is again no reason to suppose that between the units of consciousness there would be relations resembling those of the corresponding physical complexes.

It is not, however, the correspondence of two momentary states that I am chiefly interested in, but the alleged correspondence between the laws of sequence, the patterns of succession, in the two series. We are told that the succession of physical states is ordered by physical law, and hence that neither necessity nor purpose enters in. Hence, if the succession of mental states reflects this succession as a series of by-products of it, it too can show no traces of such determination. It seems to me clear, on the contrary, that necessity and purpose do play parts in determining the succession of mental states, and the rest of this paper will be devoted to showing that they do.

Look first at the process of inference. This is normally a temporal process in which thought proceeds from premise to conclusion. There may be any amount of obscurity, muddle or inconsequence in it; some inferences, so-called, supply examples of that mere association to which, according to one school of psychology, all inference reduces. But logicians have often doubted whether anything less than valid inference should be called inference at all, and in any case we shall confine ourselves to that. A valid inference is one that follows the track of necessity connecting ground with consequent, or premise with conclusion. And the question we have to ask is whether, when thought does move successfully along this track, the track itself is ever an aid to holding us upon it, whether necessity ever determines or helps to determine, the course of the inference that passes along it. I think it does.

One could illustrate the point from any valid inference. I reach into the ragbag of memory and pull out a jingle that seems in some remote past to have puzzled my boyhood:

> Brothers and sisters have I none,
> But this man's father is my father's son.

The question was, what is the relation, if any, of "this man" to me? I had forgotten the answer and had to find it afresh. The process I followed in doing so is no doubt typical. I started by ruling out this man's being a brother, for I was told in the first line that I had no brothers or sisters. I then turned to the statement about the man's father. That father, I was assured, was my father's son, which meant that he must be among my father's children. But in being told that "brothers and sisters have I none," I was being told also that my father had no child but me. If this man's father was my father's child, and my father had just one child, namely me, then I must be this man's father, and he must be my son.

I have completed here a simple line of reasoning. What account of this reasoning would be given by the epiphenomenalist? He would say that my successive thoughts or judgments were by-products of successive states of my brain, that these brain-states followed an order determined wholly by the laws of physics, such laws as those of motion, gravitation, and electric conduction, and that neither in the laws nor in the processes described by them was there any trace of teleology or necessity. If these factors play no part in the physical series, and this physical series completely determines the mental series, it is obvious that they can play no part in the mental series either.

Now I think we can see by direct inspection that they do play a part in the mental series, an essential and conspicuous part. Look first at the role of purpose. In our puzzle example, I set myself to solve a problem: given certain relationships owned by "this man" and me respectively, how are he and I related? My purpose is to answer this question, and that purpose seems to determine the course of my thought. To say that it makes no difference seems merely odd. Why should anyone be tempted to say it? Perhaps because he thinks of a purposive process as one in which a future state, desired but not yet in being, acts causally in the present. I will merely say that such an interpretation is neither required nor intended. It may be thought, again, that association will serve by itself to channel the movement down the groove; starting with the thought of family relationships, it would naturally keep to these. But more is clearly needed. If association alone were at work, thought could take off from the given relationships in numberless directions. Such ramblings are no doubt useful on a Freudian couch, but they are not to be confused with reasoning. Thinking must be thinking to some purpose, and purpose is selective; it does not call up just any of the associates of an idea; it summons some because they are relevant, and inhibits others because they are not. A normally rational mind, for example, presented with this sort of problem, would not go off into speculations about the height and weight of the brothers and sisters, or "this man's" complexion, or my father's religion, because they have no bearing on the point at issue; the thought confines itself to blood-relationships, for these alone are relevant.

Not, of course, that even well-disciplined minds as a rule go straight to the goal. *Denken ist schwer.* All actual thinking involves trial and error, wasteful wanderings up blind alleys, promising paths that lead nowhere. To say that a man is rational is not to say that he is wholly rational. On the other hand, to admit that he is not wholly rational is not to say, either, that he is all at sea, a drifting and rudderless derelict. If our thoughts do often wander, we know that at times they do not, that when they do not, we have different degrees of control over them, and that when purpose is most firmly in control, our thought is the very opposite of wanton or random or merely associative; it may move swiftly and surely to its end, governed by an implicit standard of relevance. And note well that relevance is not a descriptive standard at all. One will not find it lurking among atoms or molecules; one will not find it in a purely empirical psychology; it operates as a norm or an ideal. As such, it is an unaccountable interloper in an epiphenomenalist world. Nevertheless it is there. It is so undeniably at work in our minds that without it thinking would not be thinking.

Much the same must be said about necessity. It is not the sort of relation by which the empirical psychologist, eager to cut his discipline loose from philosophy and make it a natural science, ever thinks of explaining an event. He agrees, of course, that inference is a psychological process whose steps require explanation. What sort of explanation does he give? Try him with the first example that comes to mind, which will probably be the classic "All men are mortal; Socrates is a man; therefore Socrates is mortal." Does not one move to this conclusion because the premises, apprehended a moment before, point to it in the sense of entailing or requiring it? No, comes the reply; what we have here is the rote repetition of a verbal sequence, to be explained, like other habits, by past association. Admitting that the famous example may by now have reached this level, one turns to other cases, such as that of the slave-boy in the *Meno,* in which a process of reasoning was carried through with no possibility of an explanation by habit. The probable comment then is that one is confusing implication with inference, a timeless relation connecting propositions with a temporal process connecting judgments, and that the sequence of judgments can be explained without any reference to unempirical necessities. But if one presses for the precise terms of this explanation, one finds oneself put off either with some forlorn attempt to refurbish association or with a cryptic reference, as in Santayana, to "the dark engine of nature." About the darkness one must agree. This "engine" is supposed to be governed by mechanical law, and to be unaffected by necessity or the awareness of it, and yet to go on chugging along to such excellent effect that its casually thrown-off by-products may constitute a perfect and economical demonstration, or a series of judgments in which each follows from its predecessor by self-evident necessity. And we are told that, relatively to this necessity, the following in thought of this logical line is completely accidental.

This does not sound to me like responsible science. It sounds more like the nightmare of an adolescent philosophy of science. The process of thinking is not like that. One knows that it is not, because the process is a familiar one, which we engage in daily and can observe directly. We have a better means of checking it than we have of checking the report of an army of physical particles marching blindly, uninfluenced by purpose or necessity. About these particles and their laws we are still so largely in ignorance that physicists debate whether they are material at all and whether, except in aggregates, they have any laws; matter, Russell tells us, has disappeared into "waves of probability undulating in nothingness." I do not, of course, deny the existence of these waves or their importance. I do suggest that we have a far more reliable and direct access to what goes on in our own consciousness than we have to these unobservables, and that to reject the evidence of direct inspection for an unverifiable theory about their control of mental processes is to copy the famous dog who dropped the bone in his mouth for its reflection in the river.

Is it denied that direct inspection does disclose a mental sequence affected by necessity? Then we must turn to the facts again. I think we can often see, as we come to the end of a reasoning process, that the purely logical relation between the proposition we entertained as our premise and the proposition we arrived at as our conclusion did have something to do with the emergence of that conclusion in our thought. When we add correctly a column of figures, has the fact that the figures, when added, require this amount had nothing to do with our result? We read that when a distinguished chemist named Webster was professor at Harvard, he did away with a colleague, disposing of his body in a chemical furnace. The evidence requires the reluctant conclusion that a Harvard professor may be a murderer. Or is this mere confusion? Does the fact that the evidence requires this conclusion have nothing to do with our drawing it after all? If you were to ask me why, in solving our little puzzle of a few moments ago, I concluded that I must be related to "this man" as father to son, my natural answer would be, "Because that was the conclusion dictated by the conditions of the problem." I think this natural answer is correct. If this man's father is my father's only son, then this man's father *must* be I, and to say that this "must" had no influence on the conclusion I came up with is to make it a miracle that I should have come up with it at all.

We are proposing, then, that a logical necessity be accepted as a partial cause. To be sure, this is an unusual kind of cause, for it is not an event in time, as causes are supposed to be. If one prefers to call it a fixed condition without which the course of an inference would have been otherwise, well and good; this still admits its determining role. The objection may be expected, "You surely cannot mean that the necessity linking premise and conclusion is itself a determining factor; you must mean that it is my *grasp* of the necessity; but then you are admitting that it is a mental act or event that serves as the cause." This, however, cannot be right. It illicitly transports the effect backward into the cause, and so begs the question. What is to be explained is the appearance of the conclusion in thought; but in seeing that the premise entails the conclusion, one is already thinking that conclusion, and it is this precisely that was to be explained.

One may expect the further objection that if reasoning is determined by necessity, it could never go off the track; it could never err. If it were completely so governed, that is true, as Descartes saw. But it never is. In this, as in every other causal sequence, each step is the resultant of a "pencil of forces," the joint product of a great many cooperating causes. When Newton was engaged in deducing the consequences for the moon's behavior of the law of the inverse squares, the course of his thought would have been inexplicable without the necessity in his subject matter. But Newton was a man and sometimes nodded. He was quite capable of forgetting his meals; at times he was tired or sick or angry; and when he was out of his element, he could be as superstition-ridden as a backwoods fundamentalist. When he offers us his demonstration that the Roman church is the eleventh horn of the fourth beast in the book of Daniel, we do not bow in assent; we say sadly that he must have been uninformed or senile or clouded by religious "enthusiasm." The most luminous of minds is sometimes under a cloud, and indeed, like the rest of us, moves in and out of the shadows. But if it would be absurd to argue that because Newton's thought about the moon was held in orbit by logic his thought about Daniel was equally so, it would be still more absurd to argue that because his adventures among the Hebrew prophets lacked logical guidance, the same holds of his thought in the *Principia.*

This recognition that the mind may be under constraint from very different quarters helps us to understand why the epiphenomenalist is so given to denying its rational direction. He will recognize constraint from only one side, from the side of the body. He is right, of course, that thought is affected in its vividness, even in its sequence and consistency, by the state of the brain. But thought, besides having bodily conditions, has an epistemological object, and this the epiphenomenalist is strangely prone to forget. That this object of thought may give rise to mental effects seems plain, however hard it is to fit this fact into the epiphenomenalist account. If I see lightning strike a tree across the road, I feel fear, and the rise of the fear is surely caused by the experience of a very special kind of object. And just as the character of an object may affect my feeling, so it may affect the direction of my thought. Suppose that, contemplating a square with diagonals, it occurs to me that these diagonals must bisect each other and that the four triangles so formed must be the same in shape and size. Here it seems obvious that one condition of my having these insights is the presence before me of an epistemological object with certain necessities in its structure; if I go on to apprehend some of these necessities in the structure of the square, it is because they are there to grasp. Of course that is not the whole explanation of my grasping them, but it is surely an essential part. Unless this conditioning of thought by its object is allowed, reasoning becomes inexplicable. If it is allowed, epiphenomenalism has been once for all left behind.

The reasonings so far cited have not involved values, except so far as knowledge itself is a value. But thought in the realm of values may exhibit the same sort of rational guidance as thought about fact; one would find it hard to see otherwise what rational conduct meant. Take any case of trying to decide reflectively what one ought to do. A man is making his will, and he wants to provide for his children in the way that will be best for them. His son John has an expensive ambition to become a doctor; Jane is married to a millionaire; James is crippled by polio. What should the father do? He considers the needs of each child, and the advantages to be secured by this disposition and that; he takes into account the expectations of each, and what justice seems to require; and at the end he may, if he is fortunate, be able to say: "I am clear that I ought to do *x*." I see no reason to say that this is not a necessary inference. No doubt this kind of thinking is more likely to be drawn off course by self-interest and emotion than most reflections about fact, but I should follow common sense in several convictions about it: (1) that there is such a thing as valid thinking in morals; (2) that one's conclusions as to what one ought to do are at times arrived at because the evidence points to and requires them; (3) that one's conclusion as to what one ought to do may make a difference to what one does. None of these positions is really compatible with epiphenomenalism.

I incline toward a like view in aesthetics. A colleague who ought to know better has told me that if I were to put a smudge on canvas and go on from there as the spirit moved, I should probably produce a work of art. That depends, I suspect, on what one means by "spirit." If it means the first impulse of an incompetent person, as it would in my case, I cannot hold art so cheap as to agree. It is unlikely that the first person one meets on the street would be qualified to put arms on the Milonian Venus; what is there given would have to be completed in accordance with aesthetic requirements which, if they are less definite in their exactions than logic, at least rule out many possibilities. Not everyone could emend a text of Catullus, even in the community of scholars; for the emendations, if they are to have a reasonable chance of correctness, must issue out of that organic whole which Catullus was engaged in creating, and which his editor must try to repossess.

If we grant that the thought process is at times purposive and under rational control, we are committed to a theory of mind and body that is far removed from epiphenomenalism. We need not deny the epiphenomenalist thesis that mind has its roots in the body, if that means that certain states of the brain provide the necessary condition of certain states of mind. We must, however, deny that they are the sufficient condition. For the urges, pushes and strivings that are essential to mind are activities with ends; these ends have patterns of their own; and these patterns affect the course of their conscious realization. The patterns are not physical, nor can they be the replicas or reflections of any merely physical whole. Thinking in art and morals and even mathematics is neither the reflection in consciousness of a mechanical order in the brain nor the tracing with the mind's eye of some empirical order in its object, but an endeavour to realize in thought an ideal order which would satisfy an inner demand. The nearer thought comes to its goal, the more it finds itself under constraint by that goal, and dominated in its creative effort by aesthetic or moral or logical relevance. These relations of relevance are not physical or psychological relations. They are normative relations that can enter into the mental current because that current is truly, not just seemingly, teleological. Their operation marks the presence of a different type of law, which supervenes upon physical and psychological laws when purpose takes control.

This, it may be said, is a retreat to Aristotle. Whether it would have been welcomed by Aristotle I do not know. But it does accept the Aristotelian conviction that the life of mind, whether in the individual or in the species, is a struggle to make the potential actual, a struggle not merely for existence but for self-realization. He would have agreed, I think, that it is a struggle to escape from physical slavery into a special kind of freedom, which meant of course not lawlessness, but a following of the laws of one's real or realized nature, that is, the nature of a rational man. He would have rejected, and would surely have been right in rejecting, the conception of evolution as a process which, looked back upon from the altitude it has reached, reveals itself as a chapter of accidents. The story of the emergence of mind as a set of blind lurches by matter, all but a few of which were terminal, and of the surviving lurches being allowed to lunge and stagger on till they produced an organism that somehow floundered aimlessly through *Hamlet* and *Principia Mathematica,* seems to me a fairy tale. And how can it be denied that if there is nothing in human activity inexplicable in the end by physics, this is the story we are being told?

If we find ourselves swept away by that tale, I suggest that it is because we are suffering a sort of hypnosis, not by science—I should want to reject that emphatically—but by a philosophy of science that is dogmatic and unempirical. It is dogmatic because it accepts too uncritically the assumption that science in the end means physics. It is unempirical in the sense that it closes its eyes to a range of facts of the first importance, namely, those facts that can be ascertained about mind by directly examining its higher processes. The facts about invention, discovery, creation, dialectical thinking, are as truly facts that require explanation as any others; and to me at least they seem to be facts in which the operation of purpose and necessity is too importunate to be explained away. If it cannot be explained away, then science, instead of ignoring them, should look at them straight and steadily, and revise its methods to deal with them. The revision would have to be considerable. For science would have to start dealing with man not only as a cybernetic marvel, but also as a thinking reed.

I need hardly add that a view of this kind, so lightly sketched, leaves numberless questions unanswered. How far do you carry the purposive drive which you take as the essence of mind? Does it extend, as Stout and Whitehead appear to have thought, right down to the "inanimate" level? Does this notion of laws supervening upon others in a hierarchy imply a suspension of the lower laws as mind emerges on higher levels? Are the ends you find emerging many or one? Is aesthetic necessity quite different from logical, or are they overlapping or interdependent? Any thoroughgoing essay on the mind-body problem must be prepared to deal with such difficulties; and in this short paper I have made no attempt to deal with them. But it is not clear to me that teleology is worse off with regard to them than epiphenomenalism. It is always dangerous when confronted with any process of genuine evolution to begin at the bottom and level down, to assume that the rules obtaining there will be adequate to everything that emerges. If one does that, the temptation is almost irresistible to explain intransigent facts away. It is perhaps safer to begin at the top with the facts of our conscious life. We are not likely, if we do, to overlook matter; it will hardly let us. But it is all too easy, as the history of this problem has made clear, to overlook with disastrous results the most central facts of mind.

Yale University

THE EXPRESSIVE THEORY OF THE MIND-BODY RELATION

H. H. PRICE

THE PROBLEM I WISH TO DISCUSS, to put it in very broad terms, is this:—Anyone who believes that there is a life after death must apparently accept a dualistic theory of human personality. Again, there are some who think that the question "Is there a life after death?" is one which can reasonably be discussed, though they admit that at present we do not have enough evidence to decide it one way or the other. In that case, they must also think that the arguments against a dualistic theory of human personality are not conclusive, and that some version of the dualistic theory (not necessarily the Cartesian one) might conceivably be true.

The dualism I have in mind is a dualism of continuants, not of events. A man might agree that mental events differ in kind from bodily events, that both kinds of events occur in every living human being, and that neither kind is "reducible" to the other. If so, he admits that there is an important sort of duality within human personality. But this would not commit him to dualism in the sense which now concerns us. A dualistic theory, in the sense which is here relevant, maintains that a living human being is a compound of two entities or continuants, a mind (or soul) on the one hand and a physical organism on the other; that these two entities interact with each other all the time, so long as the physical organism remains alive; and that when the physical organism dies, this interaction comes to an end (or rather, perhaps, that dying just *is* the permanent cessation of this interaction.)

But this kind of dualistic theory is nowadays rejected by the majority of Western educated people. They would admit that our understanding of human personality is still defective in many ways; but at any rate they are sure that *this* theory of human personality is false. To put the point in rather old-fashioned language, they are sure that, whatever else may turn out to be true (and of course we must wait and see what scientists may discover in the future) at any rate the doctrine of a "soul-thing" or "psychical substance" must be false. *A fortiori* they reject the tripartite conception of human personality, suggested by some religious thinkers, both Eastern and Western, which divides it into three entities, body, mind and spirit. What then is the theory which they accept? It may be described roughly as a monistic one. Or it may be called a theory of "psycho-somatic unity."

There are, no doubt, several different versions of this theory. I wish to consider one which is not very often discussed. (I am not even sure how to formulate it.) Its starting-point is the obscure but important concept of "expression," and its fundamental contention is that no mental process can occur unless it is "expressed" by means of bodily changes of some sort or other. This is supposed to apply not only to emotional states, such as sorrow or fear or anger, but to cognitive processes as well. Descartes distinguished between the *res cogitans* and the *res extensa*. But, according to this expressive theory, *cogitatio* cannot occur apart from extension. There must be something in the spatial world, namely the "cogitator's" body, by means of which the *cogitatio* is expressed.

It might be objected that there is such a thing as silent or wholly private thinking. No doubt it is accompanied by cerebral changes, but surely it would be a mistake to regard these as "expressions" of it, in the way that overt speech or writing or gestures would be. The silent thinker might, of course, be thinking "in" mental images of some kind (verbal images or others). But surely these cannot be called expressions either. Images are not themselves bodily events, though doubtless they do have cerebral correlates.[1] And though some of them, visual images for instance, are extended, they are not located in the space of the physical world.

Nevertheless, it does seem likely that such "private" thinking is a rather late development in the life of the individual, and could

[1] Croce, if I understand him correctly, does seem to think that mental images are "expressions," for instance expressions of emotions.

not exist unless there had been an earlier stage when all his thinking *was* expressed by overt bodily changes. It might also be said, perhaps, that when a person has learned to think in this private and unexpressed way, he cannot think in that way all the time; and that some of his thoughts must still be expressed by means of overt bodily changes, or else he will cease to be a person at all.

This contention begins to look more plausible when we emphasize the "social dimension" of human personality. It might be suggested that no one can be a person unless he has social relationships with other persons, at least sometimes, nor continue to be a person unless he continues to have them, at least sometimes. The trouble with the Cartesian *res cogitans* is that it (rather than "he") could apparently be a completely solitary entity, and could get on quite well without any social relationships at all. And if so, it is surely something less than a person.

There is an important point here, but one which is not easily formulated without circularity. It is obviously circular to say that having social relations with other *persons* is part of the meaning of the term "person." Perhaps we might put it this way: we mean by "a person" a rational being who has social relationships with other rational beings. In that case it is logically possible, though it may be false in fact, that there are rational beings who (or which) are not persons.

But how could a rational being have social relationships with others unless his "inner states" (thoughts, feelings, wishes) are expressed in some way, by means of bodily states or bodily movements which others can perceive? To put it very crudely indeed, a social being must have a face—or something which serves the same purpose as a face.[2] Moreover, there could be no social relationships of a permanent kind, such as friendship or enmity, unless one can recognize another person when one meets him again after an interval. And how could you recognize him unless he had a body which you can perceive? Not only must he have a face; he must have more or less the same face over a considerable period of time.

[2] Cf. the title of C. S. Lewis's novel *Until we have faces* (it is a version of the story of Cupid and Psyche).

This version of the "expressive" theory—the version of it in which the social character of personality is emphasized—seems to me both plausible and interesting. It has the merit of approaching the mind-body problem from a new point of view, and draws our attention to questions which were not asked at all in the traditional discussions of that problem. It might also claim to do justice to whatever truth there is in Behaviorism, without committing us to the unplausible conclusion that "inner states" do not exist at all or that it makes no sense to say they do.

We notice, however, that this "expressive" theory makes no appeal to empirical facts: or if it does, they are empirical facts of a very general kind indeed, which have been familiar to all mankind for ages. This theory might in principle have been suggested at a time when nothing whatever was known about anatomy and physiology. It is a product of purely philosophical reflection. It is none the worse for that. But if it can be called a "monistic" theory, or a theory of "psycho-somatic unity" (as I think it can) it is a different sort of monistic theory from the one which is now widely accepted, and it rejects the Cartesian "two-substance" doctrine on quite different grounds. The monistic theory, or theory of psycho-somatic unity, which is now very widely accepted is certainly not independent of scientific discoveries. On the contrary, it was suggested, and is supported, by the empirical facts discovered by the biological sciences, especially anatomy and neurophysiology. All that philosophers can do about it is to "tidy it up" and try to formulate it in a clear and consistent way. The reasons which can be offered for believing it are empirical reasons. And if any reasons can be found for disbelieving it, or for doubting whether it is wholly correct, they will have to be empirical reasons too, derived presumably from the study of paranormal phenomena.

We also notice—with surprise perhaps, but we ought to have expected it—that the "expressive" version of the monistic theory of human personality does not necessarily exclude the possibility of some sort of survival after death. What it excludes is only the possibility of wholly disembodied survival. If this expressive theory is correct, a person cannot exist without having a body of some sort or other; and no mental life is possible, or at any rate no mental life of a personal kind, unless it is able to "express itself" by means of changes in some sort of extended entity. But that body need not necessarily be extended in physical space, as our present bodies are. It would serve its "expressive" purpose equally well, if it were extended (and located) in a space quite other than the space of the physical world.

Again, so far as the social aspects of personality are concerned, the expressive changes which occur in this extended entity must be such that other persons can somehow become aware of them. But this awareness need not necessarily be dependent on the complicated apparatus of sense-organs, afferent nerves and brain-centres, which we have to use now in order to become aware of "expressive" occurrences in the bodies of our neighbours.

In short, the body which any person must have in order to *be* a person need not necessarily be a physical object at all, according to this "expressive" theory. Nor does it need to have the particular sort of internal structure and the particular modes of internal operation which anatomists and physiologists have discovered inside our present physical organisms. A hyper-physical organism, such as the "astral body" postulated by the Occultists, would do just as well. So would the "radiant body" spoken of by some of the Neoplatonists. Similarly, if I am to have social relations of a permanent kind with you, I must be able to recognize you when I encounter you again after an interval. You must have more or less the same "face" as you previously had. But it would suffice if I were aware of your "face" in some clairvoyant or telepathic manner, and my recognition of it need not be dependent on the excitation of cerebral memory-traces.

Professor C. D. Broad has reminded us recently that in almost all the religious conceptions of life after death, whether primitive or civilised, it is assumed that we do have bodies in "the next world," though not physical ones.[3] This assumption, if we try to work out its implications, does no doubt require that there should be at least two quite different types of space in the universe. But it is not logically necessary that physical space should be the only space there is.

[3] *Lectures on Psychical Research* (London: Routledge & Kegan Paul, 1962), p. 408.

I conclude, then, that the "expressive" theory of the mind-body relation does not exclude the possibility of some sort of personal life after death. In this respect, it resembles the theory which Professor Ducasse himself calls "Hypophenomenalism,"[4] and differs from the kind of monistic theory (or theory of "psycho-somatic unity"), which is nowadays accepted by the majority of educated Western people. A hypophenomenalist might be expected to think that the survival hypothesis is more likely to be true than false. A holder of the expressive theory might be expected to think that it is more likely to be false than true, since there is not anything in our normal experience (as he interprets it) to prepare him for such a possibility, whereas on the hypophenomenalist interpretation of normal experience, there is. But both alike, if they follow the logic of their respective theories, would be prepared to consider any paranormal evidence which appears to favour the survival hypothesis, and neither would think that the survival hypothesis *must* be false.

Oxford University, England

[4] *The Belief in a Life After Death* (Springfield, Ill.: Charles C Thomas, Publisher, 1961), Chap. XI.

DESIRES AS CAUSES OF ACTIONS

A. I. MELDEN

THAT WE OFTEN ACT as we do because of the desires we happen to have is a matter on which, normally, we have no doubt at all, but that and in what sense this "because" is a cause is one of the philosophic issues on which virtually every possible stand seems to have been taken. How does wanting or desiring explain doing? That is to say, what sort of a "because" is the "because" in "I did . . . because I wanted . . . ?" I propose in this essay to examine some attempts to deal in Humean terms with this question, but even where my results are negative the argument may be helpful in intimating the general line to be followed in a satisfactory account of the matter.[1]

I

Let me begin by commenting upon the futility of either affirming or denying that desires are causes rather than reasons, without first clearly specifying the precise sense in which these crucial terms are employed. There may be good point to such dark sayings—those who affirm that desires are causes may wish to bring out the contrast between the explanations of actions in terms of desires and their justifications by warranting considerations; while those who deny that desires are causes may wish to mark the difference between causal explanations of non-intelligent events in nature and those explanations we commonly offer of the doings of human beings. But if these are the points of such remarks it is far better to state them clearly and to argue for them

[1] Among the attempts to defend the applicability of the Humean causal model are those by D. Davidson, "Actions, Reasons, and Causes," *Journal of Philosophy,* Vol. 60, No. 23, Nov. 7, 1963, pp. 685–700; Bernard Berofsky, "Determinism and the Concept of a Person," *Journal of Philosophy,* Vol. 61, No. 16, Sept. 3, 1964, pp. 461–475; B. Goldberg, "Can a Desire Be a Cause?," *Analysis,* Vol. 25, No. 3, Jan., 1965.

directly and in detail than to suggest or intimate them in ways that are at best misleading. For nothing is gained by classifying desires with causes rather than with reasons (or, the other way around), since not only are "reason" and "cause" blanket terms, but each in point of fact, can do the work of the other.

Consider the very different sorts of ways in which "cause" is employed. We speak of the causes of earthquakes, of the earthquakes that cause men to react in terror, of the desires, moods, purposes and emotions of persons which cause them to act as they do, and of the considerations that cause persons to behave with good and sufficient reason, that give them good and sufficient cause for what they do. So too with "reason." We speak of the reasons that earthquakes take place, of the reasons people are terrified by them, of the reasons having to do with desires, moods, purposes and emotions that people act as they do, and of the good and sufficient reasons that people have for some of the things they do and which as such establish them and what they do as justified. But parallel as these cases may be, this does not warrant the view that reasons *are* causes in any sense that implies the legitimacy of the simple substitution of the word "reason" for "cause," and conversely, without making further changes in the surrounding sentence structure. "Reason" goes with "that-clauses"; and "why-clauses"; "cause" does not. "The causes of event x" is an intelligible form of words, and so is "the reasons that event x occurs." But the simple substitution of "reason" for "cause" in the first, and "cause" for "reason" in the second results in ungrammatical constructions. But either of these intelligible forms of words will serve equally well, and only a stylistic preference would lead one to employ one rather than the other, just as it is only a matter of style—a preference for a more formal mode of speech—that would lead one to use the verb "to desire" rather than "to want."

One thing at least is clear. We do *not* speak of the causes of the doings or the actions of persons in the way in which we speak of the causes of the movements of wheels in a machine or of the fibers in one's muscles, but of what causes a person to do this or that, or of the causes he has for so acting. Here the interesting and generally neglected but important feature of our use of "cause" in the domain of human action is the apparently ineliminable reference to agents in the sentences in which the word occurs. The explosions in the cylinders of a motor produce a movement of the pistons. And the roar of the motor may cause me to clap my hands over my ears. But while the fact that we sometimes speak of the explosions causing the automobile to move should interest us no more than the fact that motors may be described in terms borrowed from the human scene as cranky or well-behaved, the distinctive fact that we do not speak of the explosions in the cylinders causing or producing a clapping of hands over ears should at least suggest the possibility that the essential reference to agents marks an important conceptual feature of our use of "cause" that is not present in those cases in which the word is applied to such natural events as the actions of motors or of the muscles of the body.

The philosopher's disdain for such matters of linguistic usage may well prepare the way for conceptual confusion. Still, linguistic considerations even when they do in fact intimate important conceptual matters at best suggest but do not in themselves provide the requisite philosophical elucidations. Let us return then to our question about the sense or respect in which a "because" that refers us to a desire offers us a cause that explains a human action. And here I must restate a point I have made elsewhere that there is not, and cannot be, any dispute over the question whether desires cause us to move our bodily parts and in so doing to perform the very many sorts of things we do.[2] Of course they do. The only intelligible and sensible question is the quite different one: In what sense is "cause" here employed? It is to the Humean answer that I shall now turn.

II

Many philosophers have supposed that Hume's schema will fit the cases in which we speak of this or that causing a person to act in such and such ways. But even here there does not appear to be any general understanding of the Humean schema. Thus the rejection of the widespread assumption of the appropriateness of this schema on the ground that there is a conceptual linkage between desiring and doing (or, as I have put it elsewhere, a

[2] *Free Action* (London: Routledge and Kegan Paul, 1961), p. 16 and p. 204 ff.

logical relation between the concepts of desire and action), has evoked the rejoinder that we sometimes fail to act on our desires.[3] But, the fact that the occurrence of a desire does not entail the agent will do anything about it is both trite and irrelevant. It may be well, therefore, to remind ourselves of the more salient features of Hume's analysis.

Hume declared a cause to be "an object, followed by another, and where all the objects similar to the first are followed by objects similar to the second."[4] Now an object, e.g., a billiard ball, will not do, produce, bring to pass or cause anything to happen as long as no change in its state is underway; it is the moving or otherwise changing object that does anything at all. Hence those who think of wanting as a Humean cause of doing identify it either with an event or with some sort of state which, together with something like a perception or passing thought, triggers the action that takes place. I want food, but in addition there must also be the sight of the restaurant, the thought that food is to be found there, and so on, if the desire for food is to provide any sort of Humean explanation of my movement to the restaurant. But however Hume's statement is to be amended or qualified by further specification of additional mental factors, a desire is thought to be some sort of mental entity—whether event, process or state is of no matter here—which is connected with the doing in which it ensues by some sort of causal law that is conceived of as a regular or invariable sequence. But given these complications and amendments, there are still further matters that need to be made clear.

First, as Hume conceives of them, cause and effect are distinct existents such that the occurrence of either is logically independent of the other. If a desire is a Humean cause of an action, that is a contingent fact, and the supposition that the former may occur in the absence of the latter is not self-contradictory.

But, second, the independent existence requirement cuts even more deeply than this. It is perfectly conceivable for Hume that

[3] See, for example, Arnold Kaufman in "Ability," *Journal of Philosophy,* Vol. 60, No. 19, Sept. 12, 1963, p. 542; and May Brodbeck, "Meaning and Action," *Philosophy of Science,* Vol. 30, No. 4, Oct., 1963, p. 322.

[4] For this and other statements, see *Treatise,* Bk. I, Pt. III, Sec. XIV.

an entity that is in fact the cause of another might not have been the cause and, therefore, might never have been followed by the latter. If desires are Humean causes of the actions in which they issue, then it is thinkable not only that in a given case a person does nothing about a desire he happens to have (such cases not infrequently do occur) but also that no desire that anyone ever has issues in anything at all including anything that anyone ever does or tries to do.

Third, causal inference is by repetition of instances. If desires explain actions in the Humean causal sense of the term, then my avowal that I am now doing what I am doing because of some specific desire I happen to have is based upon the experience I have had in the past of similar entities being followed by similar performances.

Fourth, if the causal relation is discovered by repetition of instances, it follows that each of the pairs of events we come to identify as cause and effect must be identifiable and hence describable independently of that causal property that each has with respect to the other. Unless this were true, the query "What events are invariably conjoined?" could receive no intelligible answer. The supposition, confirmation or knowledge that desires are Humean causes of doings entails that the desires have been or can be identified and recognized as the desires they are independently of their supposed or established relational property of causing or producing any actions of any sort.

But, fifth, the requirement of independent describability cuts even more deeply than this. For, as Hume and those who have followed him in adopting his causal model have supposed, every entity that does or can stand in causal relations not only has relational properties, but intrinsic properties as well. There is no room on Hume's view for the notion that an object need have only relational properties, that the properties in terms of which independent descriptions of the causes and effects can be given are properties that merely relate such entities to other actual or possible objects, times or places. Indeed, Hume goes so far as to hold that *any* internal impression or idea, being a distinct and separable object conceivably can exist by itself independently of any and all other things even including that bundle of perceptions that constitutes the self.[5] But whether or not *this* radical independence is ascribed to every entity that stands in Humean causal relations to other entities, the notion of a Humean cause does in fact involve the idea that it has a nature consisting at least in part of intrinsic features or qualities discoverable by some sort of direct inspection of it and it alone. If, then, desires are Humean causes of doings, they must be describable as the entities they are independently of any reference to the doings in which, normally, they are manifested or to any other entities with which, normally, they are associated or otherwise connected.

These are the categorial features of Humean causes. They seem innocuous enough. Certainly they are familiar to anyone who has troubled to read the *Treatise*. Traditionally they have been accepted as essential to Hume's account of causation. Whether that account can be modified by altering any of these features is another matter and I shall consider later on some moves of this sort. At this point, however, I shall turn to the question whether the causal model that Hume did in fact employ can serve to elucidate the sense in which desires are "becauses" of action, i.e., the sense in which our desires cause us to engage in our doings.

III

Let us first look more closely at the independence requirement. It goes much further than the insistence that, in any given case, from the occurrence of the event that is in fact the cause it is impossible to deduce the occurrence of the event that is the effect. For Hume's independence requirement not only stipulates that a particular counterinstance to any causal law is always conceivable, it also asks us to grant the conceivability with respect to any causal law of such counterinstances being the universal rule. If there is a Humean causal relation between our desires and our doings such that, given our desires, certain relevant doings invariably occur, then it is at least thinkable that no desire should ever have this consequence. But, since this is the alleged elucidation of the sense in which desires cause agents to do something about what it is that

[5] *Treatise,* Selby-Bigge edition, p. 207.

they want, the independence requirement amounts to the claim that it is at least thinkable that no desire of any kind ever causes any agent to do or try to do anything about it. This is not merely false, odd or fantastic; it is incoherent.

Consider standard unequivocal cases of wanting, those in terms of which we come to grasp the concept of wanting or desiring. To want something in this full-blooded sense is to want to do something in order to get it. To "want" an apple that is before one, which one can have for the asking or the taking, without penalty, liability, effort or anything else that might stay one, but not want to do anything at all to get it, is not really wanting at all but a very degenerate sort of wish. This is not to say that if one wants the apple (say, for the eating) one will of necessity do something to get it. One may do nothing about it because one wants to nurse one's hunger, or because one is weary—and it is not really worth the effort. But what sort of a desire is it when none of these or any other staying or unusual circumstances are present? Is it wanting in any sense in which we are familiar with this term if one wants but, even given the normal circumstances in which wants are manifested in deeds, one does nothing at all? The supposition does more than pose a radical change in the actual course of nature; rather, it presents us with circumstances in which our concept of a desire no longer has any application. If so, the connection between desiring and doing is conceptual or logical. That is to say, what happens in the normal case when agents act as they do because of the desires they have is no mere matter of brute fact but something that is conceptually or logically related to the concept of desire that we employ.

It is this conceptual connection of desiring and doing—a relation of ideas, as Hume put it, or as we might do so, a logical connection of concepts—that needs to be recognized. Those who have rejected the Humean causal model because of this conceptual linkage are well aware of the fact that the specific propositions *John wants x* and *John gets (or tries to get x)* are logically independent in the quite simple sense that all four truth-value combinations are possible. So too are *John is guilty* and *John is punished;* but this scarcely warrants the claim that the concepts of guilt and punishment are in no way logically related. One surely does not need to argue that it is logically impossible to be guilty without being punished (or to be punished without being guilty) in order to maintain that there is a conceptual connection, a relation of ideas, between punishment and guilt. Similarly, one surely does not need to argue that every desire must issue in action in order to argue for a logical connection between the concepts of desire and action, a conceptual connection between desiring and doing. If the complaint is that it is the use here of the word "logical" that gives rise to misunderstanding, so much the worse for the unduly restricted way in which philosophers have applied this term. Just as what happens in the normal case in the instance of punishment (and the examples may be multiplied not only in the philosophy of law and politics but also elsewhere in the philosophy of mind itself), so in the case of desires, the actions of an agent are no mere matters of brute fact generally discovered after one has already learned what a desire is—a logical accident as it were—but a matter that is logically related to and involved in the very concept of desire itself. Small wonder that attention to the doings of agents is essential in the instruction given children in how correctly to employ words like "desire" and "want"!

To all of this the reply has been that the existence of a causal relation is by no means incompatible with some relation of ideas.[6] The fact that an action is described as the imposition of punishment, and thus embodies in its description the idea of some past wrong doing, merely illustrates the familiar practice of applying descriptive terms to things which involve at least implicitly some reference to the causally related occurrences. To call something a footprint is to do more than intimate the general shape of the mark or imprint; it is also to refer us to its cause. And to label something "fuel" is to call attention to the heat produced by its combustion. Further, if the guilty go unpunished, this, like the not uncommon fact that a desire may not lead to action, merely illustrates the fact of complicating circumstances either in the presence of causally disturbing factors or in the absence of just those contributing causal conditions that normally are present and always are necessary for the production of the given effect.

[6] Cf. Davidson *loc. cit.*

These attempts to reconcile the existence of a Humean causal relation of events with an acknowledged logical relation of concepts present us, however, with a number of radically different sorts of cases that cannot be caught in the same coarse mesh. (a) The attempt to accommodate the Humean causal model to the conceptual relation of guilt and punishment is even fishier than the alleged existence of a Humean causal relation between desires and actions, so much so that any doubts about the latter move cannot be allayed by embarking upon the former. For guilt, surely, cannot be a Humean cause of anything since it hardly qualifies as the requisite sort of entity. It is neither an event nor a feeling. It is neither a content of consciousness nor is it a state of mind. It is rather a legal or a moral condition of an agent. It is manifestly distinguishable both from any *sense* of guilt that might cause a person to do anything and from the action by which that guilt may be incurred or atoned. And if guilt leads to or is followed by punishment, that would appear to be, not a matter of Humean regularity, but an institutional or social affair of agents engaged in reflection and deliberation in the course of which the response of those in authority that punishment is warranted and its measure just is of a radically different sort from anything like the stereotyped issue of any invariable sequence. (b) Nor will the footprint analogy do. A footprint is a mark made by a foot—there is no room here for the possibility that the mark was not produced in the normal way by the pressure of a foot upon the surface on which the mark appears. In the case of a desire, however, there is and must be room for the possibility that the agent does nothing about it. *This* analogy succeeds only in drawing the connection between desire and action much too tightly. And (c), as for the alleged analogy with the case of fuel and heat, that one suffers from still another defect. Fuel normally will burn and produce heat, given easily specifiable necessary and sufficient conditions. A desire, normally, will show itself in what the person does or tries to do. (Whether or not the normal case can be further specified by listing a set of necessary and sufficient conditions is still another matter. For myself I see no reason to suppose that it can except those that clearly beg the very point now at issue. But let this issue ride.) And no doubt there is a conceptual connection between fuel and heat just as there is one between desire and action. But a reference to an effect can always be divested from the description applied to any Humean cause without impugning its status as such a cause. Indeed, this is precisely the requirements of independent describability. The fuel that is coal can be redescribed as carbon and it is *as such* that it produces heat. Fathers produce their offspring—as adult males engaged in the usual sexual practices. But divest the concept of a desire of the idea of any connection with its alleged Humean effect! Unless this can be done, there can be no Humean causal relation for anyone to discover. For in order to ascertain that there is such a relation it is necessary that each term of the relation be of an identifiable kind in order to determine that in repeated instances entities of the one kind are followed by entities of the other. But what kind of entity is the desire that produces a doing? Is it a state of mind? Depression is a mental state but we know well enough how to describe it without being reduced to saying that it is the state that causes those who are in that state to act in such-and-such ways. Is it an event? In that case we ought to be able to say more than that it issues in such-and-such doings. But every attempt to describe a desire as a Humean cause of a doing where the description of the desire is divested of any reference to the doing which, allegedly, it produces, leads us, if to anything at all, only to something vaguely of the order of a felt tension or discomfort, to something neither necessary nor sufficient to establish that the content then and there felt is both a desire and the relevant Humean cause.

IV

The fact that desires, that do in fact cause agents to act in various ways, do not meet the independent describability requirement of Humean causation will perplex those who find that particular causal model especially attractive. To such philosophers, the rejection of that model may appear tantamount to the denial that generalizations like "Frustration causes aggression" are even possible.[7] Perhaps frustration generally causes, makes for, leads to or produces aggression. But even if it did so invariably,

[7] Cf. Berofsky, *loc. cit.*, p. 475.

that no more establishes that frustration is some sort of Humean content of consciousness than the fact, if indeed it is one, that knowledge makes man free shows that knowledge is some sort of internal thrust or psychical impulse. To the question "what sort of entities are desires that they cause persons to act as they do in getting or trying to get the things they desire?", our recourse should be not to those matters of superficial linguistic usage upon which our philosophical preconceptions may cause us to fasten, but to the facts in the matter that stare us in the face.

Certainly, the first thing that must strike us is the manner in which we characterize or describe our desires. Some of them we describe as persistent, fleeting or recurrent; but this hardly assists us in determining the character of the thing that persists or recurs. Some are controllable; others are so far beyond our control that the word "desire" seems far too neutral or pallid to convey that sense of urgency that overwhelms the agent and thus gives point to Plato's striking figure of the charioteer unable to control the steeds of desire. In any case these characterizations inform us, not of the presumed intrinsic features of desire but rather of their relation to other matters—the feelings, thoughts and actions of those subject to them.

Much more to the point is the intentionality feature of desires, the fact that desires necessarily are desires *for* this or that. To want —"What?"—"Nothing," is no more to want than to fear nothing is to be afraid.[8] And if what I want is the red juicy apple before me, that fact is surely essential to the desire itself. But this is paradoxical on the present account of desires as Humean causes. For as such a cause any desire must *qua* desire have intrinsic features of its own. Now even if a desire *qua* entity of any sort had intrinsic features of its own, these would seem to be distinct from its intentionality feature, the feature, namely, that consists in its connection with or relation to the object of the desire. How then can the intentionality feature be essential to the desire not merely

[8] But this is not to deny that there are borderline cases in which one fears—What?—One does not know, or wants—What?—One is not sure. We are here concerned with clear-cut, standard instances of desire. In any case "wanting nothing" is quite different from "wanting something one cannot quite say what." The latter shades off into a mere restlessness, a feeling of uneasiness.

as an entity of whatever sort it might be in its own intrinsic nature but as a desire and Humean cause of doing?

This, it will be objected, is much too fast. It is not necessary, surely, that there *be* an object that is the intentional object *of* the desire, and hence it is not necessary that there be any relation to any actual object. Some of us want the impossible including, if pessimists are to be believed, our own happiness. But still, at least there must be the thought, if not the reality, of the thing desired. Hence the essential intentionality of desires would seem to derive not from the connection between the desire and some external object but rather from its connection with thoughts and the essential intentionality feature of the latter. Now this, certainly, is not to solve but only relocate the difficulty. But leaving aside the question of what makes *this* thought a thought of *that,* and the further but related question whether we can identify a thought with some Humean or inspectible content of consciousness, how is the connection between the desire and the thought to be secured?

Here, one is reminded of Hume's ingenious but unsuccessful attempt, in his account of abstract ideas, to explain how it is that one can think of an infinitely large class of things without implying an infinite capacity of the mind to frame in that thought an idea for each of the infinitely many things thought about.[9] Hume appealed to the association of ideas in order to explain the fact that in having an abstract idea, which in its own nature is particular, one is able to think of indefinitely many other resembling entities; but this, as students of Hume will remember, serves only to reduce to contingency every necessarily true affirmative. For how, on Hume's account of the matter, can one preclude the possibility that the next idea, say, of a triangle that comes to mind by association will not be trilateral? So too with the proposed account of the intentionality feature of the desire I now have for the red apple before me: Any appeal to a mechanism that explains the *de facto* co-presence of the desire I have with the thought of the red apple must surely render contingent the connection between the two. So perhaps the desire I now have might not be what manifestly it is, namely, a desire for the red

[9] *Loc. cit.,* pp. 17–24.

apple. If, for example, I have some desire and have both the thought of the apple before me and also that of the over-ripe cheese next to it, who knows that it is the red apple rather than the cheese that I want? Do I know that I want the apple because the thought of it is pleasant and that of the cheese is not? How indeed do I know this?—for our problem reappears now in a new place, this time in the connection between thoughts and pleasure. Surely I can just as easily get these connections wrong as I can the connections between desires and thoughts. In any case does it not happen that I sometimes want things I know to be unpleasant? How then can I tell what it is that I want if that is to be achieved by connecting, relating or associating desires with something else, the thoughts of the thing in question?

Can I tell what it is that I want from the fact that something appropriate happens when I get what I want, the removal perhaps of some discomfort I feel? Could I tell that I want the apple but not the cheese from the fact that when I get the apple, the itch of desire, the felt tension or uneasiness disappears, whereas if I wanted the cheese this would not happen? But this, clearly, is a causal inference, based upon repetition of instances; and might not things have gone wrong in all sorts of ways? How could I know the first time I saw and wanted this or any other apple that it was the apple and nothing else that I wanted? And might I not have got things mixed up—connecting the uneasiness and the relief with the wrong things? Indeed, one sometimes wants the impossible but one knows *what* one wants even though one does not at that time know that it cannot be had; but how is this possible, if "knowing what one wants" means knowing what happens when one gets the thing wanted? In any case, it would render purely contingent the connection between those features that are essential to the desire as Humean cause and its intentionality feature. It is not a logical accident that desires are desires for this or that; but if the connection between desire and the object of the desire (mediated or not as one chooses by thoughts, discomforts or pleasure) can only be secured by any *de facto* relation, associative or causal, between the desire and anything else, then the intentionality feature of desires must be a brute fact about them. And it is hardly necessary to remark that this feature goes even more deeply than I have so far indicated. For if one desires an apple, necessarily one desires to do something about it. Hence the difficulty of securing the intentionality feature of a desire *for an object* reappears in the logically related case of the desire *to act*.

V

The argument, so far, has rested on the requirement of independent describability. What has been assumed is that desires are events or objects of some sort which are describable as desires simply in terms of their own intrinsic qualities or characteristics. The argument has been that the intentionality feature of a desire, not being an intrinsic characteristic, cannot be an entailed feature of such characteristics and must be secured, if at all, only by means of some *de facto* relation between it and some other entity or entities—thoughts, feelings or whatever. I have argued that all such attempts to explain the intentionality feature fail and hence that the Humean model of causation, according to which causation consists in the invariable conjunction or sequence of such independently describable events or objects, will not fit the relation between desire and action.

But why, it may be objected, must the Humean doctrine of causation be saddled with this underlying metaphysics according to which desires are entities fully explicable as the desires they are simply in terms of their *intrinsic* characteristics? Should we not, even if Hume himself did not, distinguish between causation as invariable conjunction or sequence and the metaphysical theory of the nature of desires according to which each preserves its status as desire simply and solely by virtue of its intrinsic qualities, in consequence of which each could exist as the desire it is independently of any relation in which it stood to anything else, actual or possible? If we reject this bit of metaphysical extremism, the independent describability requirement can be softened considerably. It need impose no restriction upon the type of characterizations applicable to causes or effects. These might be intrinsic, but they might also be relational. The only restriction imposed by our requirement is that any cause must be capable of being described independently of that specific causal relation in which it stands to its effect. For unless this were so, there could be no substantive answer to any question of the form "what causes or produces . . . ?" In short, one might agree with Hume that causation is constant conjunction or invariable sequence, but reject the larger metaphysical thesis that confounds the quite acceptable requirement of the describability of causes independently of their relations to their respective effects with the altogether inadmissible requirement of the describability of causes independently of any relation in which they stand to anything else. Once this is granted, the intentionality of desires may be understood as one of their essential features even though it may refer us to matters that are, so to speak, at a distance from the entities that are the desires themselves—to the things desired, and to what, in consequence, the agent wants to do at whatever distant time or place this may be.

Such a weakening of the independent describability requirement is no doubt possible. One could treat causation as constant conjunction or invariable sequence freed from the metaphysical doctrine of objects with which, in the *Treatise,* the account of causation is connected. But the attempt to deal with the intentionality feature of desires as a relational property poses insuperable difficulties. And the conception of a desire as an object whose features must be either intrinsic or relational presents us with too tradition-bound a metaphysics with which to deal adequately with the nature of desire and its role in our practical lives.

To the first point. If I want an apple must there *be* an apple such that it is true of *that* one that it is wanted by me? Any apple, within certain limits, will do; but it is not true of any particular apple that it is the one I want. And to what is my present desire related when I want something that does not exist? Thus I might want an apple knowing full well that there is none to be had, just as men want their own happiness which they do not and perhaps cannot realize. Can we suppose that the relational property that is the intentionality feature of the desire is one that relates the desire in such cases as these, not to the reality, but to the idea of the thing in question? No doubt if I do want something there must be some idea of what is wanted, otherwise we should speak not of desiring something but rather of a vague and unsettled sort of restlessness. But are we to suppose, then, that an idea is some sort of internal content of consciousness and that what makes the desire I have a desire for an apple is that it is suitably related to one such content of consciousness? But *what* relation is it that we are talking about here? And what makes this content of consciousness an idea *of an apple* rather than of anything else—In terms of what relational property are we now to make secure the intentionality feature of the object that is the idea? The whole idea that this feature of desires (and ideas) can be made intelligible in terms of relational properties between contents of consciousness—inner objects—smells fishy from beginning to end.

The trouble here is that the metaphysics of desires as internal events or contents having either intrinsic or relational properties is not a radical enough departure from the old Humean metaphysics. For, and this is our second point, what is the desire *in itself?* Here the thought involved in this piece of conceptual misconstruction is that a desire is some internal entity whose descriptions involve either intrinsic or relational properties. But what intrinsic properties can we ascribe to the desire, properties it would have no matter what else existed in its surroundings and in relation to which its status as a desire with its intentionality feature could be made good? Well, what do I experience or feel when I want something? *This* question is at least intelligible. It invites us to look to the facts in the case, to turn from obsessive metaphysical models to what we feel and think and to our states of mind—to the facts in the case. And the answer lies in what all of us already know and of which only reminders are here necessary. For sometimes there are feelings when I want something, perhaps a slight tension at the pit of my stomach or at the back of my neck, a feeling of discomfort, slight or intense, of anxiety, of anticipatory pleasure or perhaps even of nausea when, for example, I want to get out of the rocking boat on to firm ground. Sometimes "want" is too mild a word to fit the lust or craving that overcomes me when all my composure is gone and emotions and feelings and bodily sensations run riot within me. But sometimes the feelings and sensations are poles apart from anything of this sort: if they are at all relevant they are diffuse and inchoate. Sometimes my state of mind is one of exhilaration; sometimes it is composed. And so it goes. How many many different sorts of things happen then and there when one has a desire! How varied the experiences—sensations, feelings, emotions, states of mind—in which desires are manifested, for how many different sorts of interests of ours are involved in innumerably many and in unpredictably many different sorts of situations in which our desires are elicited! There is no single content of consciousness—an inner inspectible object—something that is the very kernel of the desire itself. For not only is there no single nuclear experience, but even those we do have, immensely varied as they are from one instance of desire to another, do not fit the Humean model of objects each with its own intrinsic qualities discoverable by direct inspection. The whole conception of inner objects with intrinsic and relational properties is questionable metaphysics and a prioristic psychology.

This is hardly the place to examine the language we employ in characterizing and identifying our sensations, feelings, emotions and states of mind. I shall not here attempt to argue what Wittgenstein has been at great pains to teach us, namely, that the philosophical model of inner entities each with intrinsic qualities grasped by a mental act of intuition can hardly do justice to the complex grammar of the discourse we do in fact employ in talking about our experiences. It is, no doubt, the sense of the inadequacy of this model that has led some philosophers to try still another move in order to elucidate the concept of desire—the idea of a dispositional property on the order of the fragility of glass or the malleability of gold in terms of which the behavior of these substances can be explained.[10] Such moves, I believe, are misguided, as much so as the attempt to explain the conceptual network in which our practical concepts of desire and action are fixed by employing the model of a theoretical formal theory, the basic propositions or axioms of which implicitly define the basic or primitive terms of the formal system by stipulating the conceptual structure in which each term has its place. Our concept of desire is a practical, not a theoretical, concept. In any case, I am

[10] Cf. Brandt and Kim, "Wants as Explanations of Actions," *Journal of Philosophy*, Vol. 60, No. 15, July 18, 1963, pp. 425–435. I discuss this move in my paper "Desir et Action," *Les Etudes Philosophiques*, No. 3, 1964, pp. 353–359.

concerned here with the thesis that desires are Humean causes of doings in some recognizable and easily qualified sense of that term; and it is to this theme that I now turn.

VI

Suppose there were some nuclear content of consciousness in every case of desire, each with its wholly self-contained intrinsic features. Or, to take the opposite tack, suppose every feature of any desire, including its essential intentionality, were a relational property of some sort, no other form of characterization of desires being possible. Grant only that desires are somehow describable and identifiable, that agents have them at certain times and on certain occasions. How shall we construe the relation between them and actions?

Earlier I argued that the supposition that no desire ever issues in any action is logically incoherent. That an agent normally acts on a desire seems to be a conceptual requirement. Let the exception—the inhibition of desire—be the rule and we should no longer employ our concept of desire.

Wittgenstein once commented upon this connection between concepts and the regularities of nature: "If language is to be a means of communication there must be agreement not only in definitions but also (queer as this may sound) in judgments. This seems to abolish logic, but does not do so.—It is one thing to describe methods of measurement, and another to obtain and state results of measurement. But what we call 'measuring' is partly determined by a certain constancy in results of measurement." [11] But how shall we elucidate this connection, this one between desires and the actions normally taken because of them?

One might be tempted to resolve the problem by means of a definition, by defining desires as entities normally issuing in certain appropriate forms of conduct. This might seem to trivialize the explanations of action in terms of desire, but the fact that the circumstances in any given cause were normal would be an important contingent matter conveyed by such explanations; and this would save the explanation from triviality. Still what does

[11] *Philosophical Investigations* (New York: The Macmillan Company, 1953), Sec. 242.

"normal" mean here? It must be possible to spell out the circumstances constituting normality otherwise this move would appear to be only a dodge. Perhaps this can be done by specifying the desire as the only one that then and there strikes the agent, or, given competing desires, by showing that the desire that issues in an action ranks higher in some sort of preference scale. Grant this for argument's sake. Then a desire is defined as an entity identifiable in some way which regularly issues in appropriate forms of conduct, given circumstances that are normal in some specified sense of that term. To label the entity a desire is thus to encapsulate a reference to repeated instances of entities of the given kind being followed in such-and-such circumstances by actions of a specific sort. Such an account would appear to establish a conceptual connection between desire and action while allowing for a Humean causal connection between these entities relevantly described.

But while the account does, by means of a definition, establish a conceptual connection between desire and action, it does so only by rendering problematic and even precarious every avowal of desire. Problematic, since every avowal is implicitly an inductive generalization based upon repetition of instances; and precarious, since the first time I have any specific sort of desire I shall have to wait and observe the outcome, in repeated instances, of the occurrence of entities of the independently identifiable sort which only after this fact I shall be entitled to label "desires." And if one attempts to remove this doubt and uncertainty by eliminating in the definition of "desire" any reference to the normal outcome in the action of the agent, one will not only abandon hope of securing the conceptual connection between desire and action but also merely relocate this doubt and uncertainty in the explanation of action in terms of desire. For this is an essential feature of Humean causation, that every causal explanation is based upon repetition of instances. If desires are Humean causes of doings, the assurance I have that *this* present desire of mine is the reason I perform *this* action is founded on nothing more than my past experience that entities of the former kind have been followed by the latter. And this is absurd.

I am not concerned to deny that there are cases in which there is a legitimate and intelligible doubt as to whether I really do have such-and-such a desire. Do I really want to marry the girl or is it only her money I am after? Here one can imagine circumstances in which this does express a genuine and disturbing doubt. Nor am I concerned to deny that there are cases in which I can and do doubt whether I am doing something because of such-and-such a desire. Am I taking steps to rescue my boss because of a concern to save his life or because I want the promotion the rescue will bring me? Incidents of these sorts—some of them difficult and perplexing indeed—do sometimes occur. It would be folly to suppose that desires are self-luminous objects of consciousness, entities which as Hume once put it, are what they appear to be and appear to be what they are, or that, *contra* Hume, we can discover by some sort of intellectual peek the inner bond of necessity that ties this action to that desire. But while such incidents do occur they are and must be the exception rather than the general rule. It simply makes no sense to suppose these doubts generalized, infecting every and any avowal of desire and every explanation of one's action because of one's desire.

Neither is this to deny that the occurrence of desires makes no difference of any sort to the experiences of those who have them. The point, rather, is that there is no single experience that constitutes the desire and hence no awareness of an internal event that serves as the evidence for or the ground of one's avowal of desire. Similarly, the explanation I offer of my doings in terms of my desires is not made on the basis of evidence gained by an inner observation of any regular succession of desires and doings, or of any discovery of a mysterious bond of necessitation that connects two sorts of entities. Normally there is no observation or evidence of any sort I am required to make in order to ground my avowals of desire or my explanations of my doings in terms of my desires.

VII

In my own view all of the problems we have so far encountered, in rendering intelligible the intentionality feature of desires, in making clear the conceptual connection between desire and action, in being faithful to the experience-difference that desires do make, and in rejecting the misguided request for evidence to support our avowals, arise from the basic failure to recognize the context within which alone our discourse about desires makes sense: the lives and practices of agents of the sort that you and I are. Here it is impossible to deal with these varied but related issues in detail. This I have tried to do elsewhere.[12] Nevertheless a few words on these matters may at least indicate the general line to be taken.

In an earlier section, I commented upon the fact that a reference to the agent seems to be ineliminable in our application of the term "cause" to desires: we speak not of a desire causing an action but rather of it causing a person to act. The reference to persons—to agents—is no linguistic accident, but the key to the understanding of the crucial concepts of desire, cause, and, one should add, of action itself. For, these are concepts to be understood by attending to the manner in which they are employed in the lives of agents. It is not enough, however, that we think of agents as providing the necessary residence for the occurrence of desires and actions—as if for reasons that now escape us but which, we hope, subsequent investigation will make clear, one needs a mind in which to house desires and a mind by which to make good the title of a bodily movement to the status of a human action. It is, rather, the activity of an agent in dealing with objects and with other agents in social and even moral situations that is the language-game, the context in which alone our crucial practical terms have intelligible application. That is to say, any reasonable elucidation of desire, action, and that sense of "cause" relevant to these notions, must start with and attend closely to those practical circumstances in which alone it even makes sense to affirm or deny the application of these terms.

Thus, it is in the practical activities of persons that the experience-difference made by our desires is to be understood. As agents, we do not observe entities called "desires" coming into being or passing away, although there are times when we are aware of desires welling up in us and of our being overcome by them. But even in these cases there is no nuclear entity—a

[12] In *Free Action.*

luminous content of consciousness—that strikes the inner eye of the mind. Besides, these cases are the exception, necessarily so, rather than the general rule. For, as persons who are active, not reflective and introspective, as agents in command of ourselves and of the situations in which we go about our normal business, to want this or that is to regard these in a certain way, in that way in which agents regard the things they want as things to be enjoyed or to be used in various ways and in various sorts of circumstances. The apple I want is something to be eaten and relished or . . .—and here there is no more of an end to the ways in which one thinks about it as a thing to be dealt with in some way or other than there are interests of ours that are brought to bear upon it. And since, as agents, our attention is focused upon the things that interest and concern us—the food we eat, the persons with whom we work and play and communicate—attention of necessity is directed no more to our states of mind than it is to the muscle movements in our arm or the bodily movements these bring to pass, but to the things that lie, so to speak, outside and beyond ourselves. It is in our view of objects, to be dealt with in ways conforming to out interests and in the circumstances of which we take notice that desires make a difference to our experience. Not as contents of consciousness inspected by a mind but as revealed in the manner in which we deal with things, in our expectations, anticipations, satisfactions and frustrations, in the reflections, preoccupations, moods and emotions we have in this or that related circumstance, do our desires make a difference to the character of our experiences.

For there is no single condition, necessary and sufficient, for the occurrence of a desire. What counts for this being a case of desire may be various things, no one of which is indispensable. Hence the borderline cases, the difficult and perplexing cases, even to the agent himself. For there are different sorts of criteria of desire, and to establish a place in our language for the use of this word, we need much more than a post to which to hitch some internal *quale* or Humean content. We need to be masters already of a body of discourse about thoughts, feelings, expectations, actions, satisfactions, etc., for it is in these and much more that our desires are revealed, that their criteria are to be found. And since "desire" is a term applicable to human beings like ourselves, who are sometimes perverse and relish the things of which we ourselves disapprove, but who are generally rational and often reasonable in our concerns with ourselves and with our fellows, the exceptional case rather than the general rule is the desire for the unpleasant and the harmful, and the usual, the normal case, is the desire for what is reasonable and in one or another respect desirable. This is our concept of desire, a concept that has application in the lives of persons like ourselves. Hence the conceptual connection between the desired and the pleasant and, in other respects, the desirable. That these are often and generally desired is not an accident but an essential feature of our concept of desire. In short, the conceptual ramifications of the concept of desire run wide and deep, reflecting the character of the practical context in which the term "desire" has whatever significant application it has.

I said earlier that the recognition of this context will bring home to us the character of the intentionality feature of desires no less than the connection of desire with action. To want is to want something, but not anything mentionable is wantable—It always makes sense to ask what sort of a being would want, say, to plaster his fine old Hamadan with cow-dung. For no reason whatsoever? That makes no sense. Neither does it make sense to suppose a man with a desire who does nothing about it—Why?—No reason whatsoever. But where a man's desire is for a woman or anything else, *that* is shown not by finding two objects, one labelled "desire," and the other an object or its mental surrogate, and then uncovering some hidden link between the two, but rather in the characteristic ways in which in his thoughts and moods and feelings and actions the criteria of that desire are to be found. That the traffic arrow points in a certain direction for the motorist on the highway is shown in the practices, the conduct, of motorists on the road; and that a desire is a desire for this or for that is shown in the ways in which characteristic thoughts, actions, feelings, states of mind, moods, etc. are blended in the life of the person whose desire it is.

It is no single or simple mistake that is made by those who argue for the application of the Humean causal model to the relation between desires and actions. Philosophical errors of this degree of importance are no mere slips of the intellect that distort and becloud only one small segment of the matters that interest us. It is not only that this model serves only to render dubious our status as agents by reducing each of us to a spectator of events transpiring in him—the fact that the alleged invariable sequence of events are "mine" and "yours" in some proprietory sense no more establishes that they are the activities of agents than the fact that the flow of blood occurs in a ruptured artery of mine establishes that this is an activity in which I engage. And the suggestion that these events, so related, gives us the force of that sense of "cause" that is indeed involved in our talk about desires and actions, not only suggests what is quite false, namely, that our avowals of our actions and our desires are based upon evidences provided by observations of an outer and an inner sense, but like the failure to recognize the importance of the context of persons as full-blooded agents in which terms like "desire" and "action" have their only significant application, is insatiably mischievous in the damage it does to our philosophic understanding of the logic of these practical concepts. But philosophical enlightenment is an inseparable concomitant of the recognition of the full import of a really first-rate philosophical error; and for affording us this occasion to bring us back to our good common sense with the understanding and appreciation that philosophy itself can provide we ought for this at least to be grateful to latter-day followers of Hume.[13]

University of California, Irvine

[13] I am grateful to Professors Avrum Stroll and Fred Hagen for their comments on an earlier version of this paper.

DUCASSE ON "CAUSE"—ANOTHER LOOK

RONALD E. SANTONI

Ducasse's most recent article on Causality, entitled "Causation: Perceivable? Or Only Inferred?," [1] affords another opportunity to observe the precise and lucid working of a "master of analysis" [2] in an area of philosophy in which he has made and continues to make a distinctive and enduring contribution. In this article, Professor Ducasse argues a convincing case for distinguishing between Causality as defined in theoretical physics and the view of Causality implicit in the actual use people ordinarily make of the very many common verbs of causation. In short, Ducasse contends that in theoretical physics Causality turns out to be a *dyadic* relationship *conceived* or *inferred* (but *not* perceived) to exist between *conceived* "total states *A* and *B* of a conceptual system," but that the conception of Causality entailed in the actual use of ordinary verbs of causation (e.g., "to break," "to bend," "to heat," "to kill") includes not only the *perception* of two occurrences or "concrete events" but also the *perception* of the actual causation of the one (sequent) event by the other (antecedent) event. In other words, while in theoretical physics, concrete cases of causation are *inferred* but *not* perceived to be such, ordinary use of common verbs of causation takes for granted the actual perception of causal occurrences or concrete instances of causation. For Ducasse it is an obvious fact that everyone has *perceived* (not just inferred) a particular tree branch's "being caused to bend" by "a particular bird's alighting on it," or some other concrete case of causation. Hence Ducasse maintains that

[1] Presented at the Eastern Division Meetings of the American Philosophical Association in Boston, 1964, and forthcoming in *Philosophy and Phenomenological Research.*

[2] I borrow this description of Ducasse from Raphael Demos' reference to him in his critical study of *Nature, Mind, and Death,* in *The Review of Metaphysics,* Vol. VI, No. 4, June, 1953.

"causality as *defined* in theoretical physics is patently not the relation a person has in view when . . . he employs one . . . of the many common verbs . . . of causation."

The question, of course, then arises, What exactly is the relation that a person has in view when he uses causal verbs as "to push," "to break," "to create," "to transform," "to kill," etc.? Anyone familiar with Ducasse's major works is aware of his painstaking attempts to discover the "right definition" of the word "cause" as it is actually and ordinarily employed.[3] "Causation: Perceivable? Or Only Inferred?" now serves the additional important function of providing a succinct account of Ducasse's view of the causal relation after his searching analysis of that relation has been revised, refined, and partially reformulated in the light of progressive critical scrutiny and stated objections to it. And despite the meticulousness which he has carried to the continuing discussion of causality, the question of the adequacy of Ducasse's hypothesis, both as an account of the way in which people ordinarily use and understand common verbs of causation and as a philosophical analysis of the causal relation, must remain an *open* issue.

In the discussion which proceeds, I shall endeavor to delineate a few of the problems which, even after conscientious philosophical dialectic, remain, I believe, to challenge Ducasse's most recent account of the Causality relation. Within the structure of this task, I shall contend that Professor Ducasse has failed to provide convincing replies to a number of important objections to his view of causation, notably those of Arthur Pap, and that there is serious question as to the conformity of Ducasse's hypothesis with what he takes to be the data for his philosophical analysis of Causality—namely, common verbs of causation in their ordinary use. Before turning specifically to these matters, however, it will be useful, I think, to review briefly Ducasse's latest formulation of the nature of causality.

1. *Ducasse's definition of Causation.* In "Causation: Perceiva-

[3] See, for example, *Causation and the Types of Necessity* (Seattle: University of Washington Press, 1924); *Nature, Mind, and Death* (La Salle: Open Court Publishing Co., 1951); "Of the Nature and Efficacy of Causes," *Philosophical Review,* Vol. 41, No. 4, July, 1932; "On the Analysis of Causality," *Journal of Philosophy,* Vol. 54, No. 13, June 20, 1957.

ble? Or Only Inferred?" as in *Nature, Mind, and Death* and other of his works[4] dealing with the meaning of "cause," Ducasse conceives of causation as a *triadic* relation which obtains between three terms which together constitute "what is properly called an *experiment.*" These three factors are: "(1) a concrete *state of affairs S* in which only two changes, whether simple or complex, occur; (2) one of these a change *C* occurring at a time *T;* and (3) the other a change *E* that begins to occur after change *C* has begun to occur [i.e., it is an immediately sequent event]." [5] This triadic relation between *S, C* and *E,* Ducasse insists, is not merely a *sign* that a causal relation mysteriously exists between the two changes; rather this relation *is* causation itself, and, indeed, is *perceived* by the conductor or observer of a well-performed experiment. And, relying on an earlier contention which Ducasse seems simply to assume in his most recent statement on causation, it is important to note that to say that the relation of causality obtains between *S, C* and *E* is to say that *C* in *S* is etiologically both *sufficient* and *necessary* to *E* in *S,* and conversely, that *E* in *S* is etiologically both *contingent on* and *necessitated by C* in *S.* Finally, Ducasse makes it clear that his definition of Causality, appealing only to single occurrences of *C* and *E* in *S,* requires but *one experiment* "to make evident that the particular change *C* in *S* did cause the particular change *E* in *S.*" Causation, he insists, is not to be identified with *causal law,* as too frequently is done. A causal law is an empirical deduction from *perceived* instances of causation, i.e., from a number of occurrences *each* of which was, *in its own right,* a concrete case of causation and *was perceived.*

In short, then, "cause" for Ducasse is the single change which occurs antecedently to the only other change in a given state of affairs *S,* and Causality turns out to be an *etiological,* not a logical relation, that is to say, a relation between *concrete events* in a state of affairs, not between timeless logical entities. Moreover, this definition of Causality does *not* appeal to the notion of "collections" or "kinds" of events.[6]

[4] For examples of these other works, see the preceding footnote (3).

[5] Unless otherwise noted, quotations are taken from "Causation: Perceivable? Or Only Inferred?"

[6] See, especially, section II (i) of "Causation: Perceivable? Or Only Inferred?," and also pp. 113–116, 121, of *Nature, Mind, and Death.*

In passing, it is well, in the light of what follows, to note the increased determinateness with which Ducasse now refers to the two changes involved in an instance of causation. He explicitly qualifies his reference to these changes with the phrase "whether simple or complex." No such qualification appears in his summary definition of the casual "experiment" in *Nature, Mind, and Death.*[7] Only in a later article, "On the Analysis of Causality," in which he attempts to respond to the challenging objections of Arthur Pap, does he begin to use the qualification "whether simple or complex," although on this occasion the qualifying phrase is in parentheses.

With the intent expressed above, I should now like to consider two of Pap's major criticisms [8] of Ducasse's view of Causality, and to present some of the problems which, I believe, arise in connection with Ducasse's answers to these criticisms.

2. *Pap's criticisms considered.* (a) Pap's first criticism of Ducasse's definition is expressed in the following way:

> . . . Ducasse overlooks that the observation of a solitary change preceding the event to be explained may not be the sufficient ground of the causal judgment, that it may warrant the causal judgment only in the context of a tacit argument from elimination of alternatives.[9]

Ducasse's reply to this serious criticism is, I think, disappointing and inadequate. By an appeal to his own definition of Causality, Ducasse simply rules out the possibility that a change other than the sole observed antecedent change in a set-up could be *causal* in respect to E. ". . . What Pap apparently overlooks," he says, "is that, simply under the definition of Causality stated in Sec. I . . . the supposition that C . . . was the *only* change immediately preceding E . . . automatically eliminates as alternative the hypothesis that some *other* change could be the cause of E." [10] It is unfortunate that Ducasse settles the matter here by definition rather than by philosophical argumentation. He seems to proceed

[7] See *Nature, Mind, and Death,* p. 105.

[8] In the article cited.

[9] Arthur Pap, "A Note on Causation and the Meaning of 'Event,'" *Journal of Philosophy,* Vol. LIV, No. 6, March, 1957, pp. 155–159.

[10] Ducasse, "On the Analysis of Causality," p. 423.

as though his own definition were a kind of standard for ascertaining the soundness of objections raised against his analysis of "cause." But I submit that the issue here is not one of conformity to Ducasse's definition but, rather, whether Ducasse's definition itself represents an accurate analysis of Causality, or, to employ his own philosophical framework, whether *his* definition of "cause" conforms to what people ordinarily mean when they use the word "cause" and other common verbs of causation.

Moreover, it seems to me that the force of Pap's criticism is served, *not* undermined, by the later statement from Ducasse that "Whether the only change one *observed* was the only change that *really occurred* at the time in the given state of affairs is of course a different question." And he adds: "What can be said about it is only that the more carefully we look for additional changes without finding any, the more *probable* it becomes that there were no others."[11] If Ducasse means what he appears to be saying here, surely one is entitled to ask whether a change which *really* might have *occurred* but was *not* observed might actually have been the *cause* of E in that situation, and surely Pap has grounds for being concerned with the warrant or sufficiency of evidence for a causal judgment. For if there is no assurance that the only observed change was the only change that *really occurred* then there is no *a priori* reason to assume that the only observed antecedent change in the situation was the *cause* of the immediately sequent event. And for Ducasse to answer in the *following* way does not bail him out of his difficulty. He says:

> To analyze the concept of Causality is one task; and to identify empirically concrete exemplifications of it is another task. The outcome of the latter always remains theoretically precarious in some degree. But this is nothing peculiar to Causality. Rather, it is a feature of every attempt to identify in experience concrete cases of something one has defined abstractly—for example, Straightness, or Equality, etc.[12]

For two reasons I maintain that this reply does not eliminate, but rather *adds to,* Ducasse's difficulty. *First,* I submit that,

[11] Ducasse, "On the Analysis of Causality," p. 424. See also *Nature, Mind, and Death,* pp. 106–107.

[12] *Ibid.*

contrary to what he suggests in this quotation, Ducasse's *analysis* of Causality *depends* on the identification of *empirically concrete exemplifications* of Causality. It is true that the "data" or "empirical facts" of Ducasse's analysis are, here as elsewhere, phrases in which the term in question is actually and *ordinarily* employed,[13] but it is also true that, on Ducasse's own insistence, the actual employment of the term, in each of the *data,* is in reference to a concrete, discernible occurrence. In "Causation: Perceivable? Or Only Inferred?" for instance, he makes it clear that the data for his analysis of Causality are illustrations of the usage of common verbs of causation by people when they are trying *to describe ordinary occurrences which they perceive.*[14] Hence, given Ducasse's methodological procedure for the analysis of a term, as well as his specific view of the (ordinary-language) *data* for the problem of causality, it is baffling to find Ducasse suddenly making a sharp distinction between the *analysis* of causation and the *identification* of concrete exemplifications of cause, as though the former had nothing to do with the latter. *Secondly,* it seems to me that, far from refuting Pap's criticism, Ducasse's admission of the theoretical precariousness connected with identifying concrete exemplifications of causality supports Pap's question concerning the sufficiency of Ducasse's grounds for judging instances of Causality, and gives weight to his suggestion that, against the implications of Ducasse's definition of Causality, the ascertaining of "cause" must involve the "elimination of alternatives." For if the outcome of the "identification" of "empirically concrete exemplifications" of Causality is *always* theoretically precarious and if the possibility of there being other "additional" immediately antecedent changes in a situation is *not* ruled out by *definition,* then there is no *a priori* reason to assume that the only *observed,* (immediately) antecedent change in the situation must be the cause of the sequent event E.[15] As Ducasse himself has

[13] See Ducasse's *Nature, Mind, and Death,* pp. 102–103. For the most up-to-date account of Ducasse's methodology, see his article, "Philosophy Can Become a Science," *Revue Internationale de Philosophie,* Fasc. I, No. 47, 1959, pp. 1–14.

[14] See beginning of Section II in "Causation: Perceivable? Or Only Inferred?"

[15] It is interesting to note that in *Nature, Mind, and Death* Ducasse's view does not appear adverse to this conclusion. On p. 106 he says: "We are aware, of course, that we might be mistaken in believing that the first change we observed was the only change that occurred in the given state of affairs at that time. . . ."

pointed out in a related context, ". . . Theoretically, all that observation can yield is probability. . . ." [16] It is true that "the more carefully we look for additional changes without finding any, the more probable it becomes that there were no others," but this does *not* logically entail either (1) that there are no other changes or (2) that the elimination of alternative hypotheses could not be required in the judging of what is the cause of E in S.

Thus I conclude that Ducasse's answer is laden with difficulty and is inadequate as an attempt to meet Pap's "first criticism." I proceed now to a consideration of Pap's subsequent objection.

(b) Pap's next criticism is that, according to Ducasse's analysis of the causal relation, an event E immediately preceded by a *number* of concurrent changes in a situation S cannot, without contradiction, be said to be *caused* at all. For, says Pap, "if one antecedent event is causally irrelevant to E, then all of them are, since a change which is one of several concurrent changes in S cannot be said to be the *only* change in S," that is to say, cannot be said to be the single change which occurs antecedently to the only other change in a given situation S. But, Pap challenges, according to the *ordinary meaning* of "cause," it is surely *not* self-contradictory to suppose that an event immediately preceded by a number of changes is *caused*.[17]

Ducasse's reply to this objection is ingenious but, I think, questionable and unconvincing. It rests heavily on the qualification "whether simple or complex" which, as I indicated in passing at the end of section 1, Ducasse contributes at this point to his definition of Causality, and which he preserves in his latest formulation of the causal relation. In essence, he argues first that what actually follows from his analysis is not at all what Pap suggests, but "only that the change in S, which immediately preceded the event, was then a complex change; for in order that at a time T a change C in S be the *single* change there, it does not have to be a *simple* change." [18] In other words, Ducasse is here affirming a distinction between a *single* change and a *simple* change, and is noting that for him a *single,* total change in a state

[16] Ducasse, *Nature, Mind, and Death,* p. 119.

[17] Quotations and criticism in this paragraph are taken from Pap, "A Note on Causation and the Meaning of 'Event,' " p. 158.

[18] Ducasse, "On the Analysis of Causality," p. 424.

of affairs may well be *complex*. This being the case, Ducasse is maintaining that Pap's example of "concurrent changes" is but an example of "complex change," and hence does not contradict either his hypothesis concerning Causality or common, ordinary usage of "cause." This contention represents the first part of Ducasse's reply, and seems also to be what Ducasse has in mind *earlier* when, in *Nature, Mind, and Death,* he speaks of events (and states of affairs) as "taken in their full determinateness and entirety," [19] and *later* when he disputes Margenau's talk about "partial causes." [20]

The second part of Ducasse's answer concerns Pap's inference that (on Ducasse's hypothesis) "if one antecedent event is causally irrelevant to E, then all of them are," etc. Says Ducasse emphatically: "Any appearance that this conclusion follows is due only to the ambiguous phrase, 'causally irrelevant to,' which invites confusion between etiological *sufficient to* (i.e., 'cause of') and etiological *necessary to* (i.e., 'condition of')." [21] To support his point, he contends that to say that the single immediately antecedent complex change, *abc,* in situation S, was *sufficient to* cause the only other single complex change, *def,* implies that it was sufficient to cause all the parts of *def,* but does not imply that the entirety of *abc* was a *necessary* condition of, for example, part *d* or part *e* of *def.* For, indeed, adds Ducasse, no contradiction is involved in supposing, for instance, that if part *a* of *abc* had not been present, then the remaining *bc* would have been sufficient to bring about, say, *de, df,* or *ef.*[22]

Ducasse's latter point is obviously dependent on the soundness of his former contention, namely, that a *single* change can be a *complex* change as well as a *simple* one. Otherwise, it is clear, Ducasse would not be able to talk (for example) about part *a* or *bc* of a single antecedent change *abc* or part *df* of a single sequent

[19] Ducasse, *Nature, Mind, and Death,* p. 124.

[20] I refer specifically to section 2 of chapter 8 of Ducasse's forthcoming book tentatively entitled, *An Analytical Philosophy of Knowledge.* I am indebted to Professor Ducasse for allowing me the privilege of reading some unpublished manuscripts relevant to this paper.

[21] Ducasse, "On the Analysis of Causality," p. 424. See extended discussion of this distinction in *Nature, Mind, and Death,* pp. 108–118.

[22] *Ibid.*

change in a causal experiment. For this reason, I shall now focus on the first part of Ducasse's reply and attempt to show a remaining weakness in his position here.

To support his contention that the single antecedent change in a state of affairs might well be *complex,* Ducasse refers to an illustration of the breakage of a window occurring immediately after the impact of a brick on it.[23] He hypothesizes that at the instant the brick strikes the window pane, the pane is also "struck" by air waves generated by the singing of a canary nearby. Although Ducasse disowns the notion that, on his analysis, "the singing of the canary was involved as a cause of the breaking of the window," [24] he maintains that when one asks what *caused* the whole of the "completely determinate" sequent change in the state of affairs, then, indeed, the song of the canary, the exact shape, position, speed of the brick, as well as every other part of the "specificity" of the antecedent occurrence or event, is "causally relevant to one or another part or feature" of the sequent event. And "when," says Ducasse, "events and states of affairs are taken thus in their full determinateness and entirety, the earlier of the two only changes in the given state of affairs is not only sufficient but also necessary to the later change . . . ;" [25] that is to say, it is the *cause* of the latter.

Now I wish to submit that the way in which Ducasse employs "change" and "event," both in his answer to Pap and in his other writings cited above, may well involve a departure from ordinary language and render inadequate his definition of causality. For, to resort to Ducasse's illustration, I contend that in ordinary language the singing of a canary, or the impact on the window of the air waves coming from the canary's song, would *itself* be referred to as an "event" or "change" in a situation or state of affairs. More explicitly, if, as Ducasse suggests, we are to view causality in terms of an *experiment,* then I maintain that any observer or conductor

[23] Ducasse, "On the Analysis of Causality," pp. 425–426 especially; see also Ducasse, *Nature, Mind, and Death,* p. 123; "Demos on 'Nature, Mind, and Death,' " pp. 292, 293.

[24] Demos, critical study of *Nature, Mind, and Death,* p. 570. Ducasse's disclaimer appears on p. 293 of "Demos on 'Nature, Mind, and Death.' "

[25] Ducasse, *Nature, Mind, and Death,* p. 124.

of an experiment would, in the conditions of experiment and using ordinary language in an ordinary way, acknowledge the singing of a canary, for instance, as a "change" or "event" [26] in the (given) state of affairs. I doubt that Professor Ducasse would wish to deny this. Yet if he were to admit that in the situation under consideration the singing of the canary was a separate "event" or "change" (let us say a "simple" change), as ordinary-language usage would seem to suggest, then he would have to allow that there was more than one "immediately antecedent change immediately adjacent to" [27] the sequent event, "breaking of window pane," for the brick's striking the window is clearly another one. But for Ducasse to make such an allowance would be to go against his own analysis of cause as the *only* antecedent change or event which immediately precedes the only other (sequent) change or event in the given situation. Ducasse attempts to evade this route by insisting, as we have seen, that the events or changes involved in the Causality relationship (or experiment) are always *concrete,*[28] that a concrete change (or event) may well be complex, and thus (for example) that the canary's singing may be regarded as a part of the full, *concrete, complex,* antecedent change in the state of affairs. But Ducasse's effort to lump together the brick's striking the window pane and the singing of the canary into an antecedent *concrete* event and *complex* change, although ingenious, does not alter ordinary language's recognition of a canary's singing, for instance, as an "event" or "change." In fact, his act of amalgamation here seems arbitrary in the light of ordinary-language usage, and suggests the possibility that the notion of a "complex change," when it clearly seems to unite instances of what ordinary language would regard as separate changes or events, might be a questionable innovation devised mainly to insure conformity of his definition of Causality with cases com-

[26] In discussing and defining Causality, Ducasse seems to use the two words "change" and "event" interchangeably. See "Causation: Perceivable? Or Only Inferred?;" also, "On the Analysis of Causality," p. 423, and *Nature, Mind, and Death,* pp. 105–113 and 106, especially.

[27] This expression is used by Ducasse in "Demos on 'Nature, Mind, and Death,'" p. 492.

[28] See, especially, p. 425 of "On the Analysis of Causality."

monly cited as instances of causation by people using ordinary language.

In short, then, Ducasse's attempt to respond to Pap's second criticism appears to leave him in a troublesome and frustrating position. In keeping with his "empirical inquiry" into the meaning of terms,[29] Ducasse has relied on ordinary language to give him the data from which he could formulate an accurate definition of "cause." Having offered a definition or "induction generalization" in respect to the way in which "cause" has been used in representative ordinary-language examples, he is confronted with Pap's question about the possibility of an effect being preceded by more than one immediately antecedent change in the state of affairs. Ducasse replies by turning Pap's alleged "more than one change" into a *"complex* change." But, against Ducasse, ordinary language, to which Ducasse is unquestionably committed both for the data and verificational test of his philosophical inquiries, suggests the recognition of a canary's singing, for example, as an event or change of itself, not just part of a *complex* change. However, for Ducasse to heed ordinary-language usage on this point would be to challenge his own definition of Causality as the *only* immediately antecedent change in a situation. And he seems to offer no criterion according to which a separate, let us say, *simple,* change may at times be regarded as part of a *complex* change or *concrete* event, and at other times not so regarded. So Ducasse seems to be left in a position where he claims to have reached his definition of the causal relation by an analysis of ordinary-language usage, but where his definition [30] cannot withstand some of the subsequent testimony of ordinary language. Surely this position is not comfortable for one whose philosophical procedure takes pride in the conformity of its findings with ordinary-language meanings.[31]

I conclude, then, that as masterly, as painstaking, as persistent as

[29] See Ducasse, *Nature, Mind, and Death,* p. 55, for example.

[30] I refer, of course, to his most recent formulation of the definition in "Causation: Perceivable? Or Only Inferred?"

[31] Both Pap and Demos also make this kind of point in respect to other matters in the articles cited above.

Ducasse's searching and continued analysis of Causality has been, it remains problematic in a number of respects and fails to give compelling answers to *at least* a couple of major objections directed against it. These shortcomings, however, do not alter my fundamental respect for much of Ducasse's exemplary and lucid philosophical analysis, or my impression that the philosophical world as a whole owes a debt of gratitude to C. J. Ducasse for his original and distinctive contribution to the clarification and solution of the so-called problem of Causality.

Denison University

PICTURES AND MAPS

VINCENT TOMAS

I

IN THE *Philosophy of Art*,[1] C. J. Ducasse observes that for most paintings (he has in mind "representational" paintings) "we may distinguish three typical modes of interpretation." [2]

In the first mode, we abstract from what is depicted (e.g., "a bowl of fruit") and from "the fact that the flat lines, colors, and shapes, on the two-dimensional surface of the canvas represent volumes and the relations of volumes in a three-dimensional space world having *depth*." [3] We attend solely to a flat design of colors, lines, and shapes. In the second mode of interpretation, "the lines, colors, and shapes on the flat canvas are taken as representing volumes and the relations of volumes in three-dimensional space, while at the same time the dramatic nature of the entities of which these are the volumes is still abstracted from and ignored." [4] When paintings are interpreted in either of these ways—as designs in two dimensions or in three—it is true, as has been said, that "a well-painted turnip is as good as a well-painted Madonna."

Ducasse continues:

> The third typical mode of interpretation of a painting, and the most natural to the majority of persons, is that in which the attention is focused not on the design aspect of it, but upon what is usually called the *subject-matter* represented. The varicolored pattern on the flat canvas is now interpreted as representative not only of volumes of certain shapes having certain relations in deep space, but *of dramatic entities* of familiar kinds, having in-

[1] *Philosophy of Art* (New York: Dial Press, 1929).

[2] *Ibid.*, pp. 209–210.

[3] *Ibid.*, p. 210.

[4] *Ibid.*, p. 211.

> dividual traits of their own differentiating them from other entities of the same kinds. An orange, for instance, as a dramatic entity (instrument), is something of vastly different aesthetic import from a bomb, which in size, shape and color might conceivably be much like the orange, and would therefore as design-element have essentially the same aesthetic import. Again, from the design standpoint, a live dog, and the same dog in the same place and posture but dead and stuffed, are strictly equivalent and interchangeable. But from the dramatic standpoint they are so far from being equivalent that they even have hardly any resemblance at all.[5]

From the dramatic standpoint, that is to say, it seems quite false that "a well-painted turnip is as good as a well-painted Madonna."

The *Philosophy of Art* was published in 1929, when the "retreat from likeness" was still gathering momentum. What Ducasse calls dramatic entities, i.e., agents or patients "in action of one sort or another, and dramatic instruments (positive and negative)," [6] which we may see in representational paintings interpreted in the third mode, were being said by *avant-garde* critics and aestheticians to be irrelevant to the aesthetic appreciation and appraisal of a work of art. Ducasse noted:

> But in modern times the design aspect seems to have been so violently rediscovered by some artists and critics as wholly to monopolize their attention—with the result that they became totally blind to the fact that the dramatic aspect of the objects represented also has aesthetic import, and indeed taps a realm of aesthetic feelings fully as vast as that touched by design, or vaster, and of probably greater significance in the lives of human beings as such. If painting were to leave out the representation of dramatic entities and confine itself to color and pattern, it would thus enormously and quite wantonly restrict the range of feelings that it is capable of expressing. We hear it said, of course, that the "proper" elements of effect for painting are color, shape, and the representation of plastic form. But this is nothing but a pious opinion or personal preference arbitrarily erected into a dogma by faddists in the realm of aesthetics. It only illustrates the danger in which the craftsman ever is, par-

[5] *Ibid.*, pp. 212–213.
[6] *Ibid.*, p. 208.

ticularly if he has not very much to express, of coming to think that the tools and tricks and technical devices which he must of course have and constantly practice himself in, are not made to be used but only to be played with and displayed. Common sense, however, tells us that any element of effect is proper for painting, which painting can successfully use; and there are hundreds of years of the successful use in painting of the representation of dramatic entities as sources of aesthetic feeling, to vindicate the practice.[7]

While it is true that the exclusion of subject-matter as a proper element of effect in painting for many was an unsupported dogma, the fact remains that there were, before 1929 and since, many who did not merely proclaim manifestoes but who advanced what they thought were good arguments to justify the exclusion. Of these, one of the most influential and the one with the most *prima facie* cogency is to the effect that the third mode of interpreting a painting *excludes* taking the aesthetic attitude toward it—that the feelings tapped by contemplation of the dramatic entities represented in (some) paintings are necessarily non-aesthetic and are disruptive of genuine aesthetic appreciation and are irrelevant to the aesthetic criticism of art. As José Ortega *y* Gasset summed it up in a semi-classical way in 1925 (in *La Dehumanizasión del Arte*), "preoccupation with the human content of a work of art is in principle incompatible with aesthetic enjoyment proper."

Among the contentions made in support of Ortega's conclusion is that, as Ducasse puts it, "paintings which attempt to represent anything more than lines, colors, and plastic form become illustrations; and this is supposed somehow to damn them beyond the possibility of aesthetic redemption." [8] We need not rehearse the reasons given as to why illustrations, *qua* illustrations, cannot function as aesthetic objects, nor does Ducasse really deny that they cannot. He defines "illustration" as

essentially a translation of the import of a description into concrete visual terms. It is thus fundamentally a means of satisfying curiosity more adequately than is possible by an abstract de-

[7] *Ibid.*, p. 215.
[8] *Ibid.*, p. 220.

> scription. In other words, to be an illustration is to be an answer to the question, What does . . . look like? [9]

An illustration, that is to say, is used as a source of information about the subject of it, in much the same way that a map is normally used as a source of information about the region it represents. Thus, according to Ducasse, if, when looking at Rembrandt's *Old Woman Cutting her Nails,* "we say or think: 'So that is what an old woman cutting her nails looks like,' then it is obviously functioning for us as an illustration." [10] James McNeill Whistler would have put it that we are then not looking *at* the picture, but *through* it, at some human fact, and that our appreciation is not of the picture but of the human fact.

Ducasse's answer to the Whistler type of objection is extremely compressed but, I believe, essentially correct and important. He writes:

> . . . if we take what the picture depicts, not as a piece of information, but as an object of aesthetic contemplation, then the picture is not for us an illustration. A picture representative of dramatic entities is thus not intrinsically either an illustration or not. Whether it is depends wholly on how we take it.[11]

My purpose in the remainder of this paper is to elaborate upon this answer and to bring out some of its implications. But first, some preliminary observations.

As has been noted, Ducasse refers to "what the picture depicts" and to its being "representative of dramatic entities." Consider Velasquez's *Pope Innocent X,* interpreted in the third mode. How shall we describe what it depicts—the dramatic entity that it represents? How we will answer will depend, in part, on our mental set, knowledge, and associations. Probably most of us would agree to the correctness of a description beginning, "A firm-willed man. . . ." [12] According to Ducasse, this (represented

[9] *Ibid.,* p. 220.

[10] *Ibid.,* p. 220.

[11] *Ibid.,* pp. 220–221.

[12] If one recognized the ecclesiastical vestments as those worn by popes, one might apprehend instead "a firm-willed pope." Similarly, a person with no knowledge of symbolism might apprehend a certain figure in a work of religious art as "a bearded old man holding a key," while a person with such knowledge might apprehend "St. Peter."

or depicted) object to which I am attending, namely, "a firm-willed man" and *not* "a pattern of lines and colors," may be taken in two ways, as an object of aesthetic contemplation or as an illustration. Suppose we take it as the former. We then attend simply to "a firm-willed man" and, since this for us is not "a piece of information," we are not believing or disbelieving anything because of it, e.g., that there exists or once existed a firm-willed man. Now, suppose that we want to take it as an illustration. The first thing to be noted is that the portrait itself (what we see within the frame) does not inform us of what in particular it is an illustration. If we extract from it the "information" that Pope Innocent X was a firm-willed man, we do so only with the help of the brass plate, inscribed *Pope Innocent X,* affixed to the frame, or some equivalent of the inscription which functions for us as an index. It should also be noted that the very *same* dramatic entity which is before our minds when we regard the portrait aesthetically in the third mode is also present when we regard it as an illustration. It is this *already* represented entity which, with the help of some index, *qua* illustration represents for us the historical pope who sat for the portrait. There is the dramatic entity represented by the colors adhering to the canvas, and there is, external to the picture, the pope of flesh and blood represented by the dramatic entity "in" the picture.

To fix these two kinds of representation in our minds, I will say that the pattern of colors adhering to the canvas *categorically* represents, when interpreted in the third mode, the dramatic entity partially described as "a firm-willed man"; and this, which is categorically represented, may, though it need not, *conditionally* represent something "outside" the picture, such as the pope himself.[13] And I shall argue that it is largely because of a failure to distinguish between these two kinds of representation that the claim that all representation is always irrelevant in visual art for so long seemed so plausible. Why it is not really at all plausible I will try to show in a somewhat indirect, yet I believe illuminating, way by comparing pictures with maps.

[13] Monroe Beardsley has made essentially the same distinction, using the terminology "depicts" and "represents." See his *Aesthetics: Problems in the Philosophy of Criticism* (New York: Harcourt, Brace, and Co., 1958), p. 270 and *passim.*

II

It sometimes seems illuminating for us to think of representational paintings and statues as if they were in important respects analogous to maps. For example, E. H. Gombrich, in his *Art and Illusion: The Psychology of Pictorial Representation,*[14] often makes use of the analogy.

He writes:

> . . . the correct portrait, like the useful map, is . . . not a faithful record of a visual experience but the faithful construction of a relational model.[15]

As Gombrich points out, a useful, i.e., accurate map is not necessarily one that looks like the region it represents. Mount Everest does not look like the contour lines which represent it on a map of the Himalayas. Rather, a useful map is one from which a competent map reader will derive no false information about that region. Similarly, according to Gombrich,

> to say of a drawing that it is a correct view of Tivoli does not mean, of course, that Tivoli is bounded by wiry lines. It means that those who understand the notation will derive *no false information* from the drawing . . .[16]

In the same vein,

> The map maker will generally represent water by blue and vegetation by green. Where the purpose of the map demands a distinction between fields and forests, he will introduce a further articulation of his greens and select the darker for the woods. But beyond the indication of this difference, the "real" tones of the particular scenery will obviously not concern him.
>
> If one reads Schäfer's analysis of Egyptian conventions, one is more often reminded of such conventionalized representations than one is of child art. The Egyptian painter distinguished, for instance, between a dark brown for men and a pale yellow for women's bodies. The real flesh tone of the person portrayed obviously mattered as little in this context as the real color of a river matters to the cartographer.[17]

14 National Gallery of Art, Washington. (New York: Pantheon Books, 1960).
15 *Ibid.,* p. 90.
16 *Ibid.,* p. 90.
17 *Ibid.,* p. 120.

Imagine two maps of one and the same mountain region, in one of which the mountains and valleys are represented by means of hatching, and in the other of which they are represented by means of contour lines. Despite the different conventions in accordance with which the two maps are drawn, each might convey to a map reader who understands the conventions exactly the same information. In that case, the maps would be equally accurate (or inaccurate) as representations of the mountainous region.

Gombrich juxtaposes two views of Derwentwater, one by Chiang Yee, done in "the Chinese idiom," and the other by an anonymous lithographer, which is "a 'picturesque' rendering from the Romantic period." [18] A little later he asks,

> Need we infer . . . that there is no such thing as an objective likeness? That it makes no sense to ask, for instance, whether Chiang Yee's view of Derwentwater is more or less correct than the nineteenth-century lithograph in which the formulas of classical landscape were applied to the same task? [19]

Then he observes, as we did in the case of the two maps of a mountainous region, that the

> difference in styles and languages need not stand in the way of correct answers and descriptions. The world may be approached from a different angle and the information given may yet be the same.[20]

On the other hand, for some of us it seems very misleading to speak of paintings and statues, even the so-called representational ones, as being in any really important respects analogous to maps. Consider the famous exchange between Matisse and a lady who, while visiting his studio, remarked, "But surely the arm of this woman is much too long." Matisse replied, "Madam, you are mistaken. This is not a woman. This is a picture."

This makes a good story. But what is the theoretical point of it? To make the theoretical point apparent, it is necessary to be a bit pedantic. The visiting lady, we have no reason to suppose otherwise, knew that what she saw on the easel was a picture, not a

[18] *Ibid.*, pp. 84–85.
[19] *Ibid.*, p. 89.
[20] *Ibid.*, p. 90.

woman, and doubtless Matisse very well knew that she knew it. But her remark about what she saw in the picture suggests that for her the picture was virtually a map. She was making the same point to Matisse that she would have been making to a cartographer if, while looking at a map he was making, she had said, "But surely the peninsula of this continent [think of Florida] is much too long." She was suggesting that Matisse's picture, if it remained as it was, would convey false information. It is not impossible that Matisse appreciated all this, so that what he meant by his reply was: "Madam, you are mistaken. This is not a map. This is a picture."

When Whistler quarrelled with Ruskin, one of the points at issue between them was whether pictures were to be treated as if they were maps, although, of course, this is not how either of them put it. Whistler believed that Ruskin treated them so, and he had weighty reasons to justify his belief—all those passages in *Modern Painters* where Ruskin in effect says that Turner's paintings convey much information about nature while paintings by other artists convey misinformation. In his "Ten O' Clock" lecture, Whistler referred to critics who encourage people to "look through" a picture, which after all is not transparent like a window. What might it mean to "look through" a picture? I suggest that it means to use a picture in the way that we ordinarily use a map—to get information about something "outside" it that is not presented but only represented by it. We are "looking through" the drawing of Tivoli, with its wiry lines, when we are extracting from it the information that Tivoli is bounded by hills.

Now we may ask a sticky question. Are we "looking through" Whistler's famous painting in the Louvre when we behold in it "a serene old lady seated in a chair" rather than "an arrangement in grey and black"? Suppose that we were to say to someone that indeed we do see "a serene old lady seated in a chair," and that he were to reply, "Sir, you are mistaken. This is not a map. This is a picture." Would he then be scoring a hit off us, in the same way that Matisse scored a hit in his reply to his visitor? Again, do extremist devotees of non-objective art score a hit when they contend, as Ortega did, that representational paintings are "squinting art?" (Because, according to Ortega, when we try to look at them as if they were pictures, not maps, we get "cross-eyed.") In general, reverting to what was said in the first section, are those formalists right who contend, like Ortega, that "preoccupation with the human content of the work of art is in principle incompatible with aesthetic enjoyment proper"?

I believe that the correct answer to each of these questions is in the negative. As we shall see, there are important respects in which representational works of art *are* similar to maps. At the same time we shall see that there are important respects in which some maps are unlike other maps. My conclusion will be that when we, whose interest in works of art is aesthetic, speak of representational works of art as contrasted with non-representational works, such as those painted by Kandinsky and Mondrian, we do not mean that some works represent whatever they do in the way that, under ordinary conditions, a map of Rome for us represents the actual city of Rome. Rather, we mean that they represent something in the way that a map of a non-existent region represents "a region," and does so without conveying to us any "information," veridical or otherwise. I am afraid that this last statement is somewhat cryptic, but in what follows I hope to make clear the point that is intended.

III

If a map is being used for, say, a military purpose, it is appropriate to ask whether it is an accurate or an inaccurate representation of a region. A soldier or sailor will not regard a map as accurate if, from a scrutiny of it, a person who knows how to read maps is caused to have false beliefs about the region the map for him represents. For example, scrutiny of a certain map will cause every competent map reader to believe that the distance by certain roads from a certain cross-roads in Anzio to Piazza Venezia in Rome is 58.9 kilometers. The map does not accurately represent the distance between the two places if it is false that, by the route in question, the ground distance between the cross-roads in Anzio and Piazza Venezia is 58.9 kilometers. Furthermore, "according to the map," if one were to travel this route toward Rome from Anzio, one would go generally north. Just north of

Anzio there would be a cemetery east of the road, and 2.5 kilometers further on there would be another cemetery, also east of the road, at the beginning of a wooded area that extends on either side of the road for 6 kilometers. To the degree that the actual ground distances and terrain features are not as they are represented on the map, i.e., to the degree that what is "according to the map" is not the same as what would be "according to the terrain" if one were to observe the ground itself and to measure directions, distances, elevations, etc., the map is inaccurate.

Of course, the usage of "representation" in connection with maps is not precise and firmly fixed. If a soldier has been led by his map to expect woods which are not on the ground where they should be according to the map, or to fail to expect a defile which is suddenly there on the ground although it is not shown on the map, he might say that the map inaccurately represents the region. Or, he might say that the map fails to represent the region, or that it only purports to represent it. (Not, of course, at the time he was suddenly confronted by the defile, but later, when he was telling about it.) By and large, however, "representation" does not seem to be an all-or-none concept. Ordinarily, we allow a map to be a representation of a region even if it contains some misrepresentations, provided that it is not *all* misrepresentations and completely inaccurate.

An important point to be noticed is that *qua* representation of an actual region a map is no good at all unless one correctly believes that it is a map of a specific region. What for the map-maker is the most accurate possible map of Rome and its vicinity will completely befuddle someone in Paris who knows how to read a map, who wants to get about in Paris, and who believes that the map in his hand, which (for the map-maker) is of Rome, is a map of Paris. (The most accurate possible map of Utah Beach was only befuddling to the soldier who, unbeknownst to himself, happened to land on Omaha.) A person who mistook a map of Rome for a map of Paris would be befuddled not only if he were to act on the basis of the beliefs he acquired from studying the map if he tried to get about in Paris; he would be befuddled also even though he never went to Paris but only conceived the capital city of France as the city whose streets, parks, monuments, river, and adjoining areas are laid out in the way that are those of the capital city of Italy. Then, if we were both talking about or referring to the capital city of France, we would not be thinking exactly the same thing. For instance, suppose that the man remarks, "The river meanders through the capital city of France in an interesting way," and that we reply, "Yes, it does." We then each have a thought we formulate in the same words—each of us thinks that the river meanders through the capital city of France in an interesting way. Yet, his thought is not the same as ours, as is indicated by the fact that if we were to catch on to what he was thinking, we would say, "You are not thinking of the interesting way the Seine meanders through Paris, but of the interesting way the Tiber meanders through Rome." Hence, for a map either to represent "at all" a region, or to represent it "accurately on the whole," it is not sufficient notwithstanding what in some places C. S. Peirce claimed, that it should merely be an "icon" of a region. It is necessary that the person who reads the map should make the correct connection between it and whatever region it is of.

In the case of most maps and under most circumstances, we make this connection by reading words printed outside or inside the margins of the map. For instance, in the case of the map referred to above, one initially comes to believe that it is of Rome and its vicinity (not of Paris or the moon) by reading its title *Roma e le Sette Strade* which is prominently printed "outside" the map in the margin in the upper left-hand corner. One could arrive at this same belief without this title (suppose that one has the map but that the upper left-hand corner has been torn off). One might notice that, adjacent to the largest dark, "densely built up area," there appears the word "Roma."

Now let us suppose that not only has the corner of the map been torn off, but that all the words and numerals on it are erased, leaving everything else the same, including the conventional signs for cemeteries, churches, primary and secondary roads, under- and over-passes, railroads, woods, swamps, water, and so on. The absence of all place names and other words would not prevent us from reading the map. We would still understand this curving blue line as "river," this rectangle with a cross inside as "cemetery," and this irregular green patch as "a wooded area, probably a park." As we scrutinized the map in all its detail there would develop in our mind a relatively determinate idea of a city and its neighborhood, quite distinct from the equally determinate idea of a different city we get when we study a map of Paris or New York. And the map, though wordless, would still remain an icon of Rome and its environs. But could it then for us *represent* Rome?

Whether it could would depend on the general antecedent knowledge in the light of which we read the map. If we had lived in Rome, so that we knew its streets and river and bridges and their spatial relations to one another, no doubt we would recognize that the "city" before our mind when we read the map was in certain respects similar to Rome: that in Rome the Tiber meanders in just the way we are made to think that the river meanders when we read the map; that Via Appia Antica runs in just the way the map makes us think a certain road does; and so on. After a number of such recognitions, we would be confident that the map was of Rome, although on it the word "Rome," or any other word, does not appear. Or, without ever having been in Rome, we might recognize "Rome" when we read the map if we had studied other maps of Rome, in the way that we immediately recognize "Florida" or "Italy" when we see certain familiar outlines on paper. Or, without ever having seen before a map of Rome, we might come to think of Rome instead of just of "a city" when we read the map through thinking: "That river meanders in just the way Gibbon says the Tiber does; that road runs just as straight as Gibbon says Via Appia Antica does; that. . . . Why! This is a map of Rome!"

What if we had never been in Rome, never seen maps of Rome, and also had never read *The Decline and Fall* or anything else about Rome? In that case, it seems, our wordless map could no longer, for us, represent Rome (unless arbitrarily). By hypothesis, we would lack all clues as to what region the map is of, and there would be nothing to turn our thoughts towards Rome, rather than towards Paris or some place else. We could still read the map as well as we did before. From it we could still get the idea of "a city and its neighborhood," a region which we could describe in great detail. We could go on indefinitely describing the complicated network of streets, the course of the river, the locations of the bridges that span the river, the relative sizes and locations of parks and other open spaces, the locations of airports, railroads, churches, cemeteries, and so on. But, knowing nothing about Rome, we could not recognize the similarities between the "city" before our mind when we read the map, and Rome. Nor could we learn about Rome from the map, since there would be nothing on it or in us which, as it were, invites us to regard the idea of "a city" that we get from the map as at the same time an idea of Rome. In these circumstances, that orientation of the mind toward the Eternal City by virtue of which the map could be said to represent Rome for that mind would be lacking.

In these same circumstances, would the map for us represent if not Rome in particular, then some city or other? That is, would we believe that, although its name and location happen to be unknown to us, there is a city whose streets, river, parks, etc. are laid out in the same manner as those of the "city" before our mind when we read the map? If we did believe this, our belief would be gratuitous. For, in precisely the same way that we read maps of Rome or of other actual regions, we can read equally detailed and equally or perhaps more interesting maps of Treasure Island, Lilliput, Erewhon, Wonderland, and other non-existent regions. As we scrutinize in all its detail a first-rate map with the title *Treasure Island* prominently printed in the margin, there develops in our mind a relatively determinate idea of an "island" —with its very irregular coast line, its barrier reef, its sheltered bay at the mouth of the one river, whose source is near the summit of Spy-Glass Hill, its lowlands and marshes and the dense woods that encroach on the beaches, the absence on it of all roads and bridges and other evidences of the presence of man except for the stockade there, on the low ground near the swamp, and the spot marked by a mysterious X. When we who have read Robert Louis Stevenson read this map and notice the title, we do not connect the map with some actual geographical region, for we have good reasons for believing that there is no such region—no actual island with just such an irregular coast line, such a hill, and such a stockade. If the title were torn off and all the words were erased, we might still take this map to be of Treasure Island through thinking, "That hill dominates the surrounding terrain in just the way Stevenson says Spy-Glass Hill does; that bay looks just as sheltered as the one Stevenson says the *Hispaniola* dropped anchor in; that stockade. . . . Why! This is a map of *Treasure Island!*" But we still would not believe that there is such an island.

What if we had never read Stevenson? Would our wordless map then for us represent some island or other? Would we believe that there is an island, whose name and location happen to be unknown to us, having the characteristics of the "island" before our mind when we read the map? If we did believe this, our belief would be gratuitous and false. In the same way, if we who knew nothing about Rome believed that there is some city like the "city" we envisaged when we read the wordless map of Rome, our belief, though true, would be gratuitous.

In ordinary speech, we are likely to say that *Roma e le Sette Strade* represents Rome and its vicinity, and that *Treasure Island* represents Treasure Island, even though in the first case we believe that the map can give us information about an actual region while in the second case we disbelieve that it can. We are inclined to treat both maps as representations and to take care of the radical difference between them by saying that one represents an actual region while the other represents an imaginary region. If we do not feel uncomfortable when we do this, it may be because we would also hold it to be appropriate to ask whether the map of Treasure Island is accurate. For it to be accurate, it would have to conform to Stevenson's description of Treasure Island. For example, if Spy-Glass Hill as shown on the map had an elevation of 5,000 feet and a volcanic crater on its peak, the map would be in so far an inaccurate representation, since what would be "according to the map" would not be the same as what is "according to Stevenson."

There are maps, however, about which it is pointless to ask whether they are accurate or not, for there is nothing—no actual region and no antecedent description of an imaginary region—to which they can conform or fail to conform. In my boyhood I drew many such maps, and I have heard of grown men who do the same thing. My maps were completely fanciful. On the first few, the presence and location of every feature was capricious. But very soon these were decided in accordance with a feeling that the region evoked by a map would be "more interesting," or "more mysterious," or perhaps "more desolate," if such and such details were added, subtracted, or modified. Some of these later maps were very elaborate affairs. They were extremely detailed, and they were meticulously drawn and colored on great lengths of butcher's paper in accordance with the conventions of cartography. It is easy to imagine a similar map produced by a professional cartographer with a good imagination who had gotten the bug to create cities, islands, continents, or universes to suit himself. When confronted with one of these maps, say one with "Sinistrevia" prominently printed in the margin, a competent reader of maps would no doubt have an exhilarating experience. As he scrutinized this entirely made-up map there would develop in his mind a relatively determinate idea of "Sinistrevia," a much more exciting place, we may be sure, than even Treasure Island. If he knew the conditions under which this map was made, what, if anything, would this map represent for him? Not any actual region, and not some fairly determinate imaginary region described in some novelist's or poet's book, but just—"Sinistrevia," that region which appears before one's mind when, and only when, one reads this map or later remembers it.

In the light of what we know about this map, it is pointless to ask whether it is an accurate representation of Sinistrevia. We know that there is no region, and no description of a region, to which the map must conform if it is to be accurate. Apart from the map, so to speak, there is no Sinistrevia. The characteristics of the latter are precisely what the map shows them to be. If the cartographer before he published his map had decided to replace the Matterhorn-like mountain which, we may suppose, is a prominent feature of Sinistrevia with a great crater, one could not object that this would introduce an inaccuracy into the map. Sinistrevia is precisely as the map represents it. If the map had been changed, then Sinistrevia would have been changed.

But it we alter a map of Rome, so as to show a crater in place of the Capitoline, we alter only the map, and the idea of a city we get from this map, but we do not alter Rome. And in a way, if we alter an "accurate" map of Treasure Island, so as to make it an island with a great crater where before there was Spy-Glass Hill, we do not alter Treasure Island. For educated English-speaking people, Treasure Island has certain characteristics which resist being tampered with, and they would all regard as inaccurate any map of Treasure Island which was unfaithful to Stevenson's description and their own conception of the island which they got from reading Stevenson. Stevenson, of course, could have altered Treasure Island if he had wished to do so, prior to the publication of his story. But now there are certain features of Treasure Island almost as well known to English readers as are some of Long Island to native New Yorkers, and they are just as unchangeable by fiat or by considerations of taste.

On the other hand, it would be appropriate to say, when our imaginary cartographer erased the contour lines showing a Matterhorn-like mountain in Sinistrevia and redrew them so that instead there showed a moon-like crater, "I like a mountain there better," or, "The crater fits in better with all the rest," or something of this sort. We might even say, without violating English (though conceivably the judgment expressed might be contrary to good taste), "The altered version of the map is a better (or worse) representation of Sinistrevia than the previous one." But if someone were drawing a map of Rome or Treasure Island, any consideration appealing to what one likes better or to what seems to fit in better with all the rest when the question was, "What shall I put here, a hill or a crater?" would be beside the point. In the two latter cases, what should appear on the map is to be decided by appeal to what appears on the region the map is intended to represent—by appeal either to what are the characteristics of some actual region or of some imaginary region which is in the public domain.

IV

A while ago it seemed safe enough to write, "Ordinarily we allow a map to be a representation of a region even if it contains some misrepresentations, provided, of course, that it is not *all* misrepresentations and completely inaccurate." We seem now to have reached a point where we are allowing a map (of Sinistrevia) to be a representation of a region although we grant that it is in principle impossible for it to misrepresent that region. A map represents Rome to us if it produces in us an idea of "a city" which is in certain respects similar to the idea of Rome we would get from Rome itself, and if we believe that it does—to the degree that we are extracting from it what we take to be information about Rome. But a map "represents" Sinistrevia to us *merely* if it produces in us an idea of "a region," even though we are *not* extracting from it any geographical information or misinformation.

I have just written that the map "represents" Sinistrevia. The key word was placed between quotation marks to indicate the fact that it is no longer functioning in quite the same way that it did when, in the circumstances described earlier, it was said that to a soldier a map represents Rome and its vicinity. It is not easy to formulate just what the difference is between the two cases. One reason for the difficulty is that the words we want to use to formulate it, such as "information," "of," and "about," undergo analogous shifts in meaning. For instance, if one says as I just now did that under ordinary circumstances a map of Rome will convey information about Rome, and were then to go on to say that a map of Sinistrevia will not convey information about Sinistrevia, this might be misleading. For, after all, when we take a look at the latter map does it not convey to us the information that in Sinistrevia there is a Matterhorn-like mountain to the north of a great desert? The reply to this is: In a sense, Yes; and in a sense, No. What misleads us now is "information."

Consider a sentence uttered by a certain Tommy Atkins, "I went into a public house to buy a pint of beer." Does it convey information? Yes, if one is reading it in a newspaper under the by-line of a reliable police reporter. One is then informed that a witness, Tommy Atkins, testified that he had done a certain thing from a certain motive. But no, if one reads the sentence under the by-line of Rudyard Kipling. When Kipling uses this sentence, he is not conveying information in the literal sense of the word, but fiction. For him, and for us, it is a fictional sentence, not an assertion that something really happened. (The mistake that

Matisse was pointing out to his visitor was that she was taking his picture to be like an assertion made by a police reporter, not like a fictional sentence uttered by a poet.)

Similarly, for the soldier who presupposes that Italy exists and is anxious to find out what it is like, his map asserts to him that in Italy Rome is to the north of Anzio—it conveys to him this bit of information. But for us, who do not presuppose that Sinistrevia exists but on the contrary know that it is a made-up region, the map does not assert that Sinistrevia exists and that in it there is a mountain to the north of a desert. It does not invite us to stock our minds with geographical misinformation. Rather, it invites us merely to behold or to have before our mind "a mountain to the north of a desert in Sinistrevia."

There are, then, these two senses of "representation" (which does not mean that there are no others), the sense in which if something is a representation it is conveying, or professing to convey, information to someone, and the sense in which if something is a "representation" it is not professing to convey information but only an object for our contemplation. Let us refer to the former as *conditional* representation and to the latter as *categorical* representation. Thus, to the soldier a certain map conditionally represents Rome, while to us a certain map categorically represents Sinistrevia.

To readers familiar with A. C. Bradley's "Poetry for Poetry's Sake," [21] it will be obvious that the two senses of "representation" correspond to the two senses of "about" as used in statements such as "Milton's poem is about the Fall of Man." As Bradley pointed out, this remark may be understood to mean that the poem has a certain *subject:* that conception of the Fall of Man which we have independently of our reading Milton's poem, and which we would have even if we were never to read his poem but only, say, the Old Testament. Or, it might be understood to mean that the poem has a certain *substance,* which although it also is referred to as "the Fall of Man" is "in" the poem and nowhere else and hence is available only to readers of the poem. Two poems may both be about the same subject, e.g., the Fall of Man as we conceive it

[21] *Oxford Lectures on Poetry* (London: Macmillan and Co., Ltd., 1909).

from having read the Old Testament, and yet the substances of each, despite their generic similarity, will be determinately radically dissimilar. The determinate conception of "the Fall of Man" that we get from reading poem *A* will be different from the one we get from reading either poem *B* or the Old Testament. Similarly, two or more pictures may conditionally represent the same thing to someone, and yet what they categorically represent may be very dissimilar. Compare Michelangelo's *Expulsion from the Garden* with the *Expulsion* by Massaccio and the one by Tinteretto. Or, compare a *Crucifixion* by Perugino with Grunewald's.

Before (in a logical sense of "before") the map labelled *Roma e le Sette Strade* can conditionally represent the actual city called Rome to us, it must categorically represent something to us. It must first produce in us an idea of an urban region. Otherwise, we will have no idea such that it can serve us as an idea of the actual urban region called Rome. We have seen, in what precedes, that there could be conditions under which this same idea might serve us as an idea of the actual city called Paris, and that then the map will be a source not of information about Rome (however careful the cartographer was), but of misinformation about Paris.

However, the more interesting point for aesthetics is that under certain conditions this very same map will for a viewer of it conditionally represent nothing and only categorically represent something. One might, after all, look *aesthetically* at *Roma e le Sette Strade.* True, we do not ordinarily do this with maps, any more than we ordinarily read history books as if they were novels. But we *can* do it, by taking toward them the aesthetic attitude. If we choose, we can help to even up the score with people who are inclined to treat pictures as if they were maps by occasionally treating maps as if they were pictures. Now, were we to regard *Roma e le Sette Strade* in the way we are regarding a painting when our attitude is aesthetic, although there would develop in our mind a relatively determinate idea of "an urban region and its neighborhood," we would not be taking this idea as a vehicle of knowledge about actual Rome, actual Paris, or any other place. The map would then not be presenting us with information to be believed. It would only be presenting us with a region to be contemplated, a region which, as we have seen, we could describe in great detail. And were we to do so, our intention would not be to describe Rome, the cartographer's *subject.* Our intention would be to describe the *substance,* to use Bradley's term, of the map, or what is categorically represented by it irrespective of what might be conditionally represented by it if our attitude were different.

In the same way, when one looks aesthetically at Whistler's painting in the Louvre, and then describes what one is contemplating as "a serene old lady sitting in a chair," one is not intending to describe Whistler's mother. For one is not "looking through" the picture at Whistler's mother but only into the picture at this "serene old lady sitting in a chair."

Let us now return to Velasquez's *Pope Innocent X,* of which art historians and critics often say, "It represents Pope Innocent X." When they do, what, exactly, are they saying about the portrait?

I fancy that a good deal of the time what they mean is analogous to what is meant by a man who says, "This map represents Rome and its vicinity" when he is looking at a map with *Roma e le Sette Strade* prominently printed in the left hand corner. Would they have said that the portrait represents Pope Innocent X if, before they had seen it, the brass plate on the frame had been removed, in the way that the title of a map might be torn off?

Consider what we see when we look inside the frame, as when we look into a mirror. If we were to begin to describe it by saying, "A firm-willed man. He has a mustache and small beard, and . . . ," anyone standing beside us would agree that the description, so far as it goes, fits what is there to be seen. Moreover, this same description would fit what is there to be seen even if the picture were labelled *Pope Alexander VI, Portrait of an Unknown Prelate,* or merely *No. 324.* Moreover, once more, when we take leave of Velasquez's picture and walk down the hall in the Doria Gallery, we encounter a marble bust by Bernini. Of this bust, historians and critics who have read the brass plate below it also say, "It represents Pope Innocent X." But if we look aesthetically at this bust by Bernini, we are not at all tempted to begin a description of what we are contemplating by saying, "A firm-willed man." Quite the contrary. In Bernini's bust we aesthetically see, I would say, a rather "weak-willed man."

Which of the two descriptions fits what G. B. Pamphili was like between 1644 and 1655 when, as Innocent X, he reigned on St. Peter's throne? Which description conveys information about Pamphili and which conveys misinformation? Such questions can arise only if the two works are being responded to as conditional representations—as maps in the paradigm sense of the word. They are what a historian writing a book about thc papacy might ask himself if he went into the Doria Gallery not for aesthetic enjoyment but to look for clues as to what Pamphili was like while he was the pope. But if we look at representational pictures and statues aesthetically, no such considerations arise to worry us. For us, Velasquez's portrait categorically represents "a firm-willed man," Bernini's bust categorically represents "a weak-willed man," and the question which of these representations is accurate will not arise because the notion of a categorical *mis*representation is self-contradictory.

V

Of the two senses of "representation" which have been distinguished, clearly it is categorical representation which is of primary interest in aesthetics, and it is the proper sense in which to contrast a "representational picture" with a "non-objective picture." Most aestheticians will agree that while we are in the aesthetic attitude, a picture is not conditionally representing anything to us. If it were, this would be an indication that we have forsaken the aesthetic attitude for some other. From this fact, together with the assumption that the appropriate attitude in which to view and appraise works of art is the aesthetic, extreme formalists have derived the conclusion that representation is irrelevant to all works of visual art and even traditional paintings should be appreciated only as designs. But it is only conditional representation that is irrelevant. Unfortunately, as a perusal of the formalist literature and the manifestoes of some modern artists makes clear, categorical representation, too, is held to be irrelevant. The "retreat from likeness" was a rebellion not only against conditional representation, but against categorical representation as well.

As I have tried to show, apprehension of what is categorically represented by a work of visual art—the "dramatic entities" of Ducasse or the "human content" of Ortega—seems to be perfectly compatible with aesthetic appreciation of the work. It may even be that *in order to* apprehend that content, in all its specificity, one must necessarily be in the aesthetic attitude. Therefore, I submit that at least one theoretical argument that is used to justify the retreat from likeness as an advance toward a purer visual art, an art at last conscious of its true mission, is unsound. It makes use of the premise that whenever we apprehend dramatic entities in a picture we are "looking through" the picture. That premise, I have tried to show, is false, just as Ducasse maintained.

Brown University

THE RIDDLE OF GOD AND EVIL *

EDWARD H. MADDEN

I

It is a notorious fact that the very way a philosophical problem is formulated not only determines its possible answers but already reflects commitments. So I shall formulate the riddle of God and evil in a tentative way and comment on its structure later. The usual version of the riddle is this: If God is all-powerful and all-good, why is there so much *prima facie* gratuitous evil in the world? If he is all-powerful he should be able to remove unnecessary evil, and if he is all-good he should want to remove it; but he does not. Apparently he is either not all-powerful or not all-good. Christian theologians, however, have offered numerous and ingenious reasons why this conclusion does not follow. They believe that they can show that God's omniscience and goodness and the existence of evil are compatible.

In this age of analysis the next move is usually an effort to clarify the terms of the argument, and the starting place is usually the concept of evil. Having formulated the problem one is invariably asked, "What do you mean by 'evil?' Give us an example of evil or, better, a definition of the term." It is important in my strategy not to answer this question. We have forgotten what Socrates knew so well. Clarification sometimes comes as a result of dialectic, not always as a neutral prologue to it. Specifically, in this case, it is unwise to answer the question for several reasons. First, it is impossible to give an example of evil because there is no paradigm case where all will agree that the

* For a most interesting analysis of this riddle cf. Professor Ducasse's "The Problem of Evil," Chapter 16 of his *Philosophical Scrutiny of Religion* (New York: Ronald Press, 1953).

concept is correctly applied. Several of the solutions to the problem of evil entail that evil is only an illusion, an appearance, and hence that there is no paradigm case for its correct use. I qualify evil by "prima facie" precisely for this reason. I want to avoid ruling out a possible solution by the way the problem is formulated.

Second, it is strategically unwise to attempt an explicit definition of "evil," since one gets involved thereby in *other* philosophical problems, which are important in their own right, to be sure, but solutions to which are unnecessary for advancing the discussion of the present riddle. What I have in mind is this. A promising approach to the definition of "evil" would distinguish between intrinsic and instrumental evil. By "intrinsic evil" is meant "painful or unpleasant experience." By "instrumental evil" is meant "the cause of painful or unpleasant experience." From these definitions it follows that things other than pain which are ordinarily called evil—e.g., lying, stealing, cheating, getting drunk, and so on—are evil only because they tend, directly or indirectly, to produce pain. Yet one might wish to argue, and with good reason, that lying and stealing, e.g., are intrinsically evil and would remain so whether or not they produced any painful consequences. But whatever view one takes on this issue, he has been diverted from the original problem. He has got involved in the question of what constitutes the proper analysis of "evil" and loses sight of the fact that whatever position one takes on this issue the riddle of God and evil remains the same. Hence, in the formulation and discussion of the riddle I shall mean by "evil" simply the whole set of undesirable things and experiences which all of us, minus our philosophical views, would prefer to avoid.

II

The Christian apologist has offered a great number of solutions to the riddle, but the most influential ones are these: evil is punishment for sin, is God's warning to man, is necessary for understanding and appreciating good by contrast, tests men's faith, builds character, results from natural causes in a world that is good on the whole, results from man's misuse of free will, fits into an ultimate harmony. I have argued in detail elsewhere against these alleged solutions and will not cover the ground again.[1] However I have come to believe that more needs to be said about the free will and ultimate harmony views. More needs to be said both by way of clarification and criticism. After attending to certain interesting aspects of these two views, I will turn to several new arguments which try to avoid the problem by showing it to be meaningless and I will show why I think they too fail.

Descartes' version of the free will solution is one of the most interesting ones. It shares in the great philosophical tradition that proclaims evil to be simply a form of ignorance or error. According to Descartes, God has granted man both the power of willing (freely choosing his own volitions) and the power of understanding, neither of which is defective in itself. The trouble arises

> from the fact that the will is much more ample and far-reaching than the understanding, so that I do not restrain it within the same limits but extend it even to those things which I do not understand. Being by its nature indifferent about such matters, it very easily is turned aside from the true and the good and chooses the false and the evil. And thus it happens that I make mistakes and that I sin.[2]

But it need not be so. If I restrict my volition to what I know—that is, to what is clearly and distinctly reported by the understanding—then it cannot happen that I err. In so restricting myself, I use rightfully the freedom of will that God has given me.

The really interesting reply to Descartes' view requires a brief analysis of the relations between the concepts "knowing right" and "doing wrong." There are, I believe, only three possible relations between them. (i) It is impossible to know right and nevertheless choose to do wrong. This position is a corollary of Descartes' analysis. (ii) It is possible to "know" right and nevertheless do wrong in the sense that one may admit something is right but nevertheless refuse to do it out of selfish interests.

[1] Cf. E. H. Madden, "The Many Faces of Evil," *Philosophy and Phenomenological Research,* Vol. XXIV (1964), pp. 481–92.

[2] René Descartes, *Meditations,* tr. by L. J. Lafleur (New York: Liberal Arts Press, Inc., 1951), pp. 51–52. Quoted by Professor Ducasse in *A Philosophical Scrutiny of Religion,* p. 366.

(iii) It is possible to know right and nevertheless choose to do wrong in the sense that one may choose not to do something, be prompted not to do it, *precisely because he believes it to be the right thing to do*. After all, if it is impossible to reject morality no credit is involved in accepting it.

Position (i), I believe, can easily explain away (ii). The person who behaves selfishly acts ignorantly. He simply does not understand wherein his good really lies. When we really understand, when the nature of the good is properly the possession of our own minds, then we are certain to model our conduct upon it. But (i) cannot explain away (iii) where not selfishness but the very rejection of morality is the motivation. For it follows from (iii) that if one could legitimately say "I know x is right" instead of "I believe x is right" he would have stronger reason than ever for not doing it. If "moral rebellion"—the core of position (iii)—then, is an irreducible moral notion, it follows that the Cartesian interpretation of moral evil as ignorance is untenable. Moral evil is more than lack of attainment. It is something more frightening than simply not being rational.

Descartes' interpretation of moral evil as ignorance encounters this further difficulty. God might have enhanced his gift to men by not only giving them free will but also a better understanding. Then man would have known better the right things to do and hence chosen to do them. Descartes, in fact, admits this point. He acknowledges that God could have given his understanding a clear and distinct comprehension of all the things about which he would ever deliberate. To explain why God does not increase or perfect man's understanding Descartes suggests as a possibility "that the universe may be somehow more perfect because some of its parts are not free from defect while others are, than it would be if all parts were alike." [3] But Descartes offers no argument that seems to show that what is possible is, in fact, likely or probable. The notion of "perfect" implicit in this view is such an odd one—perhaps even self-contradictory—that it is difficult to see how any defense of the view could succeed.

The free will solution, however, can be reformulated to avoid

[3] *Meditations,* p. 55. Quoted by Professor Ducasse in *A Philosophical Scrutiny of Religion,* p. 368.

these difficulties. The advocate of this solution can agree that man's misuse of free will is not simply the result of ignorance but is the result of willful disobedience. He can state his view in this way: God, being omniscient, knew that man would willfully choose the wrong sometimes if he had free will; but God granted him free will anyway because not to do so would have produced greater evil. A world with only robots would be more evil than a world with freely choosing men who sometimes rebel against morality.

There are, however, difficulties with this formulation of the free will solution also.[4] (a) Even if this solution were irrefutable, it would explain the occurrence of moral evil only and would leave physical evil wholly unexplained. Free will has nothing to do with earthquakes, landslides, and floods, or with physical deformity, insanity, and disease. (b) God could mitigate the more ghastly results of man's misuse of his freedom. He could do it in a stop-gap fashion by interfering in the world occasionally to prevent a particularly terrible result. Or he could do it in a wholesale fashion by creating man with a *disposition* to act rightly even though he might choose occasionally to do evil. The latter is all that would be required for the possibility of man's freedom and moral rebellion. And yet God has not done these things. Such behavior seems to argue against either all-powerfulness or all-goodness. It is not sufficient for the theist to reply that it is likely God *does* interfere often without our knowing it to prevent terrible consequences. This reply only terrifies one by suggesting how bad the universe might have been but helps in no way to explain why it is not better than it is. And it is insufficient for the theist to reply that God could not create man with a tendency to act rightly because this would preclude the moral growth attendant upon struggle. This reply misses the point that while some people do grow through the struggle many others are crushed by it. The great struggle, then, produces both good and evil. And the nature and amount of the latter seems too high a price to pay for the former.

(c) This view assumes that free will is so intrinsically good that

[4] Cf. Madden, *op. cit.*, pp. 485–487.

its absence would be a greater evil than that produced by man's misuse of free will. But it is not immediately obvious that man in a state of free will is intrinsically better than any other conceivable state of affairs. One *might* argue that a world of happy robots would be intrinsically better than a world of miserable human beings exercising free will. It is necessary for the free will advocate to supplement his view by saying that free will is also *instrumentally* necessary to bring about the most important ends of life, namely, moral growth and the achievement of beatitude. But several new perplexing questions arise as a result of this addition. Why did not God create morally strong and beatific beings to begin with? Moreover, would the growth and achievement of some overbalance and justify the destruction and degradation of others?

III

The term "ultimate harmony" has been used uncritically to refer to similar but not identical claims.[5] Its use extends even to incompatible claims. And the nuances between claims are often subtle and difficult to detect. The "ultimate harmony" label has been attached, some time or other, to each of the members of the following medley of claims: "All's well in God's view"; "All's well that ends well"; "Evil is only an illusion"; "This is the best of all possible worlds"; and "Whatever is, is right."

(i) The claim that "all's well in God's view" is usually introduced by musical metaphors. Just as a chord when heard in isolation may sound dissonant but when heard in context sounds harmonious, so it is with evil: an event seen in isolation is called evil by man but this event seen in relation to all other events is called good by God. This analogy should not be interpreted as suggesting that there are two ways of judging events—man's and God's—and that each one is perfectly valid in its own way. Rather the point of the analogy is that God's way is "really" correct and man's way incorrect. Whenever man judges that "x is evil," he is mistaken; whatever man ordinarily calls evil is not evil after all. In God's higher morality "evil is only an illusion."

The objections to this claim are numerous, but several of them

[5] I have been guilty of this error myself. Cf. Madden, *op. cit.,* pp. 487–490.

are particularly obvious. (a) If there really is no evil in the world, then any efforts to remove *prima facie* evil are necessarily morally wrong. Any reform movement is, by its very nature, morally pernicious. This result, to most people, seems like a *reductio ad absurdum*. Yet it is quite clear that this is the (usually implicit) bridge which many people use to cross the chasm between their Christian beliefs and their extreme laissez-faire political views. (b) The fact that God would permit men to be deceived systematically would itself constitute the most staggering evil that God could have permitted. But the most philosophically fundamental criticism (c) is that God's "higher morality" has no meaning whatever. If God's higher morality is completely different from man's ordinary moral notions, then this higher morality is completely meaningless, since man has no other notions of good and evil except the ordinary ones. Consequently when a theist says that he accepts God's higher morality this claim of acceptance is vacuous. The only way for him to avoid this allegation is to claim that while man's and God's morality are not the same, nevertheless there are metaphorical or analogical bridges which help him "make the crossing" to the new meanings. However, such efforts are doomed to fail because the lacuna between man's morality and God's higher morality is absolute. The acceptance of God's higher morality entails the falsity of *every* claim that "x is evil." Consequently it entails the pointlessness of *every* correlative claim that "x is good." But if all ordinary judgments of evil and good are either false or pointless, then clearly they contain no analogical bases for understanding God's higher morality. Hence, again, the theist's claim that he accepts God's higher morality is, of necessity, vacuous. His claim is not false; it simply does not make any sense.

(ii) The claim that "all's well that ends well" is ambiguous. One interpretation is this: man calls an event evil if it has evil consequences. But his view of consequences is a short run one. God does not call these events evil because he sees their long run consequences and knows that they are good. This interpretation again entails the view that evil is only an illusion, and the arguments against the claim that "all's well in God's view" are relevant again against the present view.

The second interpretation, however, seems to me the stronger one, and the one the users of this phrase likely have in mind. It does *not* entail the view that evil is only an illusion. It claims that evil is justified by the long run, not that the concept disappears because of it. The second interpretation is this: man, seeing only short run consequences, fails to understand that present evils eventually lead to important goods. God, however, seeing long run consequences, understands that they are good enough to *compensate for,* or make worthwhile, the evils along the way. God, of course, arranged that it should be so.

There are a number of criticisms of this second, stronger interpretation of "all's well that ends well," of which the following, it seems to me, are most effective. (a) Even if it should be true that all short run evils produce long run goods, all this would prove is that the world is less evil than it would be if short run evils also produced long run evils. It would not explain why God permits the short run evils to exist. Could he not have produced the same results without any short run evil at all or, at least, with less ghastly short run evils? (b) The price that is paid for long run good is too high; the incredible amount of misery experienced by sentient beings, and its unjust distribution, ruins the value of any possible goals. The end does not justify the means. The notion that "all's well that ends well" ignores the wounds along the way. Some will never heal.

(c) The concept of the "long run" itself is not without difficulty. I see cases where evil events produce good consequences in the long run. But I also see cases where evil events only produce more evil consequences in the long run. If it be objected that I have not waited long enough in the second case, then the question arises how long the "long run" is. Either the theist gives no answer or else depends upon the tautological one that the long run coincides with the appearance of good consequences. The problem of the long run, to be sure, appears in many philosophical contexts, but it appears in a peculiarly difficult form in the present one. What I have in mind is this. The frequency advocate runs into the same problem of the long run in probability theory. The classical theorist accuses him of a tautological criterion of the long run. By way of defense the frequentist offers the concept of the mathematical limit as an independent criterion of the long run. There are still difficulties with his view, but at least he has produced an independent criterion. The trouble with the theist's view that "all's well that ends well," however, is that, by its very nature, his long run cannot be defined in any way except a tautological one.

(d) The present view, unlike the claim that "all's well in God's view," or the first interpretation of "all's well that ends well," is a meaningful one. It is perfectly possible and hence understandable that God so arranged the world that present evils result in long run goods—where "evil" and "good" have their ordinary denotations. The odd thing, however, is that the theist seems to think that if it is *possible* God so arranged things, it is *probable* that he did. This conclusion seems odd because ordinarily we do not go from the possibility of something to its probability. We only go from the possibility to the probability because we have some evidence to bridge the gap. The theist, however, is not troubled by the lack of evidence. Already believing in God, he thinks that if a certain possible arrangement of events would solve the problem of evil then it is not only probable but certain that God so arranged them. The theist, I believe, has a perfectly good right to ignore the lack of positive evidence and to bridge the gap. But he does not have the right to ignore the evidence that tends to show the possible in this case is unlikely and to bridge the gap anyway. The previous points, I believe, provide the required negative evidence and hence make the theist's usual bridging of the gap untenable.

(iii) The claims that "this is the best of all possible worlds" and "whatever is, is right" are both ambiguous. "This is the best of all possible worlds" can be interpreted to mean that this is the best of all logically possible worlds. This interpretation is equivalent to saying that the world is perfect, that evil is only an illusion. It can also be interpreted to mean that this is the best world that it was possible for God to create. On this interpretation evil is not an illusion but a real ingredient of the world. The point is that it contains the minimum amount of evil that was compatible with the creation of any world at all. "Whatever is, is right" exhibits the same ambiguity. It can be interpreted to mean that evil is only an illusion or that nothing which it is possible to put in its place would be any better.

The ambiguity in both of these claims has led to the traditional misinterpretation of Leibniz's theodicy. He is misinterpreted as making the former claims when, in fact, he is making the latter ones. For Leibniz this is the best of all possible worlds even though evil is a necessary ingredient of it. It is logically impossible for any finite thing to be perfect and hence it is impossible even for God to create a perfect world. The very act of creation entails imperfection or evil. This is what Leibnitz meant by "metaphysical evil." God's genius, however, lies in the fact that he created the world with the least amount of necessary evil in it. The amount of evil in the world, in short, is just right commensurate with there being any world at all.

Any criticism of Leibniz has two parts. First, one can criticize the notion of "metaphysical evil." Why cannot a theistic God create a perfect world? A theistic God, after all, is supposed to be all-powerful not only *within* nature but *over* nature as well.[6]
Thus God could have created any world he wished, and he could have chosen to create a perfect one. Yet the crucial question here is what one means by "perfect." If one means by "perfect world" a world infinitely better than the present one, then God indeed could not create a perfect world. But if one means by "perfect world" a world in which there is no positive evil, then God could certainly create a perfect world. This problem will arise again, so I will not pursue it further at this point. In any case, even if God could not create a perfect world, the problem remains why he should have created any world at all if he could not create one better than the present world. This is the poignant burden of Ivan's question to Alyosha: If you were God, would you have consented to create the present world if it were the best one you could create? The only relevant reply seems to be the Neoplatonic claim that existence itself is a value. But this claim, I confess, has so little hold on my affective nature and so little relevance to the way I use value terms that it is not a live hypothesis for me.

Second, one can challenge the claim that this world has the

[6] Cf. Ducasse, *op. cit.*, p. 361.

minimum amount of evil in it commensurate with the existence of any world at all. A world with *any* evil at all in it meets Leibniz's requirement of the inevitability of "metaphysical evil." To answer the question why the world needed to have as much evil as it does, one needs to say that just the present amount was required to cultivate courage, patience, and so on. This is the most incredible part of the Leibnizian view and it is the part that has led to its identification with the "evil is illusion" corollary of "all's well in God's view." The sufficient answer is that no effort to explain why the nature and amount of evil in this world is necessary is successful. Some evil always remains gratuitous and a reproach to a theistic God. Moreover, it is not just the nature and amount of evil that causes the theist trouble; the distribution of evil is also a problem. That some people live in agony while others prosper hardly seems like the "right" amount of evil. It would be more just to have less evil to even the score or even to have more evil to even the score.

IV

If efforts to solve the riddle of God and evil fail, the theist is not necessarily defeated. It may be that the problem is unanswerable because it is meaningless in the first place. I want to examine two recent interesting arguments which claim to establish the meaninglessness of the riddle and to show wherein they go wrong.

(i) The problem of evil, according to the first argument,[7] arises because the following two propositions are inconsistent: God is omnipotent and no evil can be attributed to him" and "There is a state of affairs in the world which a perfectly moral Being should not tolerate." The latter proposition is based on observation. Evil has been observed in the world and this argues against belief in a theistic God. The assumption in this argument is that the problem would disappear if the universe were different than it is —that is, the problem would disappear if there were less evil, or no evil, in the world. But it can be shown that no matter how different the world might be, no matter how the world was altered, the same problem could be formulated. Since the prob-

[7] George Schlesinger, "The Problem of Evil and the Problem of Suffering," *American Philosophical Quarterly,* Vol. I (1964), pp. 244–47.

lem violates its own assumptions, it does not arise in the first place.

That altering the universe would make no difference to the problem can be shown in the following way. If present evils were reduced to a minimum, the problem would still remain because there was still some evil. If they were eliminated altogether, the problem would still remain because deprivation of positive happiness also counts as evil. It is still the same if everyone were positively happy because the fact that not everyone is as happy as the happiest man would be evil. Still the same if everyone were as happy as the happiest man, because the happiest man can make up an endless list of items that would increase his happiness. And still the same if everyone were in a state of supreme satisfaction, because they all have infinite capacities for increasing their sources of satisfaction.

This part of the argument suggests a related way of pointing up the meaninglessness of the problem of evil. If the problem of evil can be solved only if God creates an infinitely happy world, then it is meaningless because it requires God to do what is logically impossible. It is just as logically impossible for him to create an infinitely happy world as it is for him to create the greatest integer.

By way of criticism: (a) It is true that any formulation of the problem of evil assumes that the problem would disappear if the universe were different than it is—that is, the problem would disappear if there were less, or no, evil in the world. And this assumption quite clearly is justified for anything the present argument shows to the contrary. The problem of evil centers around the question of why there is apparently *gratuitous* evil in the world, not why there is any evil at all. No one would deny that some evil is necessary or desirable. Some evil may be necessary for building character, some for understanding or appreciating good by contrast, and so on. But the problem arises because no immediately obvious explanation exists to explain the necessity or desirability of all evil. Some evil is *prima facie* gratuitous. If the universe were altered to eliminate this evil while the other still remained, the problem would not arise.

(b) The core of the problem of evil is not why God did not create a perfect world but why he did not create a better one.

(c) The argument contains a shift in the meaning of "evil" without any justification of the shift. The ordinary meaning of "evil" does not include the notion of "absence of positive good." It is understandable if a mother is grief-stricken because her child is killed, but it is not understandable if she is grief-stricken because her child is not as bright as Einstein. There may be some justification for this extension of the ordinary notion of evil, but none is given. Consequently what the argument proves is that given the extended meaning of "evil," it would be logically impossible for God to remove all evil. It does not show that given the ordinary meaning of "evil" it would be logically impossible for God to remove all evil. But the ordinary notion, of course, is the one that both the theist and the anti-theist have in mind when they are discussing the problem of evil.

(d) The argument depends upon moral assumptions which are in no way defended. That evil includes the absence of good seems doubtful on semantical grounds but that "good" is equivalent to "happiness" and that "perfect world" is equivalent to "world in which everyone is infinitely happy" seem doubtful on moral grounds. I should want to argue that there are other things good besides happiness. But, in any case, the crucial point is this: the dissolution of the problem of evil rests on the notion of the infinite demands of happiness. The problem of evil, however, can be formulated without any reference to happiness at all. It is stated without reference to any particular philosophical analysis of the nature of "good" and "evil." Hence any dissolution of the problem which depends upon a certain philosophical analysis of these terms is, by its very nature, inadequate.

(ii) The problem of evil, according to the second effort to dissolve it,[8] arises only if God is conceived to be *all*-good and *all*-powerful. If he were simply "powerful," evil could occur in spite of him. If he were simply "good," evil might occur occasionally because of him. (It is enough to call anyone "good" if he generally, but not always, acts benevolently.) The omni-predicates, moreover, must be interpreted descriptively if the problem

[8] Robert E. Larsen, "The Problem of Evil and the Language of Religion," a manuscript which the author has graciously permitted me to consult prior to its publication.

is to arise. But they cannot be so interpreted. Hence the problem does not really arise in the first place. This argument is an interesting one and requires a fair amount of detail to do it justice.

The argument begins by asserting that certain ordinary predicates are comparative in nature, either explicitly or implicitly. When we say that Goliath was bigger than David, the comparison is explicit. When we say that Hercules was very strong, the comparison is implicit: we mean that he was stronger than any of the Greeks. When the omni-attributes are predicated of God, there is a similar implied comparison. Part of the meaning of "God is all-powerful" is that God is more powerful than any man, and part of the meaning of "God is all-good" is that God is morally superior to any man. This comparative analysis suggests that predicates can be ranked in the following way: powerful, more powerful, most powerful, all-powerful. But this suggestion is faulty. The comparative analogy breaks down eventually. The move from "most powerful" to "all-powerful" is not simply a continuation of the move from "more powerful" to "most powerful." The latter move is legitimate but not the former. The ordinary comparative adjectives have meaning, so to speak, within boundaries or limits, but "all-powerful" cannot have all its meaning from such contexts because it is a limitless concept. Moreover, it refers to power which is different in kind from man's. God is not simply "most powerful," but he is the very source of power itself. Finally, unlike ordinary predicates, "all-powerful" predicated of God is the Christian's way of ascribing value to Him. It expresses on the part of the speaker a love of God and an acceptance of religious obligation. Hence from all angles we see that "all-powerful" is not like an ordinary comparative predicate (although it takes its point of departure from one of them). Hence "all-powerful" cannot be used descriptively. But since the riddle of God and evil depends upon its being so used, the riddle does not arise in the first place.

By way of criticism: (a) I agree that the problem of evil only arises when the omni-attributes are used. I agree that "all-powerful" gets part of its meaning from the ordinary predicate "powerful." I agree that the comparison eventually breaks down. Being all-powerful is not simply a limiting case of a man's power. But I deny that the remainder of the meaning of "all-powerful" is non-descriptive in nature. The rest of the meaning of "God is all-powerful" is that God's power extends to the capacity of doing anything which is not self-contradictory. This "limitless" power, so far removed from man's capacities, may well be called a power which is different in kind from man's and, in fact, the source of all power. But what is "non-descriptive" about such additional meaning? It is certainly not descriptive in the sense that it ascribes ordinary comparative properties to God—ascriptions that could be judged empirically—but it is descriptive in the sense that it imputes understandable characteristics to an unobservable entity in a completely coherent way. Since "God is all-powerful" is descriptive in this sense, and since this sort of descriptive nature is the only one necessary for stating the traditional riddle of God and evil, it follows that the riddle is not dissolved by the present argument.

(b) I agree that "God is all-powerful" might well express on the part of the speaker a love of God and a willingness to accept religious obligations. But such devotional meaning does not eliminate or change the descriptive content. Many sentences, after all, both assert a proposition and express an attitude or feeling without mutual interference. If I say that "John Smith is a busher" I may well be describing his ability along some line, but I may also be expressing my distaste for him and my unwillingness to put myself under obligation to him. Yet the latter function of the sentence does not eliminate or change its descriptive content. If there is no similarity between this example and the case of God's omnipotence there is nothing in the present argument that establishes this fact.

(c) If "God is all-powerful" and "God is all-good" are not "descriptive" expressions in any sense then they cannot be construed as expressions which are either true or false and hence cannot be construed as making any knowledge claim at all. But then a theist believes nothing which distinguishes his God from the gods of many other type religions. That the riddle of God and evil does not arise in some of these religions I willingly admit. But to become indistinguishable from something else in order to avoid a criticism of what you are seems like too high a price to pay.

State University of New York at Buffalo

A NEW LOOK AT THE PROBLEM OF EVIL

CHARLES HARTSHORNE

SOMETIME IN MY YOUTH I said to myself, "I will follow reason to the end in considering religious questions." From what I know of Professor Ducasse something similar may have gone through his mind, perhaps at a still earlier age. I have not, and doubtless he has not, consciously departed from this initial resolution. That we have come out at such different points illustrates the plight of philosophy in our culture—perhaps in any culture with individual freedom.

That a question discussed intensively for thousands of years could be seen in a significantly new light seems rather unlikely. Nevertheless, I should be surprised if the following treatment of such a question could be identified with any of the traditional ones.

What is the logical structure of the atheistic—or at least agnostic—argument from the existence of evil? Simply this: A certain assertion—that God, all powerful and wholly good, exists—is contradicted by some empirical facts. But the immediate comment of a logician should be, "An assertion capable of being contradicted by empirical facts is itself empirical in the broad sense, a contingent hypothesis, true if the facts happen to fit, false otherwise." The argument from evil makes the assumption that theism is *not* an *a priori* or necessary truth. It is to the great credit of David Hume that he saw this, and (in his *Dialogues*) admitted explicitly that, were there reason to classify theism as *a priori,* the counter argument from evil could not be relevant. No empirical evidence can negate a necessity. That there is a prime number greater than 96 could not be in conflict with any experience; it is a nonempirical truism. Nearly nine centuries ago, a great man, Bishop Anselm, argued in effect that the existence of God is likewise nonempirical, an *a priori* necessity. The divine nonexistence, he tried to show, is a contradiction, a conceptual absurdity, because even the conceivability of nonexistence is a defect and the unsurpassably excellent being could not have this defect. Moreover, since conceivability and inconceivability are not dependent upon contingent facts, a God whose nonexistence was conceivable would be tarnished by this defect, even should He happen to exist. For then He would be divine and yet not divine. Hence it is contradictory to classify the theistic question as an empirical one. I have devoted two books to this matter. We shall see if my contention can be refuted. If it is valid, the "problem of evil" is a mistake, a pseudoproblem.

It may seem to some incredible that this should be so. If it is logically impossible that empirical facts could conflict with theism, how could so many have thought that the facts of evil did so? The answer is somewhat complex, but it can be summarized fairly simply: people had a confused idea, really a self-contradictory one—though vague enough for the contradiction to escape clear detection—of the meaning of the term "God," and therefore they also had confused ideas about what is to be meant by "creature," or a being other than God. (Anselm himself shared to a considerable degree in these confusions.) A self-contradictory idea not only can but must conflict with facts, for it conflicts with everything, including itself. Confusion in the posing of a question generates confusion in the answering of it.

"God," it was held, was a being perfect in every way, and hence in power and goodness. And, it was supposed, a being perfect in power must be able to prevent anything undesirable from occurring. It was not noticed that this is already an absurdity, no matter what the facts. For X to have power to prevent anything undesirable from occurring is for X to have a monopoly on decision-making. But this monopoly is itself the most undesirable thing imaginable; or rather it is the unimaginable and indeed inconceivable absolutizing of an undesirable direction of thought. Monopoly of decision-making is in principle undesirable. On this ground Nicolai Hartmann rejected theism as unethical; and he was right if theism means what he took it to mean. Who could want anyone, even God, to make all his decisions for him? And if this occurred, how would the decisions be "his" at all? The difficulty here is logical, does not depend upon facts.

Moreover, the values of life are essentially social, involving the interactions of more or less free, truly deciding, individuals. Give one agent a monopoly of the power to decide, and there is no social situation and no value in any sense that we can grasp. My conclusion is: the idea of omnipotence, as it figures in the classical problem of evil, is a pseudo-idea; it would not make sense no matter what the empirical world happened to be like.

But once more, why was all this not seen clearly long ago? There are several reasons.

a) It is easy verbally to evade the argument by saying: Yes, God permits us to make our own decisions but, like the hypnotist (only raised to the eminent degree) or the skillful benevolent parent (with similar difference), He so influences us that we make exactly the decisions He decides upon for us, and so He is responsible for our acts, even though they are truly ours. I say that this is mere verbiage, and that no one knows what it means. God decides my decisions, you say, yet they are truly mine. This is double talk, without any clear import. No hypnotist or parent can make a single concrete decision for anyone. At most, he can see to it (with high probability, hardly with absolute certainty) that any decision the person or child makes will have a specified abstract ingredient in it, such as opening the window on a very cold day when, without the hypnotist, no such act would have occurred. Merely "opening the window" is not a concrete act. The concrete action includes just how the window is opened, just how far, at what split second, with what rationalizing explanations (if not to others at least to the person himself), with what feeling tone and sense of purpose, duty, or guilt. It is amazing how pervasive the "fallacy of misplaced concreteness" proves to be, once one sets out to notice its commission. Only a failure to distinguish between abstract features of decision and an actual process of deciding can account for the notion that hypnotic influence can, even for a second, leave a person with no open alternatives for his own adjudication. Action which in its concreteness is predecided is automatic and unconscious. It is not individual action at all. What is done in that way by "us" is collective cellular action, not human action. As Bergson and Dewey correctly saw, consciousness [and indeed even sentience] requires genuine indeterminacies, open alternatives, real ambiguities, to be determined or resolved, and it lapses when there are none. We are always, while awake, or even dreaming, deciding what no one else has decided for us. I see no basis for the notion that there can be such a thing as A's making B's concrete decisions. This I view as a logical impossibility which is not got rid of by taking A to be God.

We may go further: the theistic version of strict determinism is the most glaringly inconsistent of all. For it splits decision into two forms which differ absolutely: the divine deciding, back of which is nothing whatever (neither any necessity of the agent's nature, nor any influence of other agents), contrasted to our deciding, which is wholly determined by antecedent influence. So we have agents with no individuality of decision-making, on the one hand, and an agent whose decisions are absolutely individual, totally uninfluenced or without social character, on the other. It is playing with words to speak of "decision" or "individuality" on both sides of this absolute contrast. And if our decisions merely duplicate items in God's, what can we mean when we use our notion of deciding, formed from a purely illusory experience of *seeming* to choose between open alternatives, to characterize God's wholly genuine and absolutely independent decisions? I see in all this but a mass of undigested notions too vague or self-inconsistent to permit any useful application of rational argument. Out of such stuff has the problem of evil been generated.

b) It is easy to suppose that the necessity—if it be granted—for there to be decisions which creatures make for themselves, and not God for them, applies at most to man, or other rational animals, or perhaps also to angels. But this too, I hold, is a confusion. Being an individual at all implies some scope for individual action, some freedom to close otherwise open alternatives. Epicurus saw this when he attributed freedom not only to man, not only to animals even, but to the very atoms. In spite of the fact that one of his reasons for this generalization was a bad one (that otherwise atoms would all fall straight "downward"), Epicurus here made a metaphysical discovery, and it is instructive to see how uniformly historians of philosophy have missed the point. A sheer dualism of rational and free animals, contrasted to subrational and simply unfree ones, or of free animals contrasted to simply unfree inanimate nature, will never explain anything not better explained otherwise. Like all absolute dualisms, it "solves" problems only by introducing a more intractable one. Rational freedom is to be viewed as a special, high-level form of freedom in general, and this as inherent in the category of individuality as such, whether atomic, human, or divine.

An infant, for example, has scarcely rational freedom, but still it has freedom. It makes its own little decisions. And so does every animal, including every cell—if it is correct to view cells as little individual animals—in metazoan bodies, and even every one-celled plant, such as a bacterium, whether beneficent or otherwise in its effects upon higher organisms. Cancer cells are acting in some degree on their own, and are not simply executing divine decisions. Quantum mechanics at least fits [we need not say establishes] the view that the same principle holds for molecules and atoms, or even particles. I regard Epicurus's principle—which of course is far from materialistic, and really implies a radical revision of the doctrine Epicurus accepts from Democritus—as the only one which conforms to the spirit of science, for which any sheer dualism is at best provisional. The belief, which precedes quantum mechanics (Maxwell, Peirce, Cournot, Boutroux, Bergson), that statistical laws are the fundamental ones I take to be the only really satisfactory one. The relation of all this to the problem of evil is that, since all creatures have some freedom, all evil can and should be viewed as involving unfortunate (not necessarily or in general wicked) cases of creaturely decision. If what X decides harmonizes with what Y decides, that is good luck; if it doesn't, that is bad luck. It really is luck, for neither X nor Y, nor yet Z, even if Z is God, can simply decide that harmony shall reign. All can aim at harmony, but none can guarantee it, not because someone, say God, is weak, but because it is the very meaning of the social situation in which all value and all sentient existence consists that each must decide in some measure for himself, and that the decisions of another cannot be foreseen in their full concreteness. They cannot be foreseen, much less eternally seen by God, for until they take place they do not exist as wholly definite entities or facts. Hence each agent must take a certain chance of discord, whatever he himself decides, and however benevolent he or anyone is.

c) If all concrete decisions in the world are creaturely decisions, what is left, one may wonder, for God to decide? The difficulty of answering this question is one reason for the desperate resort to the monopoly theory of divine decision. But the question can perhaps be answered. First, God decides upon the basic outlines of creaturely actions, the guaranteed limits within which freedom is to operate. That not everything can be guaranteed does not imply that nothing can be. Every ruler decides upon certain limits within which the decisions of citizens are to fall; the cosmic ruler does this cosmically and for all creatures, from the least to the greatest. No ruler tells the ruled what concretely they are to do; he tells them rather within what abstract limits their acts are to take place. In the cosmic case these abstract limits of freedom are the "laws of nature." No creature has decided what these shall be.

Second, God decides what use to make in his own life of what happens through creaturely freedom, just how the course of cosmic history is to be interpreted and enjoyed in the divine perspective. The creatures cannot decide this, not even collectively. For no evaluation, no experience, not even God's, or least of all God's, can be dictated by its objects. This is but another way of stating our principle of freedom as inherent in individual actuality as such. There is some degree of freedom in all experiencing and valuing. God by his very essence cherishes the creatures, but just how he is to experience them does not follow "automatically" from this law of his nature alone. He has to decide with each new creature *how* to cherish it, in relation to all antecedent creatures. It is this freely decided divine appreciation which gives our lives their abiding worth. (It also reveals every flaw, and in this sense is a "judgment.") Whitehead speaks of the "immortality of the past," whereby each concrete momentary actuality of experience, though in one sense perishing or falling into the fixity of the past, yet "lives forevermore" because what God retains is the very concrete fullness or particularity of the "actual entity." This doctrine furnishes a philosophical meaning for Niebuhr's and Tillich's "end of history beyond history." It is beyond worldly history, but not beyond divine history. For, with many recent and some older thinkers, I hold that God is not simply immutable but has his own divinely excellent way of changing.

The two forms of divine decision, instituting natural laws and freely valuing the creatures, may perhaps not exhaust the divine options. But they seem to be the only ones we (or at least I) can clearly define, and neither, it seems, could be performed by a nondivine agent.

The perfection of God was supposed to imply his immunity to suffering. In other words, not only moral evil, but also aesthetic or physical evil, was excluded from his life. Accordingly God, though apparently a producer and spectator of our sufferings, was in no way a sympathetic participant in them. As Anselm said, God is not literally "compassionate," for he is not passionate at all. But this denial of sympathy to deity made it impossible to arrive at an emotionally satisfying theory of evil. With Berdyaev, Whitehead, and some others, I hold that though God does not inflict suffering upon us (rather we inflict it upon ourselves and one another), the sufferings which occur are not simply outside the divine life. Only so, indeed, does omniscience acquire a meaning. God's knowledge is concrete and intimate. It therefore unites him with the suffering creatures much more fully than any sympathy of ours can unite us with those suffering individuals we care about. God does not simply know *that* we suffer, he knows our actual sufferings in their concreteness. To say that this awareness of suffering is merely serene—pure bliss—is, like so much else in our theological tradition, well meant but confused verbiage. It is logically impossible to know suffering in its concreteness and not in some sense suffer also. It follows that, when we inflict sufferings upon one another, often innocently, we inflict them also upon God, who lovingly shares in them. I have argued elsewhere that this does not contradict the divine perfection in the sense (and no other is relevant to the problem of evil) in which there is either religious or philosophical need to attribute perfection to God.

In sum, my view of the problem of evil is: (a) it is a pseudoproblem due to a pseudoconcept of omnipotence or divine power; evil springs from creaturely freedom, and without such freedom there could be no world at all; (b) creaturely freedom capable of producing evil, at least in the form of suffering, is universal to the creation, not confined to man or rational animals, or even to animals; (c) God's supremacy consists, not in his making the creatures' decisions for them, but in his setting abstract limits of law to creaturely decisions, and in his ideally free evaluation of the results so that they acquire permanent meaning; finally, (d) God shares in all suffering since he cherishes all creatures, so that he may be seen as the ideal companion in sorrow as well as joy. God would be masochistic as well as sadistic if it were true that he deliberately caused us to suffer. But he is neither, for no concrete evil is divinely decided, whether as punishment, means of spiritual education, or in view of any other end. God sets the creatures free, within limits, because there is no other way to have creatures or any world. The risks of freedom are inseparable from freedom, and the price of its opportunities.

Without freedom there could be nothing, whether good or evil. The laws of nature do not determine events in detail, for the laws are statistical only. In setting these laws God is not decreeing this case of cancer or that case of murder, he is decreeing such and such risks of evil and such and such opportunities for good. Without the risks there could not be the opportunities, and the opportunities are divinely judged as worth the risks. To ask, "Why did this particular evil occur?" is a theologically absurd question. There is no way, beyond the statistical and causal one which science can investigate. You must rather ask, "Why was this kind of evil so much as possible?" Answer, because a certain kind and degree of freedom makes it possible, and also makes certain good things possible, and because the chance for these good things was divinely judged worth the risk of the evil things. Thus God does not adjust concrete evils and goods in some inconceivably wise way, he does not, so far as we know, manipulate concrete happenings at all. He adjusts basic kinds of possibility of good and evil as inherent in certain laws of nature. The rest is simply what the creatures happen to decide. Those who ask for a world without freedom and risk are also asking for one without opportunity. Indeed, they know not what they ask.

Are those laws of nature good which apparently make it

possible for man to destroy his kind, and even life on earth, more or less completely? What opportunities worth this dire risk can there be? We can only dimly imagine. But if the Anselmian point holds, the opportunities must be there. No really possible world, hence not ours, can contradict the divine existence.

The classical formula was: God either will not, or cannot, prevent evil. If he will not, he is cruel or callous; if he cannot, he is weak. Either way, he lacks the perfection connoted by the term "God" and is not a being worthy of worship, if indeed he exists at all. My position is, God neither will nor could monopolize decision-making, for this is logically impossible. Theologians have generally agreed that God cannot do the logically impossible, for to do that is not really to do anything. (The logically impossible is nothing extra-linguistic.) One does not limit God's power by refusing to attribute this nothing to him. To have creatures without freedom would be to have creatures which are not creatures. Divinity is supreme freedom. The absolute negation of freedom is not creaturehood but nonentity. Creaturehood is precisely the status of freedom lacking the supreme qualities of divine freedom. Between divine freedom and zero freedom there is plenty of room for all possible creatures. Those who think otherwise have a strange view of divine freedom! One or two steps down from it, they seem to suppose, lands one in no freedom. How illogical! Any number of steps down can still leave some freedom.

What then is the perfection of divine freedom or power, if it is not a monopoly of power? It is the unsurpassable freedom or power to inspire freedom in others, and to set such limits to their freedom as will maximize opportunities for good and minimize risks of evil. Power to make the laws of nature is one aspect of this. Only God can decide natural or cosmic laws. Natural laws are the only laws which are always beneficent. Not that all results are good, but that the risks of having the laws are never comparable to the advantages. With human laws this may not be so; some laws may create greater risks than opportunities.

Why does freedom involve risk? Because free beings achieve good by harmonizing with each other and cause evil by falling into conflict. Cancer cells are in conflict with normal cells, normal cells harmonize together. Cancer cells are not bad simply in themselves, but good. Internally they achieve a harmony. Tragedy, as Berdyaev says, is not so much the clash of good with evil as of good with good. This applies to the Cold War too! Given, say, three free beings, it is partly luck if the good of the one harmonizes with that of the others. Suppose A wants to be the closest friend of B, and C also wants this status. Either way there is a good, close friendship, but the two goods conflict. There are, then, incompatible possibilities of good. Moreover, what goods free beings pursue must be partly their own decision. Not even God can make this decision; for to say that a decision is a given agent's, and that the agent "makes" the decision, are one and the same assertion. What God decides with respect to me cannot be my decision. It may be an element of my decision, but no more. For the same reason all utopianism is bound to fail, because no control of others, and no self-control either, can eliminate the risk of conflict. We can compromise our conflicts, mitigate their destructiveness, and we should try to do this; but it is vain to decide that there shall be no conflicts. Voluntary self-abnegation cannot be absolute and leave anything in the individual to negate; and enforced abnegation cannot be absolute either. All order is limited or mitigated chaos; to rule is to keep anarchy in its proper subordinate place, not to get rid of it. Order and disorder are correlative terms, neither can be absolutized. Determinism is the refusal to see this, and belief in total freedom is the converse form of the same refusal.

God is needed not to put everything precisely in its place, for things must put themselves in their places; but he is needed to see to it that there are appropriate places for them to put themselves into—if they are lucky and also make a right use of their freedom. Without God, to speak *per impossibile,* individuals could not form even a disorderly world, but only a meaningless, unthinkable chaos in which there would be neither any definite good nor any definite evil. This is the same as no world. With God there is an order, a world in which good and evil can occur. However, the chances of evil are subordinate to the chances for good, so that good is the primary overarching probability. Nature is full of good, full of harmony and joy. Those who really study nature feel this.

Notice that in this philosophy freedom is the absolute principle, even though any particular freedom is always relative. Freedom is the absolute principle; for A's freedom is limited only by the freedom of C and D and so on. What limits my decision now? The decisions I and others, including atoms and cells among the others, have made in the past. Even the laws of nature are divine decisions made long ago, and freely made. (Other laws would have been possible and could have been divinely decreed. Eventually others may be decreed—instituting a new cosmic epoch.) That the freedom of one agent is limited by the freedom of others is the social structure of existence. That one's freedom now is limited by the freedom already exercised in the past is the temporal structure of existence. I cannot simply repudiate my past decisions or those of others; for they make up an important part of my memories, and without memories what am I? Experience gets its concreteness from the past. (Even perception comes from the past and is in this sense memory, as science shows, and philosophers ought long ago to have guessed, as indeed, I gather, some did.) The control of God over us is the influence of his decisions already made. Why do we accept these? Because without them we should have no basic structure or meaning to our experience or thought. In the depths of consciousness we feel and accept the divine ordering without which there could be nothing significant or definite. The worst sinner still does this in his imperfect way.

Evil, in the sense of conflict and suffering, is explained by the existence of many free beings; that there is nevertheless a basic goodness and order is explained by the existence of one preeminent or unsurpassable free being. Freedom, as socially concerned with others and the past, is thus the absolute principle of reality as such. Causality is but freedom's concern with the past, together with the universal ordering sway of eminent or divine freedom over all other freedoms. Apart from freedom there is nothing and can be nothing. With freedom there is risk as well as opportunity.

A final remark. If the problem of evil can in principle be

solved, it does not follow that the antitheist has no strong arguments. There are other difficulties in theism which I find at least more formidable. But they do not arise from empirical facts, but from the attempt, inherent in theism, to divest the idea of individuality or consciousness from the imperfections which ordinarily accompany it. The old problem of analogy: how if at all to conceive an unsurpassable yet individual form of experience, volition, or love, is still with us. To deal with this problem in all its aspects would hardly be possible in a single article. But be this problem reasonably soluble or no, it is *a priori* or conceptual, not empirical, in its nature. There are no empirical arguments either against or for the divine existence. Not that the ontological argument is the only positive argument, but that any valid argument must share with the ontological its purely conceptual character. So must any argument against theism. The divine existence is a topic falling wholly within "logic" in that broad sense which includes metaphysics as I conceive the latter (in at least partial agreement with Karl Popper). It is not a topic within empirical science (including history as a science), for this is entirely incompetent to legislate concerning it. So is mere common sense acting as amateur scientist or historian. Only the logician-metaphysician, whether expert or amateur, has *anything* relevant to say, from a rational point of view, concerning the existence and essential or eternal nature of God. (God's contingent noneternal relations to the world and man are different. With reference to them, empirical evidences, historical events, may be relevant.) Aside from metaphysics, there is only sheer faith or sheer unfaith. Empirical facts, or contingent objects of experience, may lead some to faith, some to unfaith. But in neither case is the connection a rational one. The rational ground of faith cannot be contingent or empirical, and neither can the ground of unfaith—if indeed this has a ground.

The University of Texas

FREE WILL, THE CREATIVITY OF GOD, AND ORDER

PETER A. BERTOCCI

THERE IS AN underlying assumption in this essay.* It is that no adequate philosophical account can be given of the physical, the biological, or the divine realms of being without considering how human nature is related to them. Man, I am suggesting, is to be studied not as "another instance of Nature," not as an instance of divine Being, but as the kind of being he is. He may then be related to other beings. This does not mean that, when this relating is done, man may not turn out to be another instance of God or Nature, or both together. But it does mean that the question of relationship cannot be judged before analysis of man's own experience of himself.

Hence, in what follows, limiting myself to the nature of human freedom, I shall attempt to describe free will on what seems to me to be its own terms. I shall then consider whether this analysis throws any light on the conception of divine creativity and natural law. I shall press the question: Can it be that in human freedom we have an enlightening analogy for divine creativity?

I

Quite understandably, philosophical discussion of will has concentrated on whether human will can be assigned any degree of freedom; and theological discussion has been affected by a concern to establish human freedom and autonomy as the ground of human responsibility for moral good and evil in the world. My main concern here is not to debate the issue as to whether there is free will, but, assuming limited freedom, to ask the further question: What *is* the activity of freedom? That is, what does free

* This essay is an altered version of a paper delivered at a Conference on the Self in Western and Eastern Philosophy at Wooster College in April, 1965.

activity introduce that would not be achieved without it? Yet because talk of will (human or divine) as "free" suggests arbitrary action to many psychologists, ethicists, metaphysicians, and theologians, it will be wiser to quell that fear, if I can, before proceeding to my main concern.

C. J. Ducasse's description of will illustrates not only his usual analytic insight but what seems to me to be an unjustifiable concern lest human "free" will bring sheer arbitrariness into the life of a person. I take advantage of his analysis to deal briefly with this preliminary hurdle.

To assert "free" will, says Ducasse, is in fact to assert not freedom of will but "freedom to *act* as one wills." [1] If my arm is neither shackled nor paralyzed, "I *can*" means that I am *free* to raise it or not as I will:

> under present circumstances, *volition by me to raise it is sufficient to cause it to rise;* and, to prove that such volition *is* sufficient now to cause this, I need only make the experiment: I do so and up goes the arm. . . . In sum, man, within limits, i.e., in some circumstances and in certain respects, does have *freedom to act as he wills.*[2]

I take no exception to this, nor to much of what is to follow. I quote the important passage:

> . . . man's freedom to act as he wills, which we have shown he certainly has sometimes, does not, even on the occasions when he has it, in the least imply that his *volition,* which causes his act, is itself uncaused. The fact is on the contrary that the volition is itself determined—caused to occur—by some motivating factor, for instance, by some end in view which it will serve, or by the superior attractiveness of one of the alternatives open, or by some other consideration. My volition to raise my arm a moment ago, for example, was determined by my aim at the moment to prove that such a volition would, in the circumstances then existing, suffice to cause the arm to rise.[3]

Perhaps I am making too much of a subtle shift of emphasis from the more introspective and phenomenological account of the former quotation to the interpretative one of the latter. It is

[1] C. J. Ducasse, *A Philosophical Scrutiny of Religion* (New York: The Ronald Press, 1953), p. 369.

[2] *Ibid.*, p. 370.

[3] *Ibid.*, pp. 371, 372.

one thing to say that I am free to act as I will under certain circumstances, that I feel free and find myself, often at least, able to lift my arm. But it is not the same as to *argue,* what I do not introspect, that the volition which causes my act is itself determined (caused) by some other factor in my life. This may be the case, but only some consideration other than what I introspect would lead me to say this. Among these would be the consideration Ducasse advances in the following passage:

> Indeed, to suppose that one's volitions are not determined—either by one's past experiences, or by one's tastes . . . or by the sort of situation one is in at the time, or by one's beliefs as to right and wrong, or by the difference in the consequences one believes would follow from choice of one rather than another of the courses of action one can embark on if one but wills—to suppose, I say, that one's volition is not determined by any of these considerations nor by any others, is *not* to be supposing that one's volition is then free and responsible, but on the contrary that it is *completely fortuitous, purely random, and therefore, wholly irresponsible.* For to be *acting in a morally responsible manner* means precisely that the volitions causing the acts are being *responsive to*—determined by—such considerations as those listed above; and to *treat a person as a morally responsible being* means to be assuming that punishing or rewarding him for something he has done, holding out to him threats or promises if he does certain things, pointing out to him the probable effects of alternative courses of action, and so on, *will be effective* in shaping his future volitions on relevant kinds of occasions . . . the true opposite of determinism is not freedom but pure fortuity, absolute chance.[4]

Now if I saw the situation as Ducasse sees it—either caused freedom or pure fortuity—his analysis would determine my choice of theory. But I read one meaning into "being responsive to"—and another into "determined by"—other factors in my life as a morally responsible agent. "Determined by" suggests that what leads to the final act are the inner and outer considerations and circumstances in which I am, rather than *my* choosing which of the considerations I would choose to approve and which *I* would oppose. Still, I should wish to grant that "having freedom of

[4] *Ibid.*, pp. 372, 373, 374.

choice never means that one can do *anything whatever* which one might will to do. The variety of alternative acts which one can perform if one but will is always limited, sometimes more and sometimes less so." [5]

Nevertheless, granting that the course of action in given circumstances is *influenced by* the nature of those circumstances and also by the particular total set of dispositions, past experiences, and purposes operative in me at the time, what happens is that my willing at the time (not what Ducasse calls my total "volitional nature" at the time) is itself *an added* factor in the situation I move into. Professor Ducasse anticipates my preference for saying that circumstances *influence* (rather than *determine*) volitions, and he would explain it perhaps by the hypnotic effect of the words "free will," and by my "gratuitous" assumption that determinism and free will are mutually exclusive. It would be nothing but silly banter for me to retort that there is a gratuitous assumption that free will must involve fortuity. What might be more helpful is to argue that inclinations, dispositions, circumstances do not have their *full* effect on me, wherever there seems to me to be an alternative, until *I* approve them as part of the process of working out the particular choice I make. The important point is that I am determined because I, in part at least, affect what will determine me—and not I *am* determined by factors within and without.[6]

[5] *Ibid.*, p. 375.

[6] Apart from the moral apprehensions Ducasse has, he is also concerned to undermine the theological contention of those who like myself urge that, if men are free to any degree, God cannot *make,* create, man free and morally good at the same time, since the last choice must be man's. Ducasse, however, urges: "*freedom and goodness are no wise incompatible:* man could perfectly well be free to do evil if he wills, or good if he wills, and yet be such that in fact he never prefers the evil but always the good." (*Ibid.,* p. 378.) In this passage, and when he continues, "an omnipotent creator certainly could have implanted moral goodness in his creatures, for moral goodness is goodness of intent, goodness of will—charitableness, compassion, kindness," (*Ibid.,* p. 378) Ducasse overlooks the particular meaning of moral goodness such thinkers have in mind. It is not what man wills but that *he may or may not* will either a presumable good or a presumable evil, in view of his innate and acquired disposition, that is in mind. Had God created him with a native intent to goodness, or with an invariable goodness of intent, the very meaning of *man's* moral goodness, or badness, disappears. The intention in such views is not so much to exonerate God from man's evil acts as to see what it means to say that man is free even for God (as the sequel will further explain).

It will now be clear [7] that while there is no denying that man has limited freedom, there is a factor in willing that is neglected in Ducasse's analysis which is affected by his conviction that any other view equates free will with pure fortuity. I have tried elsewhere,[8] and in part because of such considerations as Ducasse has advanced, to try to dispel this legitimate fear by a distinction between will-agency and will-power. Here I can simply suggest the view that I have in mind, and which will serve as the basis for analogy with divine creativity.

II

Willing, as I would phrase it, is a distinctive phase of the total activity that comprises personal being. To be a person is to be a complex, non-summative unity of activities: sensing, remembering, perceiving, thinking, feeling, emoting, wanting, willing, oughting, and aesthetic and religious sensitivity. The argument here does not depend on agreement about the exact nature of these activities (other than willing). For the main contention is, minimally, that to be a person is (a) to be at least a unity of these activities, and (b) that these activities, while they are assigned different names, are *not* different parts in an assembly that constitutes a person. To be a person is to be a unity of such activities, a unity defined by what these activities actually do and can do.[9] To will, then, is for the person to act in a way that can be discriminated introspectively from other personal activities; "the person wills" is the accurate mode of speech; "the will" is nothing other than one kind of, one dimension of, personal activity.

To say this is to emphasize that the will is not side-by-side, as it were, other phases of personal activity. Willing, as a certain kind of activity among the total activities of the self, simply cannot take

[7] For fuller treatment of Ducasse's view see his masterly *Nature, Mind, and Death* (La Salle, Ill.: Open Court Publishing Company, 1951), chapter 11.

[8] See *Introduction to Philosophy of Religion* (New York: Prentice-Hall, 1958), pp. 223–239, and *Free Will, Responsibility, and Grace* (New York: Abingdon, 1958), and "The Moral Structure of the Person," *Review of Metaphysics,* Vol. 14, No. 3, March, 1961, pp. 369–88, and also *Personality and the Good,* co-author R. M. Millard (New York: David McKay, 1963), Chapter 8.

[9] For our purpose here we may also neglect the question whether the "total" person is conscious or unconscious. Yet, I should want to insist that what we know about unconscious activities we can know only by inferential analogy with the conscious.

place out of connection with the other activities and structures of personality. To neglect this fact is to invite fears about arbitrary acts of will. But another distinction must be drawn if we are to see more specifically why it is that willing does not bring sheer arbitrariness into the life of a person.

The distinction is that between will-agency and will-power. The person can will (will-agency) without fully accomplishing the objective he has in mind. When the person succumbs to temptation we say that will-agency does not have power (will-power). The distinction between will-power and will-agency cannot be absolute, since an agency that has no *effective power* at all would be nothing at all. Yet the distinction points up the fact that will-power is the effective difference made by will-agency within the total situation the person confronts at a given choice-point in his life. Thus, the student who chooses to study after having formed bad study habits, may well find that his will-agency makes little headway, that is, that he has little *effective* power over the habits formed. Yet for him to make no headway does not mean that he has no will-agency at all, or even no will-power at all. The act of willing does have some effect, however little, against the formations in personality that render it "powerless" to break the habit.

To this extent we can agree with Professor Ducasse that no person wills arbitrarily, that is, that a person cannot en-act anything at will (will-power). We can also agree that he never wills outside the total context of his native and acquired capacities, that he is never impervious to the environment that impinges on him at choice-point. But what must be added to any concrete account of choice is that any behavior or conduct in which will-agency is present is caused by many factors *including the will-agency.* A person at choice-point often does not know ahead of time exactly how much his will-agency can accomplish. Nevertheless, will-*agency as felt is will-activity;* it is not *want*-activity or *thought*-activity, or *ought*-activity; nor is will-agency the by-product of other activities exclusive of willing. Will-*power,* however, in a given situation is the by-product of all the factors involved in the matrix of activities, *including willing,* that constitute the total person-personality.

Indeed, a person's personality is the unique, more or less unified, acquired joint-product of the person's activities as they interact with the total environment. The person learns or acquires a personality that expresses his mode of interaction with his environment. Yet a person as an originative unity of activities is never exhausted in whatever degree of acquired unity his personality has; the person always lives and acts on, through and in his personality: hence the composite word "person-personality" for a person at any moment in his career.[10]

III

Assuming, then, that will-agency is free within limits, but not arbitrary in a specious sense, we may ask: In what does the achievement of freedom consist? As has just been suggested, the person in willing does not act in a vacuum. The person does not will to will; he wills to think or not to think; or he wills to pursue what he acknowledges to be right or wrong. *Moral* freedom is the personal will to exert oneself in favor of, or against, what one believes he ought to do. A person uses his freedom to favor or oppose a situation in his personality-environment-matrix that his willing *at this moment of choice* did not choose. For example, will he now, faced with a problematic situation, *pursue thinking* that is self-consistent and related to the available evidence, even if he knows that the conclusions may be displeasing to his own past sentiments and those of others whose esteem he treasures? Let us assume that he can will to think about the situation. Yet his willing does not create the structure of logic and of reasonable thinking; nor does it create the evidence to be taken into account. What, then, does his willing do? What difference does it make? What does it create, if anything?

Our point is critical; the person in willing (will-agency) does not will new basic capacities into being; it takes advantage of, or it is confined to the activating of "givens" in its total person-personality. For example, willing certainly does not create the

[10] "The Psychological Self, the Ego, and Personality" in *Psychological Review*, Vol. 52, No. 2, March, 1945, pp. 91–99; and "Foundations of Personalistic Psychology" in *Scientific Psychology*, ed. by B. B. Wolman and E. Nagel (New York: Basic Books, 1965).

evidence or the rules of thinking. Nor does it at any given moment create the emotional sentiments that may be disappointed as they make themselves felt in a way that can make straight thinking more difficult. New thoughts flood in, and new feelings may come into play that would have been inconsequential otherwise, but we cannot say that willing creates these thoughts or feelings. For only thinking activity can think thoughts, and only according to implicit laws of thought; only emoting-activity expresses itself in one form of feeling or another; and only feeling-activity can take specific forms of feeling; only sensing capacities can experience sense-data. Willing, it seems clear, does not alter the basic activities of the person, or the basic rules by which they, once active, are governed, or the basic concomitants that come raining in upon the choice-situation from learned "structures."

All the more, then, what does human willing do? If it does not act out of relation to other activities and structures, unlearned or acquired, is there anything left for willing to do? Yes. Willing *at least* makes possible changes in the constellations of factors involved in a given choice situation. For example, by holding some factors in a situation in focus (or in action) when they, left to themselves, would cease being active, it changes the outcome that would otherwise have ensued. It makes a difference whether thinking can be kept thinking about the evidence, whether sentiments are kept from becoming the focus of the situation or dominating the associative process. In a word, the *minimal* difference willing seems to make is one of keeping some factors in focus and operative and "shutting off," or decreasing, the power of other factors that in turn would be more effective if willing favored them. To illustrate, if I will to hold on to the hot plate that is paining my fingers, I am keeping in focus the thinking of the goal: "this plate must not be dropped" and favoring the feeling and other states favoring that goal, and thus refuse to allow the experienced reflex "drop hot plate" from being fully enacted.

I do not suggest the above as a complete account of a very complicated situation; there are many more focal and peripheral factors (conscious and, probably, unconscious) that no doubt have an effect in my conscious matrix at any one point. But could

I articulate all of those adequately, I doubt that the basic description just given would be abrogated. *Willing is at least that* activity of personal effort which, far from producing the situation with which it is confronted at any decision point, does create a situation that would not have ensued had the decision not been made to hold firm to certain activity-contents as opposed to others. This willing is free insofar as it is not the sheer outcome of a confluence of present and past forces now operative in person-personality. But its intended effect is to alter the existent situation in accordance with a goal decided upon at that point.

IV

We have been speaking in minimal terms reminiscent of William James' doctrine of *fiat*. I am no surer than he was of "how" all this comes about. But, undaunted, I wish to go on to say that, if I read the situation aright, to will is to create. I use the word *create* and give up the words *change* and *alter* because I have a specific kind of change in mind, namely *creative change*. Creative change is more than the actualizing of potential, although it presupposes both actuality and potentiality in the creator. Creative changes is a change in a situation that would not have taken place if the situation had been allowed to "unfold" or to drift, as it were, with the outcome being no more than the consequence or outcome of interacting factors left to themselves. Creative change produces, in other words, an alteration that might well not have occurred, and, as far as we know, would not have occurred, without an activity that entered the situation in such a way as to allow a result to take place that simply would not have ensued without effort expended to this effect.

Accordingly, a person is here held to be creative in a given situation insofar as he wills in that situation an end that (ethical or not, aesthetic or not, reasonable or not) would not have taken place until he so willed (and exerted that amount of will-power). Willing, to be sure, always is willing in a personality context; but when willing takes place, it (will-agency) effects results believed to be possible in that situation but results that so far as we know would not have occurred if the willing did not endure until the end was achieved.

Much is involved in what we have said that needs further explication. But the situation to keep before us is nicely described by Professor Wilmon H. Sheldon when he says:

> The only genuine cause is one with a power quite its own, underived from what precedes, deciding so far quite by itself what it will do. Hence, when we reason we are not reasoning in isolation, but we are reasoning and not feeling! [11]

Sensitive to the dynamics of reason, feeling, and willing he continues:

> . . . Unless there were urges, lures deep or shallow, temporary or lasting, native or acquired, each with its own magnetism, there could be no choice made, no reflection as to which is better or best. And these lures stand on their own feet, actual given trends in the individual make-up. Reason doesn't create them, though it may discover them . . . Nor does will create the lures . . .*The act of will, like reason may discover new goods, but their goodness is not created by the act. Will may indeed focus attention on this or that lure, letting its force be felt so strong that its opposite lure gradually recedes from the scene. We can by our free choice let the delights of the flesh so dominate our life that the appeal of the finer and more lasting goods disappear below the horizon.*[12]

What, then, is the thesis being suggested? Willing, far from operating in a psychic-biological vacuum, is the effort of the person to deal with the given factors in a choice-matrix that would follow a line of least resistance, as it were, if the person had not directed them in the light of a new task. Willing, on the other hand, could not create the new task were thinking impossible, or were there no dispositions and trends in the total matrix of which it is a part. Willing does not take over the function of thinking, of wanting-desiring, of pleasing or displeasing; it constructs neither the laws of reason nor the intrinsic functions and sequences of emotions. Willing is like a parent who cannot be a parent without children, and who must accept certain brute facts about their actual and possible natures. However, since the parent has energies left that are not exhausted by his children, he is free to

[11] *Rational Religion* (New York: Philosophical Library, 1962), pp. 16, 17, 18.
[12] *Ibid.*, p. 18.

manage what they present to him in ways they cannot manage by themselves, and in ways still open to him.

Nothing less is involved, it seems, than to realize that the person, were he simply a *composite* of feeling, emotion, brute sense-data, oughts, and rational activities, could not will. When a person wills he does not become the senses, the retentive capacity, or the desires, or the sense-data, or the memories, or the sentiments. Yet in willing, when he is successful, he is able (will-power) to control these raw materials in the choice-matrix so that while each contributes its share, each further enters into conduct, into the formation of character and personality, in a way it would not, as far as we can tell, if left to itself. What is *new* as a result of a will, or its creative act, is not conduct in which there is no emotion, reason, memory, obligation (or something other than these), but those components of each that now constitute the person's purpose (good or bad).

Indeed, in this context, we can say that the character and personality of a person are the partial result of creative will—they are not mere changes or alterations—in the sense that they constitute the kind of unity—the degree of orchestration of dispositions and capacities—that express the self-conscious purpose of the person. In particular, a person's character is a creation of the person because, and to the extent that, he has been able to bring into being—not something which is neither desire, nor thought, nor obligation, but—something that is new, from the point of view of that person's past and present. This new partial creation, this new orchestration, was not impossible in view of actualities and potentialities in the choice-matrix; but it now exists because willing has sustained and controlled one possible focus rather than another. For example, fear that could easily express itself in cowardly flight is kept from "taking over" the conscious matrix even as other emotions like sympathy, anger, and respect, are allowed to play a larger part in an act of courage that was cautious as well as daring.

V

Is it too much to say that such creative change involves positive addition to, and subtraction from, what is? Is there not illustrated in human personality the production of a change that brings into being new qualities and formations of character and personality at the expense of others? While I grant that it would not be an accurate description to say that willing brings into being the constitutent emotions, memories, and thoughts, that it would not be accurate to say that willing merely follows the contour, trend, or dynamics of the unattended constituents, I do suggest that willing does produce something new. For willing sustains activities that might have ceased, and it activates and directs trends that might have been ineffective.

How often in our lives actions that are begun by impulse are continued when impulse is dead. For example, an act that begins in sympathy for another may still be continued when sympathy is gone (and an act begun by willing may continue from sympathy). Something *new* takes place which cannot be predicted from past or present experience, which would not take place if the person did not will action in a given situation toward a goal or end that he envisioned.

A very clear instance of willed creation in human experience is, I think, the formation of character. Something new comes into being as a person develops his character, and in two senses. First, some character-trait might never have come into the world without his willed purpose. Second, what was given at choice-point is directed into new channels, into directions or formations never known before or reached in a particular personality. Such creative change is not mechanical change involving new juxtaposition of pre-existing parts; nor is it emanation or the evolution of potential. It is the bringing into being of something which, *once created, may be interpreted* as the "lawful" bringing together of parts at some points, and "gradual" evolution at others. But did we actually find this in human experience, or are we foisting upon human experience "models of occurrence" that may indeed fit the physical and biological world but may well be questioned in the light of what seems to take place in personal being?

For, in personal "growth," in the "development" of character, the situation, however difficult to "comprehend" unless we use physical and biological analogies, outruns those analogies. In human willing something envisioned as desirable and possible in a choice-situation *is* chosen and willed into being by the person.

Furthermore, in human experience we may build from what we are, actual and potential, but we don't even know what the potential of the actual is until a new stride is made. Once the stride is taken, once the bridge from the "potential" to the actual is built, we look back and think we can see the development or the phases that "made" the "new order" that was brought into being. And of course there were potentials and parts involved, and they are included in what *was created.* Yet can such analysis keep us from granting that a person's character, at every stage in his development, is a new fact in the horizon of his life?

To repeat, a good or bad man—be he a Socrates, a Jesus, a Gandhi, a Hitler, or the heroes and criminals of everyday life—is a creation; each person, in part, creates himself—literally. Such persons show what man can become only because by firm efforts they raise structures that take them beyond the foundations and the raw materials granted them. After they create their particular new forms of life, we are able to talk about these new stretches of thought, of aesthetic, moral, and religious sensitivity, as lawful, as if they were just waiting to be realized. In fact they probably were not "hidden"; they simply did not exist, at least in the specific form in which we now see them. Such creations are not arbitrary because they were built in the context of a pre-existing situation; but they were not built "out of" it, as far as we actually know. Yet they *became,* they came *into being* because of an effort that moved whatever did exist to become new in form, quality, and pattern.

To summarize: I am trying to get at a fact that defies articulation into any of the usual forms of intelligibility, of logical or of "technical" reason. We claim to understand the ticking of a watch by taking it apart, seeing how each part functions, and then putting it back again. We claim to understand the growth of a good man by showing how this good man is a fulfillment of past and present potential. Such analysis and description does not do full justice to what actually happens in willing a character into being. I am urging that in the very nature of our experience and development of character, insofar as it is willed, we have a stark, brute kind of event that defies analysis into logical connection, temporal connection, mechanical connection, and even telic connection of the sort exhibited at the biological level. In the creative event to which I have been pointing, something comes into being because of willed effort that we *say* must have been "there" potentially, but this is *ex post facto,* only after the creative event has taken place. This fact, I think, needs more attention than it has received in the past. For as far as we know in such instances, the reach actually exceeds the grasp, and we need to be warned about explaining the *reached* as a "lawful" development from a supposedly latent past. At least this last assumption may well need to be given up in the light of what we actually experience.

Why not simply hold to what is given, the fact of creation as being the outright addition, increase, positing, of something new that is "like" the old but not the mere developing of the old. The good man is, if you will, the man generated, not simply *re*generated; the new man is built not *on* the old man, but with the old man taken into account. There are, no doubt, limits to freedom or to creation, but this is no reason for supposing that Socrates' taking the hemlock, in the spirit in which he took it, is not a new fact in his life, and in the history of the world. *It is related, but nevertheless created;* once created we can look back at the created, and often we discover its filament with the past. But the filament now there *is* there because it too was created. It too is part-product of willing by a being who knew not whether his *fiat* would realize his goal—and then finds that it did! This is freedom; this is creation in human experience, at the very core of what we hold precious in life, moral achievement.

VI

Does this analysis of human freedom and creativity afford any light at all on the problem of God as Creator? I am referring to the theistic hypothesis that God is a creator *ex nihilo,* a doctrine that has been so difficult to understand that great minds have preferred metaphysical monism or absolutism to theism.

For the purpose of this paper, I set aside the question of the ontic relation of the physical and biological realms to God, and limit myself to the question whether a doctrine of *creatio ex nihilo,* once carefully defined in relation to finite persons, and once its theoretical intent is clear, is as unbelievable and unintelligible as critics have held it to be. But why, in essence, has such a supposedly unintelligible doctrine as *creatio ex nihilo* been advanced?

The main ground for holding that God creates *ex nihilo* is to emphasize the fact that God has delegated freedom to persons, that persons are not ontologically part of God, however close their interaction with him may be, and however intimate their dependence upon him for quality in their lives. The doctrine is intended to interpret the fact that persons are free within limits, that no one else, including God, can be responsible for their own free activity. God as creator is responsible for their being free; but since the order of Nature's structures depends essentially on Him and not upon man, God is responsible for the consequences of man's willed choice. If men are free in this sense, they cannot be foci, or centers of God's center, or the energizing of His being, however their interaction with each other and with God be conceived.

But if men are free in this sense, with limited but definite delegated creativity, the whole metaphysical model of persons as modes of the divine Whole, as centers of complex Being, must be given up. For this model ultimately carries agency in all of its possible and actual directions back to Being as the One Source of all that is. In place of this model of parts-in-whole, we need to substitute the model of purposers-Purposer, that is, a model suggested by a moral system or community of persons. Even closer would be the model of an orchestra of moral agents, in which finite purposers, rooted indeed in an interactive network they themselves do not create, are yet free to cooperate with the creator-conductor, and to choose within limits different channels for effectively expressing their own freedom.

However, the importance is not so much in the model but in the metaphysical conception that it seems to me it seeks to develop. For what is involved in saying that persons are not part of God is that in some sense they are beings that God added and adds to all that is. Persons are no part of, nor do they emanate from, the rich effulgence of his being. They are independent, but not self-created, agents.

It is this fact and this kind of system, then, that *creatio ex nihilo* stipulates. The doctrine that free persons are not part of God but created by Him does not mean that God *takes nothing* (little bits of nothing, as one of my students said) and makes something out of it. Impossible, no doubt, to imagine, or even to conceive in purely logical terms, this doctrine does mean that where earlier there had been non-existence (no Socrates), there then appeared Socrates, a new being—never *as such* existent before he was born —and that he then took a hand in his own further development in relation to God, as he formed the character and personality that took the hemlock.

But the question persists: Whence would such sheer *novelty,* such addition to all there is and has been, come? I confess I have no answer if I take the usual lines of trying to imagine *how* a Socrates came into being from an earlier stage in which, even granting him being in the mind of God, he simply was not the existent that made his Apology for philosophizing before the Athenian judges in 399 B.C. All I know is that if I take the evidence at hand, a new fact, a different quality of existent, came into being, developed, chose to die for his convictions that he should obey God and yet not undermine the State or leave Athens for Boeotia.

If I am told that this fact was already among the possibilities in God's mind, I would grant it. But I would still urge that what still defies imagination and logical conception is the *how* of transforming that possibility into actual existence. In other words, I grant that the *creatio ex nihilo,* of Socrates or anything else, cannot be explained if we demand that explanation must involve explaining *how* sheer novelty can be added to what already is, if we use as a pattern of explanation either mechanical know-how or logical implication. Logical implication simply will not do, for finite freedom cannot be implied by a total network of logical relationships. And mechanical know-how is simply not forthcoming when the problem is to account for the kind of novelty that is more than the assembling of parts into a new combination.

VII

I am suggesting that in a doctrine of *creatio ex nihilo* we have cornered an ultimate fact of being that must be the basis for other explanation but is itself not explicable. And this fact of existence is not at odds with human experience, and especially that of forming character. For this reason we must turn to the claim that theists themselves have been all too ready to grant. Nowhere in experience, many theists have claimed, do we have an instance of *creatio ex nihilo*. All human creation, for example, deals with materials already at hand, and this surely does not apply to *creatio ex nihilo* which by definition means that God has no Platonic co-eternal stuff, for example, which he persuades to take on desired form. Theists have been wont to argue that in this instance it should be understandable that man, the created, should not find, in himself or in the created world, empirical ground for such a doctrine as *creatio ex nihilo*.

But this is the very point I am challenging, and which, hopefully, the earlier analysis of the concrete meaning of freedom supports. For if human freedom is at all like what we have analyzed, it does involve adding qualities and dimensions to personality that simply were not there, and would not be there now, apart from the free act. Similarly, *creatio ex nihilo* on the part of God need not involve, I suggest, anything essentially different from what is given in our own experience, although there are differences of details beyond human imagination and conception. Why do I say this?

Because it seems to me that whenever, anywhere, there is addition of novelty, when a real difference appears, the problem of *creatio ex nihilo* is on our hands—if it is a problem at all. But I also suggest that it is a problem only if the philosopher insists on trying to explain how novelty comes into being instead of conforming his theory of reality to what is given in human experience. Whether God creates, or finite persons create, there is added to what is already present. Specifically, for God to create free, finite persons is for him to bring into being, in connection with what is given in his own being, something that could not come into being, and would not come into being, without his effort. Granted that God not only creates new beings but sustains them in a network of relations hidden from our knowledge, can there be any ontological difference in the act of creation? It matters not what the *how* of creation is, for what is involved, whatever the *how*, is the novelty resulting. And for this our own acts of will, in bringing new actualities into being in our own life, provide the nearest and perhaps the best example we have in experience of what it means to say *creatio ex nihilo* (be it human or divine). At least, this is the suggestion here.

Can it be that in our thinking about this whole matter of creation we have been more affected than we realized by an understandable fear comparable to that we found in the interpretation of human free-will—a fear from which a more complete and radical empiricism could save us? This theoretical fear is represented in the presumably profound epigram, *ex nihil, nihil fit*. All that this means is that nothing is nothing, and nobody can make something out of it. But the contention here is not that nothing makes nothing, or that anyone, God or man, makes something *out* of nothing! In the world of our experience new qualities and existents come into being that are not reducible to recombinations of the old; and some things go out of being, whatever residuals are left. For these data there is no clearer description than one that points up the fact that there is something added where there earlier was nothing of that specific quality; that there is now nothing of that quality where there earlier was something.

This fear would be justified did we mean that in the beginning there was nothing, nothing, nothing, and then, behold, one day something came into being. What I actually experience, to take my paradigm, is that I, a person, exist and that I can, at certain points at least, not merely alter my being but bring into existence what was not in being until my effort made it possible. Creation presupposes some existent, and presupposes that existent as agent. Analogously, the existent, God, did not come from nothing, and He does not bring something into being out of nothing.

Thus, on the cosmic scale, when we say, "In the beginning, God," we are saying that a certain kind of self-existent Being was able to bring into being, create, new beings; He himself did not come from nothing, and He made or makes nothing *from* nothing; He created and creates—period! *In a word, creating is a kind of change produced by a kind of being who pre-exists his creative act and is co-existent with his creative act, that is, maintaining his own identity as well as sustaining the creative process toward its goal, and to its goal when he is successful.*

If we follow all of the actual data before us, therefore, and keep the creator and the creative activity related to each other, we shall find that our fears are ungrounded as far as what is given in experience is concerned. A finite person may himself die in the midst of creating, but the cosmic Person, as here assumed, is self-existent and continuous with all creativity, his own and that delegated (as to human beings). In short, what can be experientially grounded is the assertion that there is an originative structure able to create some sort of order. On this note we can turn to the relation of order and creativity.

VIII

It is unempirical, I have urged, to separate the creative act from the existential context in which it lives. And it has been argued that human creativity, while adding to *what is,* (a) works in relation to the matrix of what is given up to the creative moment, and (b) is affected by the kind of opportunities and obstacles constituting the matrix. Put it this way: *there is always some structure, some order of being, as the necessary, although not sufficient, ground of creativity.* Let us illustrate at the human level.

The sensing, remembering, thinking, feeling, wanting, oughting, and appreciating of a finite person—each of these activities has a structure and order of its own that constitutes the inner, continuing base for a person's creativity. But though necessary, each activity is not the sufficient support for the creative act itself. A person wills within the structure of abilities and dispositions which their flexibility allows; and he wills in an environment, social and physical, that has structures and possibilities of which his creative act must take account.

If, for example, I say: "I will forgive another person so that he and I can participate in a fellowship that neither of us knew before," I find myself confronting emotional dispositions and traits both in myself and in the other person that will, according to their own order, offer obstacles and opportunities with which my will to forgive must work. But my will to forgive does not "emerge" or "emanate" from my own past dispositions and present structure. To the extent that I succeed in forgiving, to the extent that the other person cooperates in the formation of the new fellowship, to that extent we are creatively willing into being a *new order.*

If this is true, we may say that to be creative, whether the act eventuate in good or evil, is to begin to build another order that bears some relation to the old order. The order may be short-lived and may not be able to resist pressures from its surrounding world. In the instance at hand, for example, my enemy and I may find in the initial stages of our new relation that hostilities are greater than anticipated, and even insuperable. Creativity, in other words, is initiated within, and presupposes a structure of order, a personal being, who remains to follow through as he confronts other orders of being, as they will to build a kind of stability that was not there before. No order, no freedom; no structures, no creativity. No unified personal structure—finite or divine—no freedom and no creativity. This means that our actual product of creativity or existence will always be a joint-product of what has been and now is.

We need always to keep in mind that in human experience when we create we never create what bears no relation at all to what already is. For example, in thinking we cannot create a logic that allows us to disregard consistency; and in emoting, we create no kind of emotion totally different from familiar kinds—we do create another emotional quality. Hence, there is little actual ground for fear lest the creative freedom we have will create discontinuities—arbitrary and fortuitous—in the structural givens of our lives.

On the other hand, if we do insist on structural discontinuity with the past, does this justify the contention that what we have called creation is not sheer novelty of the kind designated by *"ex nihilo"?* No. For to be continuous does not mean that there is no creation but only that what is created has characteristics in common with what has already occurred. The fact again seems to be that while we never know in advance exactly how much the creative process will actually accomplish, we discover, once the creative act has accomplished its purpose or any part of it, that we can often trace some continuity between the new accomplishment and the old facts! What the existence of continuity proves is not that there is no creation, but that much creation, at least, is related to some order already established. And the fact of continuity can also be understood ultimately in terms of some purpose that is being worked out in and through events that are creative.

IX

Finally, does this notion that creativity involves the addition of something new, without disregarding the order already established, help us to understand divine *creatio ex nihilo* when this involves the physical and biological realms of being?

Broadly speaking, *creatio ex nihilo* is compatible with the view that living or organic processes are not reducible completely to inorganic events. The reader may not be inclined to grant this, and, with such discoveries as DNA in mind, prefer to think of the living as another level of the physical. But such disagreement as to the point of discontinuity between the realms of matter and life is of no real significance for our purposes here. More important is it to keep the differences between what goes on in a stone, a starfish, a bone, and the frontal lobe of a brain from being neglected. Philosophical analysis here must be impressed not only by the broad differences between the inorganic and the organic, but by different classifications of entities within each realm. (If, for example, it should be the fact that different types of "physical" entities do have properties markedly distinguishing them from other "physical" beings, the philosopher may well ask how it is that such different beings constitute *an* order of physical nature—even before he faces the question of the addition of "living" beings to a "physical" realm.)

In any case, a doctrine of *creatio ex nihilo* is far from embarrassed by realms characterized by similarity and difference, or by continuity and discontinuity. If certain realms of being (such as the "physical") seem to be the necessary but not sufficient ground for new developments (the biological and mental), a theistic doctrine of creation can accommodate both regularity in change and creative novelty. For the theist can hold that a cosmic Person has the kind of unified structure that can purposely create orders of being, both in consonance with his own nature and possibilities, and in relation to the nature of created actualities and possibilities.[13]

The theist's main contention is that to talk about God creating the world *ex nihilo,* is to talk about a Being whose complex, unified nature it is to be creative also, creative in relation to his own given ontic structure. The very fact that, once the creative activity has taken place, it may be seen as a relatively continuous and even predictable order of change, itself testifies to the fact that, as Creator, God is not arbitrary in the vicious sense, but creates in orderly steps and humanly understandable fashion, with a purpose in view and in relation to givens of his own nature, as well as of the state of the created world.

Thus we press the underlying analogy, reminding ourselves of Plato's warning that in cosmological matters we are in the realm of the probable only, and that we are not here presenting the argument for such a God. God is the kind of unified being who, in creating, is himself involved in and affected by the additions (and subtractions) he makes, although such continuity-in-novelty as there is seems clearly to indicate that his nature is not exhausted in either change or creation. For to be a creator, as human experience indicates, is to be a creator within a certain structure that maintains itself in and through the creations that reflect the structure. God as a Person, as Creator, is non-changing. But *what* he creates, the quality of his own experience, will be affected by, but not controlled by, the created world.

The underlying model for reality, suggested by personal creativity, has other far-reaching possibilities. Perhaps the time is ripe to stop thinking of change and creativity against a background of

[13] On other metaphysical grounds I would prefer the hypothesis that what we know as the space-time world of sense-perception is integral to the activity of God, and not "outside" of His being. But such a personalistic, idealistic, view of the space-time world aside, I would urge in any case that the space-time world, insofar as it manifests related orders of change, may well be expressing the purpose of God's inner nature, including his capacity to create again and again. For God to create either an independent space-time world, or to be involved in the graded, orderly interrelated levels of changes as aspects of his own being, is for our purposes here not critical.

pemanence. *Creativity-and-Unity, Creativity-in-Unity, here is the ontological fact that forever marries creativity and continuity.* Instead of wondering *how* anything can be added to all there is, *ex nihilo,* we must acknowledge the category of categories: reality is a Creative Order, yes, analogous to, but not reducible to, the creative order exhibited in the finite person. If we conceive of God as the Creator-Person—both person and creator at once—what fact of existence, in the scientific, moral, aesthetic, or religious realm have we actually disregarded?

Boston University

APPENDICES

APPENDIX A

ACADEMIC HISTORY OF CURT JOHN DUCASSE

Born:	July 7, 1881, 12:05 P.M. in Angouleme, France
U. S. Citizen:	Came to U. S. A. in 1900 Naturalized citizen in 1910
Parents:	Father—Jean Louis Ducasse (d) Mother—Clementine Theoda Grolig Ducasse (d)
Married:	1921 to Mabel Lisle
Children:	None
Education:	Lycee of Bordeaux, France Abbotsholme School, England (two terms) University of Washington, Seattle, Wash.—A.B. magna cum laude, 1908; A.M., 1909 Harvard University—Ph.D., 1912
Teaching:	Instructor in Philosophy and Psychology, U. of Washington, 1912–16 Assistant Professor of Philosophy, U. of Washington, 1916–24 Associate Professor of Philosophy, U. of Washington, 1924–26 Associate Professor of Philosophy, Brown U., 1926–29 Professor of Philosophy, Brown U., 1929–58 Professor Emeritus of Philosophy, Brown U., 1958– Walker-Ames Visiting Professor of Philosophy, U. of Washington, May, 1946 Flint Visiting Professor of Philosophy, U. of California at Los Angeles, Spring, 1947 Part-time Lecturer, New York U., Fall, 1958 Part-time Lecturer, Radcliffe College, Fall, 1959 Part-time Lecturer, Boston U., Fall, 1960

Summer schools: University of California, 1925
University of Michigan, 1927
Cornell University, 1929
University of Chicago, 1931
Columbia University, 1936

Administration: Chairman of Department of Philosophy, Brown U., 1930–51

Acting Dean of the Graduate School, Brown U., 1947–49

Professional Affiliations, Offices, Honors, etc.

Chairman, Committee of Organization, Pacific Division of the American Philosophical Association, 1924

Secretary, Pacific Div. Amer. Philos. Assoc., 1924–26

Vice-President, Amer. Philos. Assoc. (Eastern Div.), 1932–33

Fellow, American Academy of Arts and Sciences, 1933–

Chairman, Committee of Organization, Association for Symbolic Logic, 1934

President, Association for Symbolic Logic, 1936–38

Delegate of the Amer. Philos. Assoc. to the American Council of Learned Societies, 1937–48

Fellow, American Association for the Advancement of Science, 1938

President, Amer. Philos. Assoc. (Eastern Div.), 1939

Member, Executive Committee, American Council of Learned Societies, 1939–41

Member, Board of Editors, *Philosophy and Phenomenological Research,* 1942–

Member, Commission of the Amer. Philos. Assoc. on Philosophy in Liberal Education, 1943–45

Member, Board of Trustees, Amer. Soc. for Aesthetics, 1943–47

President, Amer. Soc. for Aesthetics, 1945

Member, Board of Trustees, American Society for Psychical Research, 1951–

Corresponding member, Centro Literario-Filosofico "Arca del Sur," Montevideo, Uruguay, 1952

Corresponding member, (British) Society for Psychical Research, 1954

Member of Council, Amer. Assoc. of Univ. Professors, 1954–57

Member of Council, Amer. Acad. of Arts and Sciences, 1954–58

Second Vice-President, American Soc. for Psychical Research, 1957–

President, Philosophy of Science Association, 1958–61

Member, U. S. National Committee of the International Union for the History and Philosophy of Science, 1958–61

Chairman, Publications Committee, Amer. Soc. for Psychical Research, 1959

Member, Metaphysical Society of America, 1963

Lecturing:

The Howison Lecture, University of California, 1944

The Foerster Lecture on the Immortality of the Soul, University of California, 1947

The D. W. Prall Memorial Lecture, Amer. Soc. for Aesthetics, Pacific Division, 1947

The Paul Carus Lectures, Amer. Philos. Assoc., 1949

The John William Graham Lecture on Psychic Science, Swarthmore College, 1951

The 1960 Garvin Lecture on the Immortality, of Man, Lancaster, Pa., 1960

Listed in:

Who's Who in America (until vol. 28)

Leaders in Education

Directory of American Scholars

Who's Who in New England

Who's Who in the East

Minerva Weltkalender der Gelehrten

World Biography

Italian "Enciclopedia Filosofica"

Who's Who in American Education

Honorary degrees:

A. M. *ad eundem,* Brown University, 1943; D.Litt., Brown University, 1960

APPENDIX B

PUBLICATIONS OF CURT JOHN DUCASSE

Books

Causation and the Types of Necessity. Seattle: University of Washington Press, 1924. 132 pp.

The Philosophy of Art. New York: The Dial Press, 1930. xiv, 314 pp.

The Relation of Philosophy to General Education. General Education Board of the Rockefeller Foundation, 1932. 105 pp. (Printed for private circulation.)

Philosophy as a Science: Its Matter and its Method. New York: Oskar Piest, 1941. xx, 242 pp.

Art, the Critics and You. New York: Oskar Piest, 1944. 170 pp.

El Arte, Los Criticos, y Vd. Spanish translation of *Art, the Critics and You.* Buenos Aires: Editorial Argos, 1950. 188 pp.

Nature, Mind, and Death. The Carus Lectures, Eighth Series, 1949. La Salle, Ill.: Open Court Publishing Co., 1951. xi, 514 pp.

A Philosophical Scrutiny of Religion. New York: The Ronald Press Co., 1953. x, 441 pp.

A Critical Examination of the Belief in a Life after Death. Springfield, Ill.: Charles C Thomas, Publishers, 1961. xvii, 316 pp.

Contributions to Books

Contemporary American Philosophy. Vol. I. London: Allen and Unwin, 1930. *Contribution:* The chapter, "Philosophical Liberalism."

The Philosophy of G. E. Moore. The Library of Living Philosophers, edited by P. A. Schilpp, Vol. IV. Evanston, Ill.: Northwestern University Press, 1942. *Contribution:* The essay, "Moore's 'The Refutation of Idealism'."

Studies in the History of Culture. Menasha: George Banta Publishing Company, 1942. *Contribution:* The chapter, "John Herschel's Philosophy of Science."

Philosophy in American Education. New York: Harper's, 1945. Coauthor with Brand Blanshard, Charles W. Hendel, Arthur E. Murphy and Max C. Otto.

Readings in Philosophical Analysis. Ed. by Feigl and Sellars. New York: Appleton-Century-Crofts, Inc., 1949. *Contribution:* "Explanation, Mechanism, and Teleology." (Reprinted from *Journal of Philosophy,* March 12, 1925.)

Democracy in a World of Tensions. A symposium prepared by UNESCO, edited by Richard McKeon. Chicago: University of Chicago Press, 1951. *Contribution:* Chapter VI and discussion of Chapter XXXI.

Structure, Method and Meaning. Essays in honor of Henry M. Sheffer, edited by Paul Henle, H. M. Kallen, and S. K. Langer. New York: Liberal Arts Press, 1951. *Contribution:* The essay, "Francis Bacon's Philosophy of Science."

Contemporary Philosophy. A Book of Readings. Edited by J. L. Jarrett and S. McMurrin. New York: Henry Holt and Co., 1954. *Contribution:* "Standards of Criticism." (Reprinted from *The Philosophy of Art,* N. Y., Dial Press, 1930.)

American Philosophers at Work. Edited by Sidney Hook. New York: Criterion Books, 1956. *Contribution:* The essay, "The Method of Knowledge in Philosophy." (Reprint of the 1944 Howison Lecture at the University of California.)

A Modern Introduction to Philosophy. Edited by P. Edwards and A. Pap. Glencoe, Ill.: The Free Press, 1957. *Contribution:* Section 20, "Is Life After Death Possible?" (Reprint of part of the 1947 Foerster Lecture at the University of California) and Section 26, "Preperception and Freedom" (Reprint of part of Chapter XI of *Nature, Mind, and Death*).

Does Man Survive Death? Edited by Eileen J. Garrett. New York: Helix Press, 1957. *Contribution:* "What Could Survive?" (Reprinted from *Tomorrow,* Vol. 5, No. 1, Autumn, 1956).

Determinism and Freedom in the Age of Modern Science. Edited by Sidney Hook. First New York University Symposium on Philosophy. New York: New York University Press, 1958. *Contribution:* The essay, "Determinism, Freedom and Responsibility."

The Philosophy of C. D. Broad. Vol. X of The Library of Living Philosophers, edited by P. A. Schilpp. New York: The Tudor Publishing Company, 1959. *Contribution:* The essay, "Broad on the Relevance of Psychical Research to Philosophy."

Psychoanalysis, Scientific Method, and Philosophy. Edited by Sidney Hook. Second New York University Symposium on Philosophy. New York: New York University Press, 1959. *Contribution:* The essay, "Psychoanalysis and Suggestion, Metaphysics and Temperament."

Introductory Readings in Philosophy. Edited by R. Ammerman and M. C. Singer. Dubuque, Iowa: Wm. C. Brown Book Company, 1960. *Contribution:* "The Guide of Life." (Reprinted from the Phi Beta Kappa *Key Reporter,* Vol. XXIII, No. 2, January, 1958.)

Dimensions of Mind. Edited by Sidney Hook. Third New York University Symposium on Philosophy. New York: New York University Press, 1960. *Contribution:* The essay, "In Defense of Dualism."

Theories of Scientific Method, The Renaissance Through the Nineteenth Century. By R. M. Blake, C. J. Ducasse, and E. H. Madden. Seattle: University of Washington Press, 1960. *Contribution:* Chapters 3, 7, 8, 9, and 10.

Self, Religion and Metaphysics. Edited by G. E. Myers. Essays in Memory of James Bissett Pratt. New York: The Macmillan Company, 1961. *Contribution:* The essay, "What Metaphysics is Good for."

In Search of God and Immortality. The Garvin Free Lectures, Vol. II. Boston: The Beacon Press, 1961. *Contribution:* The lecture, "Life After Death Conceived as Reincarnation."

Selected Readings in Philosophy of Education. Edited by Joe Park. New York: Macmillan, 1963. *Contribution:* "What Can Philosophy Contribute to Educational Theory?" (Reprinted from *Harvard Educational Review,* Fall, 1958.)

The Range of Philosophy. Edited by H. H. Titus and M. H. Hepp. A book of readings. New York: American Book Company, 1964. *Contribution:* "In Defense of Dualism" (from N.Y.U. Symposium, *Dimensions of Mind,* 1960, N.Y.U. Press) and "Aesthetics and the Aesthetic Activities" (Presidential address to the American Soc. for Aesthetics; from *Jl. of Aesthetics and Art Criticism,* March 5, 1946).

Body, Mind, and Death. A book of readings. Edited and with an Introduction by A. G. N. Flew. New York: Macmillan, 1964. *Contribution:* "The Empirical Case for Personal Survival" (being sections from the 1947 Foerster Lecture at the University of California).

Theories of Education. Maxwell Air Force Base: Academic Instructor and Allied Officer School, Air University, U. S. Air Force, 1964. *Contribution:* "What can Philosophy Contribute to Educational Theory?" (from *Harvard Educational Review,* Fall, 1958).

Intellectual Foundations of American Education. Edited by Harold J. Carter. New York: Pitman Publishing Corp., 1965. *Contribution:* "What can Philosophy Contribute to Educational Theory?" (from *Harvard Educational Review,* Fall, 1958).

Literature and Aesthetics: Tolstoi and the Critics. Edited by Holly G. Duffield and Manuel Bilsky. Chicago, Ill.: Scott Foreman & Company, 1965. *Contribution:* "What has Beauty to do With Art?" (from *Jl. of Philosophy,* vol. XXV, no. 7, March, 1928).

Brain and Mind. Edited by J. R. Smythies. London: Routledge and Kegan Paul, 1965. *Contribution:* The essay, "Minds, Matter, and Bodies."

Art and Philosophy. Essays contributed to the N.Y.U. Institute of Philosophy, October, 1964. New York: New York University Press, 1965. *Contribution:* "Taste, Beauty, Meaning, Feeling: and Reality in Fine Art and in Fiction."

Body, Mind, and Death. By F. C. Dommeyer. Stockton, Calif.: University of the Pacific Philosophy Institute Publication, 1965. *Contribution:* Counterthesis, "The Watseka Evidence."

Articles

"The Retina and Righthandedness," (in collaboration with H. C. Stevens). *Psychological Review,* vol. 19, no. 1, January, 1912.

"A Defense of Ontological Liberalism," *Journal of Philosophy,* vol. 21, no. 13, June 19, 1924.

"R. M. Blake, Sceptic," *Journal of Philosophy,* vol. 21, no. 19, Sept. 11, 1924.

"The Non-Existence of Time," *Journal of Philosophy,* vol. 22, no. 1, Jan. 1, 1925.

"Explanation, Mechanism, and Teleology," *Journal of Philosophy,* vol. 22, no. 6, March 12, 1925, Reprinted in *Readings in Philosophical Analysis,* edited by Herbert Feigl and Wilfrid Sellars. New York: Appleton-Century-Crofts, 1949.

"A Liberalistic View of Truth," *Philosophical Review,* vol. 34, no. 6, Nov., 1925.

"Liberalism in Ethics," *International Journal of Ethics,* vol. 35, no. 3, April, 1925.

"On the Nature and the Observability of the Causal Relation," *Journal of Philosophy,* vol. 23, no. 3, Feb. 4, 1926.

"A Neglected Meaning of Probability," *Proceedings of the Sixth International Congress of Philosophy,* 1926.

"Mind and Its Place in Nature: Discussion," *Philosophical Review,* vol. 36, no. 4, July, 1927.

"Terminological Anarchy," *Philosophical Review,* vol. 37, no. 2, March, 1928.

"What has Beauty to do With Art?," *Journal of Philosophy,* vol. 25, no. 7, March 29, 1928.

"Is Art the Imaginative Expression of a Wish?," *Philosophical Review,* vol. 37, no. 3, May, 1928.

"The Place of Philosophy in an University Education," *Brown Alumni Monthly,* vol. XXX, no. 6, Jan., 1930.

"Of the Spurious Mystery in Causal Connections," *Philosophical Review,* vol. 39, no. 4, July, 1930.

"On our Knowledge of Existents," *Proceedings of the Seventh International Congress of Philosophy,* 1930.

"Art History, Criticism, and Esthetics," *Creative Art,* vol. 9, no. 1, July, 1931.

"Some Questions in Aesthetics," *The Monist,* vol. 42, no. 1, Jan., 1932.

"Graduate Work at Brown," *Brown Alumni Monthly,* vol. XXXII, no. 6, Jan., 1932.

"Of the Nature and Efficacy of Causes," *Philosophical Review,* vol. 41, no. 4, July, 1932.

"The Aim and Content of Graduate Training in Ethics," *International Journal of Ethics,* vol. 43, no. 1, Oct., 1932.

"Symposium in Honor of the Seventieth Birthday of Alfred North Whitehead." Cambridge: Harvard University Press, 1932. Pp. 7–10.

"On the Attributes of Material Things," *Journal of Philosophy,* vol. 31, no. 3, Feb. 1, 1934.

"Is Scientific Verification Possible in Philosophy?," *Philosophy of Science,* vol. 2, no. 2, April, 1935.

"Mr. Collingwood on Philosophical Method," *Journal of Philosophy,* vol. 33, no. 4, Feb. 13, 1936.

"Introspection, Mental Acts, and Sensa," *Mind,* vol. 45, no. 178, April, 1936.

"Verification, Verifiability, and Meaningfulness," *Journal of Philosophy,* vol. 33, no. 9, April, 1936.

"The Meaning of Probability: Discussion," *Journal of the American Statistical Association,* vol. 31, no. 193, March, 1936.

"Are the Humanities Worth Their Keep?," *American Scholar,* vol. 6, no. 4, Autumn, 1937.

"The Animal with Red Cheeks," *American Scholar,* vol. 7, no. 3, Summer, 1938.

"The Esthetic Object," *Journal of Philosophy,* vol. 35, no. 12, June 9, 1938.

"Symbols, Signs and Signals," *Journal of Symbolic Logic,* vol. 4, no. 2, June, 1939.

"Philosophy and Natural Science," *Philosophical Review,* vol. 49, no. 2, March, 1940.

"Concerning the Status of So-Called 'Pseudo-Object' Sentences," *Journal of Philosophy,* vol. 37, no. 12, June 6, 1940.

"Some Critical Comments on a Nominalistic Analysis of Resemblance," *Philosophical Review,* vol. 49, no. 6, Nov., 1940.

"The Nature and Function of Theory in Ethics," *Ethics,* vol. 51, no. 1, Oct., 1940.

"Propositions, Opinions, Sentences and Facts," *Journal of Philosophy,* vol. 37, no. 26, Dec. 19, 1940.

"Truth, Verifiability, and Propositions about the Future," *Philosophy of Science,* vol. 8, no. 3, July, 1941.

"Some Observations Concerning the Nature of Probability," *Journal of Philosophy,* vol. 38, no. 15, July 17, 1941.

"Objectivity, Objective Reference, and Perception," *Philosophy and Phenomenological Research,* vol. 2, no. 1, Sept., 1941.

"Art Appreciation and the Curriculum," *Bulletin of the Association of American Colleges,* vol. 27, no. 3, Oct., 1941.

"Is a Fact a True Proposition?," *Journal of Philosophy,* vol. 39, no. 5, Feb., 1942.

"Concerning Professor Bogholt's Criticism of my 'Disposal of Naturalism,' " *Philosophical Review,* vol. 51, no. 2, March, 1942.

"Some Comments on C. W. Morris's 'Foundations of the Theory of Signs,' " *Philosophy and Phenomenological Research,* vol. 3, no. 1, Sept., 1942.

"Correctness vs. Occurrence of Appraisals," *Journal of Philosophy,* vol. 39, no. 5, Feb. 26, 1942.

"Aesthetic Contemplation and Sense Pleasure," *Journal of Philosophy,* vol. 40, no. 6, March 18, 1943.

"Liberal Education and the College Curriculum," *Journal of Higher Education,* vol. 15, no. 1, Jan., 1944.

"Propositions, Truth and the Ultimate Criterion of Truth," *Philosophy and Phenomenological Research,* vol. 4, no. 3, March, 1944.

"On Our Knowledge of the Meaning of Words," *Proceedings of the Congrès International de Philosophie Consacré aux Problemes de la Connaissance,* Port-au-Prince, Haiti, 1944.

"Facts, Truth and Knowledge," *Philosophy and Phenomenological Research,* vol. 5, no. 3, March, 1945.

"Some Comments on Professor Nagel's Latest Remarks," *Philosophy and Phenomenological Research,* vol. 5, no. 3, March, 1945.

"Some Comments on Professor Sellars' 'Knowing and Knowledge,' "

Philosophy and Phenomenological Research, vol. 5, no. 3, March, 1945.

"The Subject-Matter Distinctive of Philosophy," *Philosophy and Phenomenological Research,* vol. 6, no. 3, March, 1946.

"Aesthetics and the Aesthetic Activities," *Journal of Aesthetics and Art Criticism,* vol. 5, no. 3, March, 1947.

"Some Comments on Professor Wild's Criticisms of My View on Semiosis," *Philosophy and Phenomenological Research,* vol. 8, no. 2, Dec., 1947.

"Some Comments on Professor Wild's Preceding Remarks," *Philosophy and Phenomenological Research,* vol. 8, no. 2, Dec., 1947.

"Aiken's 'Criteria for an Adequate Aesthetics': Discussion," *Journal of Aesthetics and Art Criticism,* vol. 7, no. 2, Dec., 1948.

"Graduate Preparation for Teaching," *Journal of Higher Education,* vol. 19, no. 9, Dec., 1948.

"Some Observations Concerning Particularity," *Philosophical Review,* vol. 58, no. 6, 1949.

"Causality," *Collier's Encyclopedia,* vol. 4, 1950.

"Cynicism," *Collier's Encyclopedia,* vol. 6, 1950.

"Deductive Probability Arguments," *Philosophical Studies,* vol. 4, no. 2, Feb., 1950.

"Reality, Science and Metaphysics," *Synthese,* vol. 8, nos. 1–2, 1950–51.

"Qu'est-ce que la Philosophie?", *Synthese,* vol. 8, nos. 6–7, 1950–51.

"Whewell's Philosophy of Scientific Discovery," (Two articles.) *Philosophical Review,* vol. 60, no. 1, Jan., 1951, and no. 2, April, 1951.

"Mr. G. N. M. Tyrrell's 'Man the Maker,'" *Journal of the American Society for Psychical Research,* vol. XLVI, no. 4, Oct., 1952.

"The Macdonald 'Spook' Collection," *Bulletin of the Hartford Seminary Foundation,* no. 14, Dec., 1952.

"Philosophy, Education, and the Nature of Man," *Journal of the Phi Beta Kappa Society,* vol. XXXI, no. 4, Dec., 1952.

"Causality, Creation, and Ecstasy," *The Philosophical Forum,* Boston University Annual, vol. XI, 1953.

"Scientific Method in Ethics," *Philosophy and Phenomenological Research,* vol. 14, no. 1, Sept., 1953.

"A Terminal Course in Philosophy," *Journal of Higher Education,* vol. XXIV, no. 8, Nov., 1953.

"Professor Demos on 'Nature, Mind, and Death,'" *Review of Metaphysics,* vol. VII, no. 2, Dec., 1953.

"Some Questions Concerning Psychic Phenomena," *Journal of the*

American Society for Psychical Research, vol. XLVIII, no. 1, Jan., 1954.

"How Does One Discover What a Term Means?", *Philosophical Review,* vol. LXIII, no. 1, Jan., 1954.

"Are Religious Dogmas Cognitive and Meaningful?", *Academic Freedom, Logic and Religion,* being the symposia at the 1953 meeting of the Eastern Division of the American Philosophical Association, University of Pennsylvania Press, 1953. Also published in *Journal of Philosophy,* vol. LI, no. 5, March 4, 1954.

"International Conferences of Parapsychological Studies," *Journal of the American Society for Psychical Research,* vol. XLVIII, no. 4, Oct., 1954.

"The Philosophical Importance of 'Psychic' Phenomena," *Journal of Philosophy,* vol. LI, no. 25, Dec. 9, 1954.

"On the Function and Nature of the Philosophy of Education," *Harvard Educational Review,* vol. XXVI, no. 2, Spring, 1956.

"Concerning the Language of Religion," (Discussion) *Philosophical Review,* vol. LXV, no. 3, July, 1956.

"Science, Scientists, and Psychical Research," *Journal of the American Society for Psychical Research,* vol. L, no. 4, Oct., 1956. (Reprinted in *Manas,* vol. X, no. 18, May 1, 1957.)

"On the Analysis of Causality," *Journal of Philosophy,* vol. LIV, no. 13, June 20, 1957.

"Physical Phenomena in Psychical Research," *Journal of the American Society for Psychical Research,* vol. LII, no. 1, Jan., 1958.

"Che Cosa Potrebbe Sopravvivere?", *Luce e Ombra,* anno 58, no. 2, March–April, 1958.

"What Can Philosophy Contribute to Educational Theory?", *Harvard Educational Review,* vol. XXVIII, no. 4, Fall, 1958.

"What has Science Done to Religion?", *Centennial Review,* vol. III, no. 2, Spring, 1959.

"Causality and Parapsychology," *Journal of Parapsychology,* vol. XXIII, no. 2, June, 1959.

"Philosophy Can Become a Science," *Revue Internationale de Philosophia,* Fasc. 1, no. 47, 1959.

"How Good is the Evidence for Survival After Death?", *Journal of the American Society for Psychical Research,* vol. LIII, no. 3, July, 1959.

"Life, Telism, and Mechanism," (Address to 1957 *Interamerican Congress of Philosophy*), *Philosophy and Phenomenological Research,* vol. XX, no. 1, Sept., 1959.

"How the Case of *The Search for Bridey Murphy* Stands Today," (being a chapter of *The Belief in a Life After Death* pre-published as an article), *Journal of the American Society for Psychical Research,* vol. LIV, no. 1, Jan., 1960.

"The Doctrine of Reincarnation in the History of Thought," (being a chapter of *The Belief in a Life After Death* pre-published as an article), *International Journal of Parapsychology,* vol. II, no. 3, Summer, 1960.

"Filozofia nauka i moralność," Ameryka No. 26 (America Illustrated), Pub. *in Polish* by U. S. Information Agency, Washington, D. C., March, 1961.

The same paper, but *in Russian,* in No. 28 of America Illustrated, March, 1962.

"The Sources of the Emotional Import of an Aesthetic Object," (Comments on a paper by Hayner entitled "Expressive Meaning in Art"), *Philosophy and Phenomenological Research,* vol. XXI, no. 4, June, 1961.

"Some Comments on Prof. Dommeyer's Criticisms," (Comments on a paper by Dommeyer entitled "A Critical Examination of C. J. Ducasse's Metaphilosophy"), *Philosophy and Phenomenological Research,* vol. XXI, no. 4, June, 1961.

"Concerning the Uniformity of Causality," (Comments on a paper by Richard Gale entitled "Professor Ducasse on Determinism"), *Philosophy and Phenomenological Research,* vol. XXII, no. 1, Sept., 1961.

"Concerning the Logical Status of Criteria of Morality," (Comments on R. Santoni's comments on Dommeyer's criticisms), *Philosophy and Phenomenological Research,* vol. XXIII, no. 1, Sept., 1962.

"What Would Constitute Conclusive Evidence of Survival," *Journal of the Society for Psychical Research,* vol. 41, no. 714, Dec., 1962.

"Comments by C. J. Ducasse," (on A. G. N. Flew's criticism of the preceding item, entitled "The Platonic Presuppositions of the Survival Hypothesis"), *Journal of the Society for Psychical Research,* vol. 42, no. 716, June, 1963.

"Early History of the Association for Symbolic Logic," (co-author Haskel B. Curry), *Journal of Symbolic Logic,* vol. 27, no. 3, Sept., 1962.

Contribution to a Symposium: Symposium on "The Future of Parapsychology," reported on in *International Journal of Parapsychology,* vol. IV, no. 2, Spring, 1962.

"Hypnotism, Suggestion, and Suggestibility," *International Journal of Parapsychology,* vol. V, no. 1, Winter, 1963.

Addendum to "Early History of the Association for Symbolic Logic," (co-author Haskel B. Curry), *Journal of Symbolic Logic,* vol. 28, no. 4, Dec., 1963.

" 'Substants,' Capacities, and Tendencies," *Review of Metaphysics,* vol. XVIII, no. 1, Sept., 1964.

"Art and 'the Language of the Emotions'," *Journal of Aesthetics and Art Criticism,* vol. XXIII, no. 1, Fall, 1964.

"Causation: Perceivable? Or Only Inferred?," *Philosophy and Phenomenological Research* (not yet published).

Published Lectures

The Method of Knowledge in Philosophy. The Howison Lecture for 1944. *University of California Publications in Philosophy,* vol. 16, 1945.

Science: Its Nature, Method, and Scope. David Wight Prall Memorial Lecture, 1947. Piedmont, California: The Prall Memorial Foundation, vol. 3, no. 1, 1947.

Is a Life After Death Possible? The Agnes E. and Constantine E. A. Foerster Lecture on the Immortality of the Soul, 1947. Berkeley: University of California Press, 1948. (Reprinted in *Newsletter of the Parapsychology Foundation,* vol. 3, no. 1, Jan.–Feb., 1956.

Nature, Mind, and Death. The Carus Lectures, Eighth Series, 1949. (See books.)

Paranormal Phenomena, Nature, and Man. The First John William Graham Lecture on Psychic Science, 1941. *Journal of the American Society for Psychical Research,* vol. 45, no. 4, Oct., 1951.

Christianity, Rationality, and Faith. A John Hershel Morron Lecture, at Hamilton College, 1954. *Review of Religion,* vol. XXII, nos. 3–4, March, 1958.

Metoda poznawcza filozofii (a translation into Polish of the University of California 1944 Howison Lecture). Published by East Europe Institute, 1958.

Es Posible la Vida despues de la Muerte? Libreria "Mercurio," Buenos Aires, Argentina, 1958. (Spanish translation of the 1947 Foerster Lecture at the University of California; published also in *La Conciencia,* Buenos Aires, vol. IX, no. 156, July–Aug., 1957.

Life After Death Conceived as Reincarnation. The 1960 Garvin Free Lecture on the Immortality of Man, at Lancaster, Pennsylvania. Published in *In Search of God and Immortality,* The Garvin Lectures. Beacon Press, Boston, 1961.

Newspaper and Magazine Articles

"Significant Form," *The Nation,* vol. 122, Feb. 3, 1926.

"Words of Cheer for Worms," *The Nation,* vol. 123, Sept. 8, 1926.

"Seven Popular Dialogues on Various Questions in Aesthetics," *The Providence Journal,* Jan. 5, 19, Feb. 2, March 2, 30, April 20, June 15, 1927.

"Six Discussions of Current Art Exhibits," *The Providence Journal,* 1930.

"A Philosopher Considers the Price of Liberty," *The Providence Evening Bulletin,* 1930.

"A Dialogue on the Fine Arts," *The Town Crier,* Providence, R. I., 1935.

"Conditions of Social Progress," *The Providence Evening Bulletin,* 1939.

"Has Science Increased Race Happiness?", *The Providence Evening Bulletin,* April 14, 1939.

"What is the War Doing to our Morals?", *The Providence Sunday Journal,* Aug., 1943.

"Discussion," (in *Modern Review,* vol. II, no. 2, Feb., 1948) of M. Dynnik's article "Contemporary Bourgeois Philosophy in the United States," published in *Modern Review,* vol. I, no. 9, Nov., 1947.

"The Introductory Course in Philosophy," *Philosophers' Newsletter,* no. 40, 1950. (Guest editorial.)

"Patterns of Survival," *Tomorrow* Magazine, vol. I, no. 4, Summer, 1953.

"Knowing the Future," *Tomorrow* Magazine, vol. III, no. 2, Winter, 1955.

"The John William Graham Collection of Literature of Psychic Science," *Books at Brown,* vol. XVIII, no. 1, May, 1956.

"On the Whole Beneficial to Serious Studies" (contribution to a Symposium on Seven Questions concerning "The Search for Bridey Murphy"), *Tomorrow* Magazine, vol. 4, no. 4, Summer, 1956.

"What Could Survive?", *Tomorrow* Magazine, vol. 5, no. 1, Autumn, 1956. (Reprinted as chapter 3 of Part I, of book *Does Man Survive Death?,* ed. by Eileen Garrett, Helix Press, New York, 1957.

"The Guide of Life," *The Key Reporter* (Phi Beta Kappa News-letter), vol. XXIII, no. 2, Jan., 1958. "Mr. Ducasse Replies," *The Key Reporter,* vol. XXIII, no. 3; April, 1958, (A reply to a letter from a reader to the editor concerning "The Guide of Life.")

"Sanity in Education," in *Educational Summary,* Crofts, Sept. 12, 1958.

Reviews

De la Matière à la Vie. Henri Colin. *Journal of Philosophy,* vol. 25, no. 6, March 15, 1928.

Essai Critique sur L'Esthetique de Kant. Victor Basch. *Journal of Philosophy,* vol. 26, no. 2, Jan. 17, 1929.

Psychologie de l'Art. Henri Delacroix. *Philosophical Review,* vol. 38, no. 4, July, 1929.

Mind and the World Order. C. I. Lewis. *The Symposium,* vol. I, no. 2, April, 1930.

Aesthetic Judgment. D. W. Prall. *Philosophical Review,* vol. 39, no. 3, May, 1930.

Beauty. Helen Huss Parkhurst. *International Journal of Ethics,* vol. 41, no. 3, April, 1931.

Foundations of Geometry and Induction. J. Nicod. *Journal of Philosophy,* vol. 28, no. 17, Aug. 13, 1931.

Scientific Method in Aesthetics. Thomas Munro. *Philosophical Review,* vol. 40, no. 4, July, 1931.

Collected Papers of Charles S. Peirce. C. Hartshorne and P. Weiss, editors; vol. III, *Exact Logic. Saturday Review of Literature,* vol. 10, 1933.

A Bibliography of Aesthetics and of the Philosophy of the Fine Arts from 1900 to 1932. Compiled and edited by W. A. Hammond. *Philosophical Review,* vol. 43, no. 1, Jan., 1934.

Collected Papers of Charles S. Pierce. C. Hartshorne and P. Weiss, editors; vol. IV, *The Simplest Mathematics,* and vol. V, *Pragmatism and Pragmaticism. Saturday Review of Literature,* vol. 11, 1934.

Beauty and Human Nature. A. R. Chandler. *Journal of Educational Research,* vol. 29, no. 1, Jan., 1935.

A Guide to Reading in Aesthetics and Theory of Poetry. G. N. Belknap. *Philosophical Review,* vol. 45, no. 1, Jan., 1936.

A Study in Kant's Aesthetics. Barrows Dunham. *Philosophical Review,* vol. 45, no. 1, Jan., 1936.

Collected Papers of Charles S. Peirce. C. Hartshorne and P. Weiss, editors; vol. VI, *Scientific Metaphysics. Saturday Review of Literature,* vol. 13, 1936.

A Modern Book of Aesthetics. M. Rader. *Philosophical Review,* vol. 46, no. 1, Jan., 1937.

Essai sur la Creation Artistique. Liviu Rusu. *Philosophical Review,* vol. 46, no. 2, March, 1937.

Wesen und Wesenserkenntnis. Wilhelm Pöll. *Philosophical Review,* vol. 47, no. 2, March, 1938.

Linguistic Aspects of Science. Leonard Bloomfield. *Journal of Symbolic Logic,* vol. 4, no. 3, Sept., 1939.

L'Instauration Philosophique. Etienne Souriau. *Philosophical Review,* vol. 49, no. 4, July, 1940.

An Essay on Metaphysics. R. G. Collingwood. *Philosophical Review,* vol. 50, no. 6, Nov., 1941.

Prefaces to Inquiry. W. R. Gondon. *Philosophic Abstracts,* vol. 2, no. 9, Spring, 1942.

The Philosophy of Bertrand Russell. P. A. Schilpp, editor. *Journal of Higher Education,* vol. 16, no. 2, Feb., 1945.

Signs, Language, and Behavior. Charles Morris. *Erasmus Speculum Scientiarum,* vol. 1, no. 7, Jan., 1947.

Analysis of Knowledge and Valuation. C. I. Lewis. *Philosophical Review,* vol. LVII, no. 3, May, 1948.

Matter, Mind and Meaning. Whately Carington. *Journal of the American Society for Psychical Research,* vol. 44, no. 1, Jan., 1950.

Second Sight in Daily Life. W. H. W. Sabine. *Journal of the American Society for Psychical Research,* vol. 44, no. 3, July, 1950.

Very Peculiar People. E. J. Dingwall. *Journal of the American Society for Psychical Research,* vol. 44, no. 4, Oct., 1950.

The Problem of Knowledge. E. Cassirer. *U.S. Quarterly Book Reviews,* vol. 6, 1950.

On the Psychology of Artistic Enjoyment. Sylvi Honkavaara. *Personalist,* vol. 32, no. 3, July, 1951.

The New Renaissance of the Spirit. V. A. McCrossen. *Personalist,* vol. 32, no. 2, April, 1951.

The Biography of a Ghost Hunter. Harry Price. *Journal of the American Society for Psychical Research,* vol. 45, no. 3, July, 1951.

Aesthetic Theories of French Artists. C. E. Gauss. *U. S. Quarterly Book Reviews,* vol. 7, 1951.

The Philosophy of Religion. W. S. Morgan. *Journal of the American Society for Psychical Research,* vol. 45, no. 2, April, 1951.

The Clairvoyant Theory of Perception. M. M. Moncrieff. *Journal of Parapsychology,* vol. 15, no. 4, Dec., 1951.

Explorations in Altruistic Love and Behavior. P. A. Sorokin, editor. *Journal of the American Society for Psychical Research,* vol. 46, no. 1, Jan., 1952.

The Maggid of Caro. H. L. Gordon. *Journal of the American Society for Psychical Research,* vol. 46, no. 2, April, 1952.

The Meaning of Beauty. Eric Newton. *Personalist,* vol. 33, no. 4, Oct., 1952.

The Sensory Order. F. A. Hayek. *U. S. Quarterly Book Review,* vol. 9, no. 2, June, 1953.

Tout l'Occultisme Dévoilé. Robert Tocquet. *Journal of the American Society for Psychical Research,* vol. 47, no. 4, Oct., 1953.

The Physical Phenomena of Mysticism. Herbert Thurston, S. J. *Journal of the American Society for Psychical Research,* vol. 47, no. 3, July, 1953.

Religion and the Modern Mind. W. T. Stace. *Philosophy and Phenomenological Research,* vol. 14, no. 1, Sept., 1953.

The Physical Phenomena of Mysticism. Henry Thurston, S. J. *Philosophy and Phenomenological Research,* vol. 14, no. 2, Dec., 1953.

New World of the Mind. J. B. Rhine. *Tomorrow* Magazine, vol. 2, no. 2, Jan., 1954.

The God of the Witches. Margaret A. Murray. *Journal of the American Society for Psychical Research,* vol. 48, no. 1, Jan., 1954.

Religion, Philosophy and Psychical Research. C. D. Broad. *Philosophical Review,* vol. 62, no. 2, April, 1954.

Great Systems of Yoga. Ernest Wood. *Journal of the American Society for Psychical Research,* vol. 48, no. 3, July, 1954.

In Search of the Hereafter. R. M. Lester. *Journal of the American Society for Psychical Research,* vol. 48, no. 4, Oct., 1954.

Ghosts and Poltergeists. Herbert Thurston, S. J. *Journal of the American Society for Psychical Research,* vol. 49, no. 1, Jan., 1955.

The Nature of Human Personality. G. N. M. Tyrrell, *Journal of Parapsychology,* vol. 19, no. 1, March, 1955.

Parapsychologie. R. Amadou. *Journal of the American Society for Psychical Research,* vol. 49, no. 2, April, 1955.

The Imprisoned Splendour. Raynor C. Johnson. *Journal of the American Society for Psychical Research,* vol. 49, no. 3, July, 1955.

Physical and Psychical Research: An Analysis of Belief. C. C. L. Gregory and Anita Kohsen. *Philosophy and Phenomenological Research,* vol. XVI, no. 1, Sept., 1955.

Man's Place in A Superphysical World. W. W. Coblenz. *Journal of the American Society for Psychical Research,* vol. 50, no. 2, April, 1956.

The Search for Bridey Murphy. Morey Bernstein. *Journal of the American Society for Psychical Research,* vol. 50, no. 3, July, 1956.

The Unknown, Is It Nearer? E. J. Dingwall and J. Langdon-Davies. *Journal of the American Society for Psychical Research,* vol. 50, no. 3, July, 1956.

The Search for Bridey Murphy (with a new chapter by W. J. Barker). Morey Bernstein. *Journal of the American Society for Psychical Research,* vol. 50, no. 4, Oct., 1956.

Some Aspects of the Conflict Between Science and Religion. H. H. Price. *Journal of the American Society for Psychical Research,* vol. 50, no. 4, Oct., 1956.

Mind in Life and Death. Geraldine Cummins. *Journal of the American Society for Psychical Research,* vol. 51, no. 1, Jan., 1957.

Clock Without Hands. R. Edwin. *Journal of the American Society for Psychical Research,* vol. 51, no. 1, Jan., 1957.

Quand la Médecine se Tait. R. Tocquet. *Journal of the American Society for Psychical Research,* vol. 51, no. 1, Jan., 1957.

Traité de Parapsychologie. René Sudre. *Tomorrow* Magazine, vol. 5, no. 3, Spring, 1957.

Extrasensory Perception: The 1955 Ciba Foundation Symposium. Tomorrow Magazine, vol. 5, no. 2, Winter, 1957.

Parapsychology, Frontier Science of the Mind. J. B. Rhine and J. G. Pratt. *Philosophy East and West,* vol. 7, nos. 3–4, Oct.–Jan., 1958.

Les Calculateurs Prodiges et leurs Secrets. R. Tocquet. *Journal of the American Society for Psychical Research,* vol. 52, no. 4, Oct., 1958.

Les Grands Médiums. R. Amadou. *Tomorrow* Magazine, vol. 6, no. 3, Summer, 1958.

Nothing So Strange. A. Ford and M. Harmon Bro. *Tomorrow* Magazine, vol. 6, no. 3, Summer, 1958.

Personal Identity and Survival (the Thirteenth Myers Memorial Lecture). C. D. Broad. *Journal of the American Society for Psychical Research,* vol. 53, no. 1, Jan., 1959.

F. W. H. Myers' Posthumous Message. W. H. Salter. *Journal of the American Society for Psychical Research,* vol. 53, no. 1, Jan., 1959.

Toward a Perspective Realism. E. B. McGilvary. *Philosophical Review,* vol. 68, no. 2, April, 1959.

Four Modern Ghosts. E. J. Dingwall and T. H. Hall. *Journal of the American Society for Psychical Research,* vol. 53, no. 2, April, 1959.

Psi Cognition. K. Ramakrishna Rao. *International Journal of Parapsychology,* vol. 1, no. 1, Summer, 1959.

Phénomènes de Médiumnité, Lévitations et Fantômes. R. Tocquet. *Journal of the American Society for Psychical Research,* vol. 53, no. 4, Oct., 1959.

Phénomènes de Médiumnité, Lévitations et Fantômes. R. Tocquet. *International Journal of Parapsychology,* vol. 2, no. 1, Winter, 1960.

Report on Five Years of Activities, January 1, 1954 to December 31, 1958 (of the Parapsychology Foundation, Inc.) *International Journal of Parapsychology,* vol. 2, no. 2, Spring, 1960.

Causality. Mario Bunge. *Isis,* vol. 51, Part 1, no. 163, March, 1960.

Les Fantômes du Trianon. A. Moberly and E. Jourdain. *Tomorrow* Magazine, vol. 8, no. 1, Winter, 1960.

The Meaning of Death. H. Feifel, editor. *Journal of the American Society for Psychical Research,* vol. 55, no. 1, Jan., 1961.

Les Hommes et les Astres. Michel Gauquelin. In *Tomorrow* Magazine, vol. 9, no. 2, Spring, 1961.

Human Personality and its Survival of Bodily Death. F. W. H. Myers; edited by Susy Smith, with foreword by Aldous Huxley. *Journal of Philosophy,* vol. LVIII, no. 20, Sept. 28, 1961.

A Life After Death. S. Ralph Harlow. *Journal of the American Society for Psychical Research,* vol. 55, no. 4, Oct., 1961.

Mysticism and Philosophy. W. T. Stace. *Journal of Philosophy,* vol. LIX, no. 12, June 7, 1962.

Philosophical Reasoning. John Passmore. *Philosophy,* vol. XXXVIII, no. 146, Oct., 1963.

Lectures on Psychical Research. C. D. Broad. *Philosophy and Phenomenological Research,* vol. XXIV, no. 4, June, 1964. (Discussion) *Philosophical Review,* vol. LXXIII, no. 3, July, 1964. (Review)

Venture Inward. Hugh Lynn Cayce. *Journal of the American Society for Psychical Research,* vol. LIX, no. 1, Jan., 1965.

Realms of Meaning. Philip H. Phenix. *Teachers College Record,* vol. 66, no. 4, Jan., 1965.

INDEX OF PROPER NAMES